Lecture Notes in Computer Science   11338

Commenced Publication in 1973
Founding and Former Series Editors:
Gerhard Goos, Juris Hartmanis, and Jan van Leeuwen

Ting Hu · Feng Wang
Hongwei Li · Qian Wang (Eds.)

Algorithms and Architectures for Parallel Processing

ICA3PP 2018 International Workshops
Guangzhou, China, November 15–17, 2018
Proceedings

 Springer

Editors
Ting Hu
Memorial University
St. John's, NL, Canada

Feng Wang
Wuhan University
Wuhan, China

Hongwei Li
University of Electronic Science
and Technology of China
Chengdu, China

Qian Wang
School of Cyber Science and Engineering
Wuhan, China

ISSN 0302-9743   ISSN 1611-3349   (electronic)
Lecture Notes in Computer Science
ISBN 978-3-030-05233-1   ISBN 978-3-030-05234-8   (eBook)
https://doi.org/10.1007/978-3-030-05234-8

Library of Congress Control Number: 2018962485

LNCS Sublibrary: SL1 – Theoretical Computer Science and General Issues

This Springer imprint is published by the registered company Springer Nature Switzerland AG
The registered company address is: Gewerbestrasse 11, 6330 Cham, Switzerland

Preface

Welcome to the proceedings of the 18th International Conference on Algorithms and Architectures for Parallel Processing (ICA3PP 2018), which was organized by Guangzhou University and held in Guangzhou, China, during November 15–17, 2018. This year, the program consisted of two workshops covering two important aspects of parallel processing technology in the cloud and big data era:

(1) ICA3PP 2018 Workshop on Intelligent Algorithms for Large-Scale Complex Optimization Problems
(2) ICA3PP 2018 Workshop on Security and Privacy in Data Processing

The aim of these workshops is to provide a forum to bring together practitioners and researchers from academia and industry for discussion and presentations on the current research and future directions related to parallel processing technology. The themes and topics of these workshops are a valuable complement to the overall scope of ICA3PP 2018, providing additional value and interest. We hope that all of the selected papers will have a good impact on future research in the respective field.

The ICA3PP 2018 workshops collected research papers on the related research issues from all around the world. All submissions received at least two reviews during the review process. According to the review results, 24 papers were selected for presentation at the conference.

The success of the ICA3PP 2018 workshops depended on the work of many individuals and organizations. We therefore thank all workshop organizers for their hard work in designing the call for papers, assembling the Program Committee, managing the peer-review process for the selection of papers, and planning the workshop program. We would also like to express our gratitude to the members of the Program Committee for the time and effort that they invested. Sincere thanks are due to Springer for their help in publishing the proceedings. Our special thanks to the Organizing Committees of ICA3PP 2018 for their strong support, and especially to the program chairs, Prof. Jaideep Vaidya and Prof. Jin Li, for their guidance.

Lastly, we thank all participants of the ICA3PP workshops for their contribution. We hope that you will find the proceedings interesting and stimulating. It was a pleasure to organize and host the ICA3PP workshops 2018 in Guangzhou.

November 2018

Ting Hu
Feng Wang
Hongwei Li
Qian Wang

Organization

ICA3PP 2018 Workshop on Intelligent Algorithms for Large-Scale Complex Optimization Problems

Workshop Chairs

Ting Hu	Memorial University of Newfoundland, Canada
Feng Wang	Wuhan University, China

Workshop Program Committee

Zhaolu Guo	Chinese Academy of Sciences, China
Rutvij H. Jhaveri	VM Institute of Technology, India
Wei Li	Jiangxi University of Science and Technology, China
Hu Peng	Wuhan University, China
Qi Rao	Peking University, China
Yu Sun	Guangxi University, China
Weihua Zhou	University of Southern Mississippi, USA

ICA3PP 2018 Workshop on Security and Privacy in Data Processing

Workshop Chairs

Qian Wang	Wuhan University, China
Hongwei Li	University of Electronic Science and Technology of China, China

Workshop Program Committee

Debiao He	Wuhang University, China
Zoe L. Jiang	Harbin Institute of Technology (Shenzhen), China
Ximeng Liu	Singapore Management University, Singapore
Jian Shen	Nanjing University of Information Science and Technology, China
Haomiao Yang	University of Electronic Science and Technology of China, China

Contents

ICA3PP 2018 Workshop on Security and Privacy in Data Processing

ICA3PP 2018 Workshop on Intelligent Algorithms for Large-Scale Complex Optimization Problems

An improved Grey Wolf Optimizer (iGWO) for Load Balancing in Cloud Computing Environment

Bhavesh N. Gohil[1]([✉]) and Dhiren R. Patel[1,2]

[1] S. V. National Institute of Technology, Surat 395007, Gujarat, India
{bng,dhiren}@coed.svnit.ac.in
[2] VJTI, Mumbai, India

Abstract. Load balancing in any system aims to optimize throughput, resource use, imbalance load, response time, overutilization of resources, etc. An efficient load balancing framework in cloud computing environment with such features may improve overall system performance, resource availability and fulfillment of SLAs. Nature-inspired metaheuristic algorithms are getting more popularity day by day due to their simplicity, flexibility and ease implementation. The success and challenges of these algorithms are based on their specific control parameter selection and tuning. A relatively new algorithm motivated by the social hierarchy and hunting behavior of grey wolves is Grey Wolf Optimizer (GWO), which is having least dependency on the control parameters. In the basic GWO, 50% of the iterations are reserved for exploration and others for exploitation. The perfect balance between exploration and exploitation is overlooked in GWO. The impact of perfect balance between two guarantees a near optimal solution. To get over this problem, an improved GWO (iGWO) is proposed in this paper, which focuses on the required meaningful balance between exploration and exploitation that leads to an optimal performance of the algorithm. Simulation results based on exploitation and exploration benchmark functions and the problem of load balancing in cloud demonstrate the effectiveness, efficiency, and stability of iGWO compared with the classical GWO, HS, ABC and PSO algorithms.

Keywords: Artificial Bee Colony · Cloud computing
Grey Wolf Optimization · Harmony Search Algorithm · Load balancing
Particle Swarm Optimization

1 Introduction

The metaheuristic algorithms are efficient in solving real-world problems. Particle Swarm Optimization (PSO) [1], Artificial Bee Colony (ABC) [2], Harmony Search (HS) [3], etc. are some of the well-known algorithms. For most of such algorithms, the performance is dependent on their algorithmic-specific control parameters. Required tuning of such algorithm-specific parameters to achieve optimized results is a difficult and time-consuming task. Hence, it's required to think for algorithm-specific parameter free optimization algorithm with same or improved performance. Also, No Free Lunch

© Springer Nature Switzerland AG 2018
T. Hu et al. (Eds.): ICA3PP 2018 Workshops, LNCS 11338, pp. 3–9, 2018.
https://doi.org/10.1007/978-3-030-05234-8_1

(NFL) theorem [4] logically proves that no algorithm can solve all optimization problems, but the average ranking of all algorithms for different problems is the same. Though a number of optimization algorithms exist for optimization problems, the NFL theorem encourages researchers to use Grey Wolf Optimization for the same.

GWO [5], a newly developed population-based metaheuristic algorithm. GWO mimics leadership hierarchy and hunting behavior of grey wolves. In order to be successful, an optimization algorithm needs to establish a perfect ratio between exploration and exploitation. In this paper, an improved version of GWO (iGWO) is proposed to balance the exploration and exploitation trade-off in classical GWO algorithm.

The remainder of this paper is organized as follows: The proposed iGWO algorithm is explained in Sect. 2. Load balancing in Cloud using iGWO is presented in Sect. 3. Section 4 depicts the simulation results and comparison. Concluding notes with the future scope are mentioned in Sect. 5.

2 An improved Grey Wolf Optimizer (iGWO)

The grey wolf is a part of canidae family. Grey wolves are considered as apex predators, meaning that they are at the top of the food chain. Grey wolves mostly prefer to live in a pack. The group size is 5–12 on an average. They have a very strict social dominant hierarchy. In GWO algorithm, four categories of wolves are considered. The leaders are called alphas. They have a responsibility for decision making for hunting, place of sleeping, wake up time, etc. Their decision must be followed by the troop. Betas have the second level in the hierarchy. They help alphas in their activities. In the absence of alpha, the beta is the best candidate to become alpha. Omegas are the lowest ranking grey wolves. They have to follow the instruction of other dominant wolves. Other wolves are called deltas. The Grey wolves have an exciting characteristic of group hunting. As per Muro et al. [6], there are three phases of grey wolf hunting: (i) tracking, chasing and approaching the prey (ii) pursuing, encircling and harassing the prey until it stops moving and finally (iii) attack the prey.

In GWO, the switching between exploration and exploitation is performed by the modified values of a and A. In that, 50% of the iterations are reserved for exploration and others are reserved for exploitation. Relatively more exploration is related to too much of randomness and too much of exploitation is similar to too little randomness, which will probably not give optimized results. Thus, there must be a logical balance between both the phases. In basic GWO, the value of a decrease from 2 to 0 linearly using the following equation:

$$a = 2\left(1 - \frac{t}{T}\right)$$

Where T indicates the total number of iterations and t is the current ongoing iteration. Our proposed iGWO employs relatively less exponential value for the decay of a over the course of iterations as mentioned below:

$$a = 2\left(1 - \frac{t^{0.95}}{T^{0.95}}\right),$$

Using this proposed function of a, the number of iterations used for exploration and exploitation are 48% and 52%, respectively. Also, the position vector of a grey wolf in basic GWO is guided equally by the positions of α, β and δ wolves as follows:

$$X_g(t+1) = \frac{X_\alpha + X_\beta + X_\delta}{3}$$

But, the most dominating wolf among the group is α followed by β and δ. Therefore, in the proposed iGWO, more weight is given to the α followed by β and wolves to find the position vector of a grey wolf as follows:

$$X_g(t+1) = \frac{2 * X_\alpha + 1.5 * X_\beta + X_\delta}{4.5}$$

But, the most dominating wolf among the group is α followed by β and δ. Therefore, in the proposed iGWO, more weight is given to the α followed by β and wolves to find the position vector of a grey wolf as follows:

$$X_g(t+1) = \frac{2 * X_\alpha + 1.5 * X_\beta + X_\delta}{4.5}$$

3 Load Balancing in Cloud Using iGWO

Existing metaheuristics algorithms [7–17] required to tune their algorithmic-specific control parameters. Tuning of such parameters to generate optimized results is a tough and time-consuming task. In this paper, an improved version of Grey Wolf Optimization [4], a newly developed optimization algorithm having the least dependency on the control parameters is used for load balancing in the cloud amongst its Physical Machines.

In [11, 15, 17–19], the load on Physical Machine (PM) in the cloud is calculated based on the resource utilization. But PMs may be of different resource capacities and hence, a PM with less capacity of resources is considered to be heavily loaded compared to PM with high capacity of resource for the same workload. Thus, we use the average remaining resources capacity of PM [16] to calculate the load of it. If the average remaining resources capacity is the same on all PMs of cloud, the load is balanced.

Following objective function is used to calculate the load imbalance level (IL) of a cloud cluster. By having IL, the load differences of PMs with its mean are identified. This makes it easy to identify the type and size of VMs to be moved/migrated to achieve load balancing and maintaining Service Level Agreement (SLA) standards.

ILminimize = min

$$\left(\sqrt{\sum_{i=1}^{n} \tfrac{1}{n} (PMiRemCPU - PMC_C \mu RemCPU)^2} + \sqrt{\sum_{i=1}^{n} \tfrac{1}{n} (PMiRemRAM - PMC_C \mu RemRAM)^2} \right.$$
$$\left. + \sqrt{\sum_{i=1}^{n} \tfrac{1}{n} (PMiRemNWB - PMC_C \mu RemNWB)^2} \right)$$

Here, the entire physical cluster is considered to calculate the workload instead of the only number of VMs in PM. To find the load imbalance metric, the objective function is applied, which attempts to minimize the imbalance load between each PM in the cluster.

To find the value of the objective function, each position of the grey wolf is mapped into the utilization of resources like CPU, RAM, and NW bandwidth of Physical Machines (PMs). The minimum value of the objective function (best fitness) is stored as an alpha score and the corresponding value of variables are stored as alpha position. Similarly, second best fitness and positions are stored as beta score and beta position followed by third best fitness and position are stored as delta score and delta position. In the next step, the search agents update their positions as per objective function. This process continues up to a maximum number of iterations.

4   Simulation Results and Comparison

To measure the performance of any load balancing technique, it's important to evaluate to what extent the imbalance level amongst PMs of heterogeneous capacities in the data center is minimized. For the evaluation, the degree of imbalance was measured against the different number of iterations, number of search agents, the number of PMs and number of runs. The evaluation was simulated in MATLAB environment.

The degree of imbalance (fitness function's value) was measured against the various number of Iterations, Search Agents, PMs and Runs. To measure the degree of imbalance against a different number of iterations for all the algorithms, a simulation environment was set up with 60 PMs in the datacenter, 100 SAs in search space and a different number of iterations with 10 different runs.

From the results of Table 1, it has been observed that GWO outperforms other algorithms against all the iterations. It has also been observed that the iGWO converges near optimal as increases the number of iterations. To measure the degree of imbalance against a different number of PMs for all the algorithms, a simulation environment was set up with different number of PMs, 100 search agents in search space and 100 iterations with 10 different runs.

From the results of Table 2, it has been observed that iGWO outperforms other algorithms for all the PMs. To measure the degree of imbalance against a different number of search agents in search space for all the algorithms, a simulation environment was set up with 60 PMs in the datacenter, a different number of search agents in search space and 100 iterations with 10 different runs.

Table 1. The degree of imbalance against number of iterations

Algos.	Number of iterations						
	100	150	200	250	300	350	400
HS	7.746	4.577	4.517	4.418	4.331	4.271	4.248
ABC	4.640	4.173	3.835	3.501	3.169	2.899	2.667
PSO	2.580	2.306	2.220	2.212	2.124	2.128	2.049
GWO	1.090	0.655	0.443	0.329	0.280	0.238	0.203
iGWO	**1.077**	**0.594**	**0.416**	**0.328**	**0.278**	**0.231**	**0.201**

Table 2. The degree of imbalance against number of PMs

Algos.	Number of PMs					
	10	20	40	60	80	100
HS	1.06	2.06	3.59	4.71	5.77	6.61
ABC	0.30	1.14	3.03	4.70	6.04	7.18
PSO	0.10	0.57	1.68	2.51	3.21	3.78
GWO	0.06	0.14	0.53	1.13	1.86	2.51
iGWO	**0.05**	**0.13**	**0.48**	**1.09**	**1.69**	**2.44**

From the results of Table 3, it has been observed that iGWO outperforms other algorithms for all the search agents. It has also been observed that the iGWO converges near optimal as increases number of search agents. To measure the degree of imbalance against a different number of runs for all the algorithms, a simulation environment was set up with 60 PMs in the datacenter, 100 search agents in search space and 100 iterations with a different number of runs.

Table 3. The degree of imbalance against number of search agents

Algos.	Number of search agents							
	50	100	150	200	250	300	350	400
HS	4.53	4.72	4.88	4.95	5.04	5.07	5.10	4.53
ABC	4.67	4.68	4.61	4.63	4.54	4.53	4.52	4.67
PSO	2.79	2.51	2.34	2.24	2.20	2.08	2.07	2.79
GWO	1.54	1.07	0.92	0.87	0.77	0.72	0.65	1.54
iGWO	**1.46**	**1.04**	**0.90**	**0.84**	**0.68**	**0.65**	**0.63**	**1.46**

From the results of Table 4, it has been observed that iGWO outperforms other algorithms for all the runs. It has also been observed that the iGWO converges near optimal as increases number of runs.

Table 4. The degree of imbalance against number of runs

Algos.	Number of runs					
	5	10	15	20	25	30
HS	3.55	3.60	3.59	3.57	3.55	3.59
ABC	2.96	3.05	3.07	3.05	3.06	3.04
PSO	1.67	1.67	1.67	1.66	1.69	1.66
GWO	0.55	0.53	0.52	0.53	0.52	0.53
iGWO	**0.46**	**0.51**	**0.48**	**0.49**	**0.48**	**0.50**

5   Conclusion

This paper proposed an improvement to the Grey Wolf Optimizer named iGWO and applied it for load balancing in the cloud which is a challenging and NP-hard problem. Different experiments carried out in terms of average value of an objective function(IL) against a different number of PMs, Search Agents, Iterations, and Runs for HS, ABC, PSO, original GWO and iGWO with their best-identified control parameters. The results prove that the proposed algorithm is found to be very effective due to near global optimal and fewer chances in local minima stagnation. An iGWO is simple to implement because it does not require to tune algorithm-specific parameters like other metaheuristics algorithms viz. HS, ABC, PSO, etc. An iGWO benefits from relatively less exploration than exploitation in comparison to HS, ABC, PSO, and original GWO. The results prove the effectiveness of iGWO to existing metaheuristic algorithms including GWO and it has an ability to become a useful algorithm for solving real-world optimization issues. This work can be extended to check other performance objective functions and multi-objective functions of load balancing in the cloud.

References

1. Kennedy, J., Eberhart, R. C.: Particle swarm optimization. In: IEEE International Conference on Neural Networks, Perth, Australia, pp. 1942–1948 (1995)
2. Karaboga, D., Basturk, B.: Artificial bee colony (ABC) optimization algorithm for solving constrained optimization problems. In: Melin, P., Castillo, O., Aguilar, Luis T., Kacprzyk, J., Pedrycz, W. (eds.) IFSA 2007. LNCS (LNAI), vol. 4529, pp. 789–798. Springer, Heidelberg (2007). https://doi.org/10.1007/978-3-540-72950-1_77
3. Geem, Z.W., Kim, J.H., Loganathan, G.V.: A new heuristic optimization algorithm: harmony search. Simulation **76**(2), 60–68 (2001)
4. Wolpert, D.H., Macready, W.G.: No free lunch theorems for optimization. IEEE Trans. Evol. Comput. **1**, 67–82 (1997)
5. Mirjalili, S., Mirjalili, S.M., Lewis, A.: Grey wolf optimizer. Adv. Eng. Softw. **69**, 46–61 (2014)
6. Muro, C., Escobedo, R., Spector, L., Coppinger, R.: Wolf-pack (Canis lupus) hunting strategies emerge from simple rules in computational simulations. Behav. Process. **88**, 192–197 (2011)

7. Li, K., Xu, G., Zhao, G., Dong, Y., Wang, D.: Cloud task scheduling based on load balancing ant colony optimization. In: Sixth IEEE Annual China Grid Conference, pp. 3–9 (2011)
8. Liu, Z., Wang, X.: A PSO-based algorithm for load balancing in virtual machines of cloud computing environment. In: Tan, Y., Shi, Y., Ji, Z. (eds.) ICSI 2012. LNCS, vol. 7331, pp. 142–147. Springer, Heidelberg (2012). https://doi.org/10.1007/978-3-642-30976-2_17
9. Dasgupta, K., Mandal, B., Dutta, P., Mondal, J.K., Dam, S.: A genetic algorithm (GA) based Load balancing strategy for cloud computing. In: First International Conference on Computational Intelligence: Modelling Techniques and Applications, vol. 10, pp. 340–347. Elsevier (2013)
10. Dhinesh Babu, L.D., Venkata Krishna, P.: Honey bee behaviour inspired load balancing of tasks in cloud computing environments. Appl. Soft Comput. 13(5), 2292–2303 (2013)
11. Kruekaew, B., Kimpan, W.: Virtual machine scheduling management on cloud computing using artificial bee colony. In: Internation Multiconference of Engineers and Computer Scientists (IMECS), Hong Kong, pp. 12–14 (2014)
12. keshk, A.E., El-Sisi, A.B., Tawfeek, M.A.: Cloud task scheduling for load balancing based on intelligent strategy. Int. J. Intell. Syst. Appl. 6, 25 (2014)
13. Rastkhadiv, F., Zamanifar, K.: Task scheduling based on load balancing using artificial bee colony in cloud computing environment. IJBR 7(5), 1058–1069 (2016)
14. Florence, P., Shanthi, V.: A load balancing model using firefly algorithm in cloud computing. J. Comput. Sci. 10(7), 1156–1165 (2014)
15. Gao, R., Wu, J.: Dynamic load balancing strategy for cloud computing with ant colony optimization. Future Internet 7, 465–483 (2015)
16. Thiruvenkadam, T., Kamalakkannan, P.: Energy efficient multi dimensional host load aware algorithm for virtual machine placement and optimization in cloud environment. IJST 8(17) (2015)
17. Norouzpour, O., Jafarzadeh, N.: Using harmony search algorithm for load balancing in cloud computing. IJST 8(23) (2015)
18. Tian, W., Zhao, Y., Zhong, Y., Xu, M., Jing, C.: A dynamic and integrated load-balancing scheduling algorithm for Cloud datacenters. In: International Conference on Cloud Computing and Intelligence Systems (CCIS), Beijing (2011)
19. Wood, T., Shenoy, P., Venkataramani, A.: Black-box and gray-box strategies for virtual machine migration. In: 4th USENIX Conference on Networked Systems Design and Implementation (NSDI), Berkeley (2007)

Indexed Coinduction in a Fibrational Setting

Decheng Miao[1]([⊠]) [iD] and Jianqing Xi[2] [iD]

[1] Shaoguan University, Shaoguan 512005, Guangdong, China
tony10860@126.com
[2] South China University of Technology,
Guangzhou 510640, Guangdong, China

Abstract. This paper provided some logical structures over fibration including comprehension and equation functor, then described semantic behavior by corecursion, also represented universal coinductive rule in a fibrational setting. Comparing the traditional methods, our works do not rely on special semantics computation context, which can analyze semantics elaborately of indexed coinductive data type and described its coinductive rule.

Keywords: Semantic behavior · Coinduction rule · Fibration · Lift
Corecursion

1 Introduction

Being the dual concepts of induction, coinduction [1] is a new method to research semantic behavior in programming. Coinduction whose math basis is coalgebra [2] observes dynamic behavior from outside, it provides a complementary method for induction to enhance semantic computation. Indexed coinduction is an important kind of coinduction whose semantics computation ability is stronger; it can deal with more complex data structure in programming.

As a new field in computer science, fibration has some applications such as database system [3] and programming [4]. In a fibrational setting, indexed coinductive data type and relation category describing its semantic behavior do not coexist in the same category, but constructing some lifted functors in total category to represent semantic computation and program logics of indexed coinduction abstractly. Hermida and Jacobs did substantial fundamental research in this field [5].

2 Semantic Property of Indexed Coinductive Data Type

All discuss objects in our work are based on small category [6], more details about fibration can be found in [6]. For category $\mathbb{C}$, let *Obj* $\mathbb{C}$ to be its objects set and *Mor* $\mathbb{C}$ to be its morphisms set. From the fibrational point of view, indexed coinductive data type is a common coinductive data type with discrete indexed objects including streams, lists and stacks. Based on the works from [7], we constructed indexed fibration in a fibrational setting to analyze semantic behavior of indexed coinductive data type, and provides a universal coinductive rule.

T. Hu et al. (Eds.): ICA3PP 2018 Workshops, LNCS 11338, pp. 10–16, 2018.
https://doi.org/10.1007/978-3-030-05234-8_2

Definition 1. Let $P : \mathbb{T} \to \mathbb{B}$ be a fibration between two small categories $\mathbb{T}$ and $\mathbb{B}$, and its base category $\mathbb{B}$ has products. Let $\Delta : \mathbb{B} \to \mathbb{B}$ be a diagonal endo-functor above $\mathbb{B}$, it maps $\forall C \in Obj\,\mathbb{B}$ to product object $C \times C$. The pullback of P along Δ constructs fibration $Rel(P) : Rel(\mathbb{T}) \to \mathbb{B}$, and $Rel(P)$ is a relation fibration of P.

The property pullback-preserving of Definition 1 ensures that fiber $Rel(\mathbb{T})_C$ above C on $Rel(P)$ is isomorphism up to fiber $\mathbb{T}_{C \times C}$ above $C \times C$ on P, i.e., $Rel(\mathbb{T})_C \cong \mathbb{T}_{C \times C}$. The procedure of constructing a new fibration by a given fibration is called to be change of base. For example, we construct $Rel(P)$ by change of base in Definition 1 from P. Change of base preserves structure, such as preserves fibered terminal objects [5], that is, if P has truth functor T_P, then $Rel(P)$ has truth functor $T_{Rel(P)}$, and $T_{Rel(P)}(C) = T_P(C \times C)$.

Theorem 1. Let $P : \mathbb{T} \to \mathbb{B}$ be a fibration or bifibration between two small categories $\mathbb{T}$ and $\mathbb{B}$, and $T_P : \mathbb{B} \to \mathbb{T}$ be a truth functor of P. There $\exists I \in Obj\,\mathbb{B}$, where I is a discrete indexed object in base category $\mathbb{B}$. Let indexed functor $P/I : \mathbb{T}/T_P(I) \to \mathbb{B}/I$ be $P/I(u) = P(u) : P(Y) \to I \in Obj\,\mathbb{B}/I$ for $\forall u : Y \to T_P(I) \in Obj\,\mathbb{T}/T_P(I)$. Then indexed functor P/I is also a fibration or bifibration.

Proof. We write f^* and $^*f$ a re-indexed and an opposite functor induced by f [7] respectively. For $\forall f : C \to D \in Mor\,\mathbb{B}$, there exists a Cartesian arrow $f_X^\downarrow : f^*(X) \to X$ above f on fibration P satisfying $P(X) = D$. And there also exists a unique morphism $w : T_P(I) \to f^*(X)$ such that $v = f_X^\downarrow \circ w$ and $P(v) = f \circ h$ (Fig. 1). Let $\alpha : D \to I \in Obj\,\mathbb{B}/I$, $\beta : C \to I \in Obj\,\mathbb{B}/I$. Then $\gamma : P(u) \to \alpha = P(Y) \to D \in Mor\,\mathbb{B}/I$, $\delta : P(u) \to \beta = P(Y) \to C \in Mor\,\mathbb{B}/I$, which satisfies diagram commuting, that is, $\gamma = f \circ \delta$. In total category $\mathbb{T}/T_P(I)$ on functor P/I, there exist two objects $s : X \to T_P(I) \in Obj\,\mathbb{T}/T_P(I)$, $t : f^*(X) \to T_P(I) \in Obj\,\mathbb{T}/T_P(I)$, we have $g : u \to s = Y \to X \in Mor\,\mathbb{T}/T_P(I)$. Then there exists a unique morphism $k : u \to t = Y \to f^*(X)$ satisfying diagram commuting $g = f_X^\downarrow \circ k$. $f_X^\downarrow$ is a Cartesian arrow of f on functor P/I, so if P is a fibration, then the functor P/I is also a fibration.

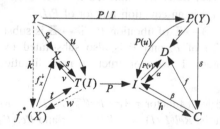

Fig. 1. Cartesian morphism $f_X^\downarrow$ of P/I above f

Let $m : Z \to T_P(I) \in Obj\,\mathbb{T}/T_P(I)$ be an object in total category $\mathbb{T}/T_P(I)$. Then $P/I(m) = \alpha$ by the definition of functor P/I. Let $f_\downarrow^Z : Z \to {}^*f(Z)$ be an opposite Cartesian arrow of f on P (Fig. 2). The diagram commutes $\alpha = \beta \circ f$ in slice category $\mathbb{B}/I$, there exists an unique morphism $n : {}^*f(Z) \to T_P(I)$ in total category $\mathbb{T}/T_P(I)$ on functor P/I, which satisfies diagram commuting $m = n \circ f_\downarrow^Z$. By Definition 4 $f_\downarrow^Z$ is an opposite Cartesian arrow of f on functor P/I, namely, if P is an opposite fibration, then the indexed functor P/I is also an opposite fibration.

Therefore, if P is a fibration or bifibration, the single-sorted indexed functor P/I is also a fibration or bifibration.

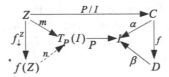

Fig. 2. Opposite Cartesian morphism $f_\downarrow^Z$ of P/I above f

Theorem 1 proves that indexed fibration P/I and fibration P have the same properties of fibration or bifibration, and also presents a construction method of indexed fibration. In fact, change of base of P along domain functor $dom : \mathbb{B}/I \to \mathbb{B}$ can construct a indexed fibration $P/I : \mathbb{T}/T_P(I) \to \mathbb{B}/I$. For $\forall \alpha : C \to I \in Obj\,\mathbb{B}/I$, the fiber $\mathbb{T}_C$ above C on P is isomorphism up to the fiber $(\mathbb{T}/T(I))_\alpha$ above α on P/I [7]. And if P has truth functor, then the indexed fibration P/I constructed by P has also truth functor.

Definition 2. Let $P/I : \mathbb{T}/T_P(I) \to \mathbb{B}/I$ be an indexed fibration, base category $\mathbb{B}/I$ has products. Let $\Delta/I : \mathbb{B}/I \to \mathbb{B}/I$ be a diagonal endo-functor in slice category $\mathbb{B}/I$. Then Δ/I maps $\forall \alpha \in \mathbb{B}/I$ to product object $\alpha \times \alpha$. The pullback of P/I along Δ/I constructs a fibration $Rel(P/I) : Rel(\mathbb{T}/T_P(I)) \to \mathbb{B}/I$, $Rel(P/I)$ is relation fibration of P/I.

Definition 3. Let $P : \mathbb{T} \to \mathbb{B}$ be a bifibration satisfying Beck-Chevalley condition [5, 7] between two small categories $\mathbb{T}$ and $\mathbb{B}$, P has truth functor, and base category $\mathbb{B}$ has product. Let $T_{P/I}$ be a truth functor of indexed fibration P/I. Then $Eq_{P/I} = {}^*(\delta/I) \circ T_{P/I} : \mathbb{B}/I \to Rel(\mathbb{T}/T_P(I))$ is an equation functor of P/I.

The truth functor $T_P : \mathbb{B} \to \mathbb{T}$ of fibration $P : \mathbb{T} \to \mathbb{B}$ is substituted by the equation functor $Eq_P : \mathbb{B} \to Rel(\mathbb{T})$ of P, and P is also substituted by its relation fibration $Rel(P)$, then by Theorem 1 we construct a new fibration $Rel(P)/I : Rel(\mathbb{T})/Eq_P(I) \to \mathbb{B}/I$.

Definition 4. Let the ad joint functor $\tau \dashv \sigma : Rel(\mathbb{T}/T_P(I)) \to Rel(\mathbb{T})/Eq_P(I)$ satisfies diagram commuting, that is, $Rel(P/I) = Rel(P)/I \circ \tau$ and $Rel(P)/I = Rel(P/I) \circ \sigma$. If $Rel(P)/I$ has a right ad joint functor $Eq_{(P/I)}$ such that $Eq_{(P/I)} = \tau \circ Eq_{P/I}$, then $Rel(P)/I \circ \tau \dashv \sigma \circ Eq_{(P/I)}$, we call $Rel(P)/I \circ \tau$ is quotient functor of indexed fibration P/I. Write $Rel(P)/I \circ \tau$ for $Q_{P/I}$, and $Q_{P/I} \dashv Eq_{P/I}$.

We construct relation fibration $Rel(P/I)$ of P/I, and equation functor $Eq_{P/I}$ and quotient functor $Q_{P/I}$ of P/I. Let F be an endo-functor in base category $\mathbb{B}/I$ on $Rel(P/I)$, $F^\perp$ be an endo-functor in total category $Rel(\mathbb{T}/T_P(I))$ on $Rel(P/I)$. If it satisfies diagram commuting $Rel(P/I) \circ F^\perp = F \circ Rel(P/I)$, and the following isomorphism holds, i.e., $Eq_{P/I} \circ F \cong F^\perp \circ Eq_{P/I}$ and $F \circ Q_{P/I} \cong Q_{P/I} \circ F^\perp$, then $F^\perp$ is a lifting equation-preserving of F about $Rel(P/I)$ in total category $Rel(\mathbb{T}/T_P(I))$.

Indexed coinductive data type vF, as the carrier of terminal F-coalgebra, is maximal fixed point of functor F. The functor F denotes syntax destructor of vF, and its morphism out observes semantic behaviors of vF from outside during its syntax destructing. Applying equation functor $Eq_{P/I}$ of indexed fibration P/I to map F-coalgebra (α, r) to a $F^\perp$-coalgebra $Eq_{P/I}(\alpha, r) = (Eq_{P/I}(\alpha), Eq_{P/I}(r) : Eq_{P/I}(\alpha) \rightarrow Eq_{P/I}(F(\alpha))$ $\cong F^\perp(Eq_{P/I}(\alpha)))$. Accordingly, $Eq_{P/I}(vF)$ is the carrier of terminal $F^\perp$-coalgebra, namely, equation functor $Eq_{P/I}$ preserves terminal objects.

Write $Coalg(Eq_{P/I})$ for functor from F-coalgebra category $Coalg_F$ to $F^\perp$-coalgebra category $Coalg_{F^\perp}$, it maps objects and morphisms in base category $\mathbb{B}/I$ on relation fibration $Rel(P/I)$ to those correspondingly in total category $Rel(\mathbb{T}/T_P(I))$ by equation functor $Eq_{P/I}$. Therefore, functor $Coalg(Eq_{P/I})$ establishes relationship between $Coalg_F$ and $Coalg_{F^\perp}$ further.

Let $(Eq_{P/I}(vF), out^\perp : Eq_{P/I}(vF) \rightarrow F^\perp(Eq_{P/I}(vF)))$ be a terminal $F^\perp$-coalgebra in total category $Rel(\mathbb{T}/T_P(I))$ on relation fibration $Rel(P/I)$. Then $out^\perp$ is a homomorphism image of out by the action of functor $Coalg(Eq_{P/I})$, that is, $Coalg(Eq_{P/I})$ $(out) = out^\perp$. Terminal property of terminal $F^\perp$-coalgebra ensures that $out^\perp$ is up to unique isomorphism, whose existence provides extremely convenience for analyzing accurately semantic behavior and depicting abstractly its co-inductive rule of co-inductive data type.

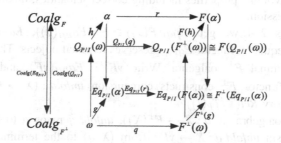

Fig. 3. Ad-joint properties of $Coalg(Eq_{P/I})$ and $Coalg(Q_{P/I})$

Similar to $Coalg(Eq_{P/I})$, write $Coalg(Q_{P/I})$ for the functor from $Coalg_{F^\perp}$ to $Coalg_F$. Then we have $Coalg(Q_{P/I}) \dashv Coalg(Eq_{P/I})$ by the ad joint property of ad joint functor in [5]. For each $F^\perp$-coalgebra $(\omega, q : \omega \rightarrow F^\perp(\omega))$, $\omega : X \rightarrow T_P(I) \in \textbf{\textit{Obj Rel}}$ $(\mathbb{T}/T_P(I))$, $Coalg(Q_{P/I})(q) = Q_{P/I}(\omega) \rightarrow Q_{P/I}(F^\perp(\omega)) \cong F(Q_{P/I}(\omega))$, that is, $Coalg(Q_{P/I})(q) = Q_{P/I}(q)$. Then $Q_{P/I}(q)$ is a homomorphism image of q by the action of functor $Coalg(Q_{P/I})$, seen if from Fig. 3. If $g : \omega \rightarrow Eq_{P/I}(\alpha)$ is a $F^\perp$-coalgebra morphism from q to $Eq_{P/I}(r)$, then the F-coalgebra morphism $h : Q_{P/I}(\omega) \rightarrow \alpha$ from $Q_{P/I}(q)$ to r is F-coalgebra homomorphism above g. Similarly, g is a $F^\perp$-coalgebra homomorphism above h.

The left ad joint $Coalg(Q_{P/I})$ of functor $Coalg(Eq_{P/I})$ makes an intuitional inter-deducible relation between F-coalgebra $Q_{P/I}(\omega)$ as its carrier and $F^\perp$-coalgebra ω as its carrier, which provides a succinct and consistent modelling method for formal description of co-inductive rule of indexed co-inductive data type, vF as carrier of terminal coalgebra. In other words, if functor $Coalg(Eq_{P/I})$ preserves terminal objects, then the lifting equation-preserving $F^\perp$ of F on $Rel(P/I)$ generates a soundness co-inductive rule.

3 Coinductive Rule

For a fibration with equation functor and quotient functor, formal description of coinductive rules and semantic behavior analysis of indexed coinductive data type are coherent [5]. Let $P : \mathbb{T} \to \mathbb{B}$ and $P/I : \mathbb{T}/T_P(I) \to \mathbb{B}/I$ also satisfy the requirements of Definition 3, Then P/I has co-inductive rule, vF as indexed co-inductive data type.

From the category theoretical point of view, co-recursive computation of coinductive data type stems from terminal coalgebra semantics [2]. For $\forall \alpha : C \to I \in Obj\,\mathbb{B}/I$, and $vF \in Obj\,\mathbb{B}/I$, we apply F to construct co-recursive operation $unfold : (\alpha \to F(\alpha)) \to \alpha \to vF$ of indexed coinductive data type in base category $\mathbb{B}/I$. For each F-coalgebra $(\alpha, r : \alpha \to F(\alpha))$, $unfold\ r$ maps r to the unique F-coalgebra morphism $unfold\ r : \alpha \to vF$ from (α, r) to the terminal F-coalgebra (vF, out). The operation $unfold$ derived from terminal coalgebra semantics is a core-cursion parameterized operation of coinductive data type, whose corecursion computation has some favorable properties including correct semantics, flexible expansibility and succinct expression.

By Definitions 2–4 we get $Eq_{P/I}(F(\alpha)) \cong F^\perp(Eq_{P/I}(\alpha))$, $Eq_{P/I}(F(vF)) \cong F^\perp(Eq_{P/I}(vF))$, and equation functor $Eq_{P/I}$ preserves terminal objects. Then $Eq_{P/I}(vF)$ is the carrier of terminal $F^\perp$-coalgebra. Write $vF^\perp = Eq_{P/I}(vF)$, and $X = Eq_{P/I}(\alpha)$. Applying endo- functor $F^\perp$ constructs corecursion $unfold : (X \to F^\perp(X)) \to X \to vF^\perp$ in total category $Rel(\mathbb{T}/T_P(I))$.

For any $F^\perp$-coalgebra $(X, q : X \to F^\perp(X))$, $unfold\ q$ maps q to the unique $F^\perp$-coalgebra morphism $unfold\ q : X \to vF^\perp$ from (X, q) to the terminal $F^\perp$-coalgebra $(vF^\perp, out^\perp)$. For $\forall \alpha \in Obj\,\mathbb{B}/I$, $\exists X \in Obj\,Rel(\mathbb{T}/T_P(I))$. The following is coinductive rule of indexed coinductive data type with universality.

$Coind_{Uni} : (X \to F^\perp(X)) \to X \to Eq_{P/I}(vF)$.

If $(X, q : X \to F^\perp(X))$ is a $F^\perp$-coalgebra over F-coalgebra $(\alpha, r : \alpha \to F(\alpha))$, then $Coind_{Uni}X\ q$ is $F^\perp$-coalgebra homomorphism over $unfold\ r$.

Example 1. The element type of stream or infinite sequence is designated by index I, such as natural number Nat, integer Int and character $Char$, $\forall I \in Obj\,\mathbb{B}$. For any stream $\alpha : S \to I \in Obj\,\mathbb{B}/I$, we can construct an endo-functor $F : \alpha \to I \times \alpha$ on $\mathbb{B}/I$, where $head : \alpha \to I$ is head function of this stream, and $tail : \alpha \to \alpha$ is tail function erased head element. For any stream property $R \in Obj\,Rel(\mathbb{T}/T_P(I))$ in total category

$Rel(\mathbb{T}/T_P(I))$ on relation fibration $Rel(P/I)$ of indexed fibration P/I, such as bi-simulation, then for another stream object $\beta : S' \to I$ in $\mathbb{B}/I$, a coinduction of α and β on bi-simulation property R is established:

Object R is relation of bi-simulation between two streams α and β, if and only if $\forall(\alpha, \beta) \in R$, $head(\alpha) = head(\beta)$, and $(tail(\alpha), tail(\beta)) \in R$.

Let the stream $Stream(I)$ be carrier vF of terminal F-coalgebra $(vF, out : vF \to F(vF))$ in base category $\mathbb{B}/I$. For each F-coalgebra $(\alpha, r : \alpha \to F(\alpha))$, it is lifted to a $F^{\perp}$-coalgebra $(X, q : X \to F^{\perp}(X))$ by relation fibration $Rel(P/I)$, which satisfies diagram commuting, i.e., $F \circ Rel(P/I)(X) = Rel(P/I) \circ F^{\perp}(X)$. The terminality of terminal F-coalgebra defines a corecursive operation *unfold r* on $Stream(I)$, which executes the judgment of indexed coinductive data type $Stream(I)$; another corecursive operation by the terminality of terminal $F^{\perp}$-coalgebra describes semantic behavior of $Stream(I)$. If q lies above r, then $Coind_{Uni}X\,q$ is a $F^{\perp}$-coalgebra homomorphism on *unfold r*, and iterating each property R in total category $Rel(\mathbb{T}/T_P(I))$ on relation fibration $Rel(P/I)$, $R \in Obj\,Rel(\mathbb{T}/T_P(I))$, we can obtain the semantic set $\{R(X,X)|X = Eq_{P/I}(\alpha), \forall \alpha \in Obj\,\mathbb{B}/I\}$, which depicts behaviors of $Stream(I)$.

In Example 1, *unfold r* describes mapping relationship between streams α and its semantic behavior intuitively. The existence of *unfold r* provides a effectual way of homomorphism from coalgebra to its terminal coalgebra, so we can establish coinduction definition principle, that is, to define function *unfold r* : $\alpha \to Stream(I)$, we only need to construct corresponding operation r on α, and let (α, r) be a F-coalgebra, $F(\alpha) = I \times \alpha$; meanwhile, the uniqueness of *unfold r* can prove two homomorphism are equivalent further. Therefore, we have coinduction proof principle, that is, to prove $m, n : \alpha \to Stream(I)$ is equivalent, we only need to prove m and n also is homomorphism from the same coalgebra (α, r) to its terminal F-coalgebra $(Stream(I), out : Stream(I) \to F(Stream(I)))$, namely, m and n also equal *unfold r*.

Example 1 proposes some fibrational tools, such as indexed fibration, equation functor and quotient functor and so on, to analyze deeply semantic behavior and coinductive rule of stream in a fibrational setting, which has math foundation for discussing semantics computation and program logics of formal languages.

4   Conclusions

Most related literatures concentrate on coinduction, but discussing to indexed coinduction is still in a preliminary stage currently. There exist some unsolved problems in semantics computation and program logic. For instance, analysis of semantics behavior and description of coinductive rule, especially the latter is almost generated automatically, which is short of solid math foundations and succinct formal description means. We discussed semantic behavior and coinductive rule of indexed coinductive data type systematically and deeply in a fibrational setting. Comparing with traditional methods such as coalgebras and category theory, the advantages of our works are as follows: we analyzed semantic behavior of indexed coinductive data type succinctly in a fibrational setting, promoted the abilities of processing and proving of programming for semantic behavior of indexed coinductive data type; we also presented and described universal coinductive rule of indexed co-inductive data type abstractly in a fibrational setting, not relying on particular computing circumstance; our works proposed solid math foundations, succinct and uniform description to semantics computation and program logic.

We modelled on slice category $\mathbb{B}/I$, but the index I only focuses on some particular single-sorted indexed coinductive data type; it is difficult to handle more complex many-sorted indexed coinductive data type, take mutual recursive as an example. Thus extending discrete index object I of single-sorted indexed fibration to indexed category $\mathbb{C}$ to construct many-sorted fibration, representing many-sorted indexed coinductive data type in $\mathbb{B}$ by index set $Obj\,\mathbb{C}$, modelling semantic behavior of many-sorted indexed coinductive data type in indexed category $\mathbb{C}$ by fibration $G : \mathbb{B} \to \mathbb{C}$, selecting different program logics pointing at different indexes are our future works.

Acknowledgements. This study is supported by Guangdong Province High School Outstanding Young Teacher Training Project, China (Grant No. YQ2014155) and Guangdong Provincial Natural Science Foundation, China (Grant No. 2018A0303130274).

References

1. Greiner, J.: Programming with inductive and co-inductive types. School of Computer Science, Carnegie Mellon University, Pittsburgh, USA (1992)
2. Rutten, J.: Universal coalgebra: a theory of systems. Theor. Comput. Sci. **249**(1), 3–80 (2000)
3. Johnson, M., Rosebrugh, R., Wood, R.J.: Lenses, fibrations and universal translations. Math. Struct. Comput. Sci. **22**, 25–42 (2012)
4. Miao, D.C., Xi, J.Q., Jia, L.Y., et al.: Formal language algebraic model. J. South China Univ. Technol. (Nat. Sci. Ed.) **39**(10), 74–78 (2011)
5. Hermida, C., Jacobs, B.: Structural induction and coinduction in a fibrational setting. Inf. Comput. **145**(2), 107–152 (1998)
6. Barr, M., Wells, C.: Category Theory for Computing Science. Prentice-Hall, NewYork (1990)
7. Ghani, N., Johann, P., Fumex, C.: Indexed induction and coinduction, fibrationally. Log. Methods Comput. Sci. **9**(3–6), 1–31 (2013)

Porting and Optimizing VASP on the SW26010

Leisheng Li[1]($\boxtimes$), Qiao Sun[1], Xin Liu[2], Changmao Wu[1],
Haitao Zhao[1], and Changyou Zhang[1]

[1] Laboratory of Parallel Software and Computational Science,
Institute of Software, Chinese Academy of Sciences, Beijing, China
{leisheng, sunqiao, changmao, haitao,
changyou}@iscas.ac.cn
[2] National Research Centre of Parallel Computer Engineering and Technology,
Wuxi, Jiangsu, China
yyylx@263.net

Abstract. VASP (Vienna Ab initio Simulation Package) is a prevalent first-principle software framework. It is so widely used that its runtime usually dominates the usage of current supercomputers. The porting and optimization of VASP to the Sunway TaihuLight supercomputer, a newly heterogeneous many-core platform based on SW26010 CPU, becomes of great importance. In this paper, we focus on the challenges in porting and optimizing VASP on the SW26010 CPU. Optimizations on three types of time-consuming kernels, which include matrix operations, FFT, and certain domain-specific computing primitives, are carried out base on thorough performance profiling. The experimental results are shown by the case of RELAX, where speedup of 2.90x and 4.48x is sustained respectively for both of the iterative diagonalization methods in VASP, RMM-DIIS (RMM) and block Davidson (DAV).

Keywords: SW26010 · Many-core CPU · Density functional theory
VASP · LDM

1 Introduction

The Sunway TaihuLight, is the first one in the world with peak performance of 125 PFlops and a sustained Linpack performance of 93 PFlops [1]. The Sunway TaihuLight supercomputer is equipped with SW26010 CPUs. Each processor includes four core-groups (CGs). Each CG includes one management processing element (MPE), one computing processing element (CPE) cluster with 64 CPEs and one memory controller (MC). The four CGs are connected via the network on chip (NoC). In terms of the memory hierarchy, each CPE has 64 KB scratch pad memory (SPM), named as Local Data Memory (LDM). The LDM can be configured as either a fast buffer or a software-emulated cache, but in most cases we need a user-controlled buffering scheme to achieve good performance. The memory controller also supports DMA (Direct Memory Access) for mutual data transportation between the LDM and the main memory.

The software-developing environment on the SW26010 CPU includes both serial and parallel programming languages. There are compilers supporting mainstream

© Springer Nature Switzerland AG 2018
T. Hu et al. (Eds.): ICA3PP 2018 Workshops, LNCS 11338, pp. 17–26, 2018.
https://doi.org/10.1007/978-3-030-05234-8_3

programming languages including C, C++ and Fortran and parallel programming modals including MPI, Pthreads, OpenACC and so on.

To make full use of its computing power, scientific and engineering computing software needs customizing and subtle optimization on the Sunway TaihuLight supercomputer. Worth mentioning is that two scientific applications on this super-computer won the ACM Gordon Bell Prize in 2016 and 2017 respectively [2, 3].

The Vienna Ab-initio Simulation Package (VASP) is a widely used materials science application for performing ab-initio electronic structure calculations and quantum-mechanical molecular dynamics (MD) simulations using pseudopotentials or the projector augmented wave method and a plane wave basis set [4]. It is of great significance to port and optimize VASP to Sunway TaihuLight.

By the time when this paper was writing, no related study on porting and opti-mizing any first-principle computing software including VASP has been reported on SW26010. Because CPU+GPU and CPU+MIC are the architectures that are compa-rable to SW26010, we study the relevant work about them. On the GPU platforms, a line of research has been done on the optimization of VASP. Maintz et al. have accelerated Block Davidson algorithm [5]. And Hutchinson et al. have boosted the exact-exchange computing kernel of VASP [6]. Later, Hacene et al. have suggested an accelerated version of VASP on the basis of CUBLAS CUFFT, and several high-performance hotspot kernels by CUDA. Based on these works, VASP has been offi-cially released Nvidia GPU-oriented acceleration version [7]. Wende et al. have developed MPI/OpenMP version based on the Intel MIC architecture [8].

2   The Performance Analysis of VASP on MPE

2.1   The Main Computing Steps of VASP

According to the literature [9], the main calculation steps of VASP are as follows:

1. Generating the trial-wavefunctions. The trial-wavefunction is a linear combination of the plane wave basis set, and in the reciprocal space, the wavefunction arrays in VASP store the coefficients of these basis functions.
2. Calculating Hartree potential, kinetic potential, exchange-correlation potential and pseudopotential, and their effect on the wavefunctions. Some of these calculations are performed in the real space, some in the reciprocal space. Fast Fourier Trans-forms (FFT) is used to transform the real space and the reciprocal space repre-sentation of the wavefunctions. Some calculations about pseudopotential can be performed either in the real space or in the reciprocal space. And for large systems, it is common that these calculations are preferably performed in the real space due to higher efficiency. Because of this, in this paper we only consider the case where computation is done only in the real space.
3. Performing subspace diagonalization and iterative diagonalization. Two algorithms, RMM and DAV, are then used in the iterative diagonalization Subspace diago-nalization, which are described in detail in the reference [10].
4. Computing the occupied states and the new free energy.
5. Computing the new charge density and the mixed density.

6. Computing the total energy difference and judge whether self-consistent convergence is achieved.

The analysis of the hotspots of VASP in references [5–8] corresponds to the above steps. However, the results in the above research are based on the Intel X86 platform. Profiling on the SW26010 CPU needs to be done so that the performance characteristics of VASP can be revealed.

2.2 The Parameters of Compiling and Running

The Fortran compiler of SW26010 supports the whole set of features of Fortran 90, so that the source code of VASP is able to be compiled smoothly. In the first step, the original version of VASP 5.3.5 was ported merely to the MPE of SW26010. VASP depends heavily on LAPACK and BLAS with version number 3.5.0. FFT module can be implemented using FFTW, or the built-in FFTFurth code can be used. We use FFTFurth as the baseline because the CPE code is based on it. The code compilation is optimized by using option -O3.

It is found that some parameters do have great impact on the overall performance. Since each K point of the RELAX case has 96 wave functions, 24 processes are used for better load balancing. NCORE is the number of processors on which one wavefunction is distributed. It is set to 1 to avoid the data exchange of FFT transform. NSIM is the number of wavefunctions optimized simultaneously and its default value is 4.

2.3 The Profiling of VASP on MPE

The performance of VASP on MPE is profiled by instrumentation-based method. The timing code is added to each function to count the execution time of each function. In order to perform comprehensive performance evaluation and optimization of VASP, three test cases are used to profile, including the electronic structure relaxation (RELAX), the density of state calculation (DOS) and the energy band calculation (BAND). Since it is found that the calculation hotspots of the studied cases concentrate on the self-consistent iterative computation, the performance characteristics are similar. In this paper, the RELAX case is used to exemplify the achievement of this paper.

The most time consuming functions with their execution time are shown in Error! Reference source not found. There is a triply-nested loop in the EDDAV function, which can be replaced by ZGEMM. The hotspots of RMM and DAV algorithms are basically the same, so as to improve the performance of these functions can accelerate both RMM and DAV (Table 1).

For ZGEMM, an optimized BLAS library has been developed for SW26010 by ISCAS. The performance of ZGEMM in this BLAS is good enough to decrease the percentage of ZGEMM execution time to an acceptable degree. In this paper, the optimization methods for the other functions are described in detail as the next sections.

Table 1. The hotspot of VASP

Category	Functions	Step	% time of RMM	% time of DAV
Matrix operation	ZGEMM	(3)	13.19	36.46
	RPRO.DGEMM	(2)	1.24	0.06
	RACC0MU.DGEMM	(2)	0.80	1.12
FFT	FFT.X	(2)(3) (5)	15.61	11.47
	FFT.Y	(2)(3) (5)	15.53	11.36
	FFT.Z	(2)(3) (5)	16.76	12.00
Hotspots of VASP	ECCP.LOCAL	(3)(6)	4.72	0.69
	ECCP.KIN	(3)(6)	0.60	0.09
	VHMAIL	(2)	2.39	1.77
	KINHAMIL	(2)	0.29	0.20
	PW_CHARGE	(5)	0.54	0.28
	CREXP_MUL_WAVE	(2)	0.31	0.01
	WORK_MUL_CREXP	(2)	0.31	0.38

3 Optimizing FFT

The grid in VASP is three-dimensional, which leads to 3D FFT computation. The dimensions in the directions X, Y and Z are N_x, N_y and N_z, respectively. The basic steps of the optimized three-dimensional FFT are as follows:

1. Execute $N_y \times N_z$ FFTs in the X-dimension.
2. Execute $N_x \times N_z$ FFTs in the Y-dimension.
3. Execute $N_x \times N_y$ FFTs in the Z-dimension.

   The data of grid points is stored with the X-dimension, which is as the major order. The vector is expressed as $\left[x_0, \cdots, x_{n_x \times n_y \times n_z - 1}\right]$, where x_n is a complex. The elements from x_0 to $x_{n_x - 1}$ store the data of the first X-dimension and elements x_0 to $x_{n_x \times n_y - 1}$ store the data of the first XY-plane. By so doing, all of the N_z XY-planes make up the vector data of the entire grid points.

   The code FFTFurth in VASP was developed by Jürgen Furthmüller [12]. It supports FFT in certain lengths, which can be disposed into small prime numbers, such as 2, 3, 5 and 7.

   In general, the small number of grids in each dimension leads to a small scale FFT computation. Each CPE of SW26010 owns 64 KB LDM, which can accommodate 4096 double complexes. For most VASP cases, the computation of FFT in one dimension can be calculated in the LDM of one CPE, since that one CPE can accommodate several one-dimensional FFTs.

   The number of X-dimensional FFTs is $N_y \times N_z$ and they are distributed among the 64 CPEs in the way shown in Fig. 1. The data is continuously stored so that DMA can achieve a high efficiency for both reading and writing. The more data is accessed by DMA, the higher the utilization of the bandwidth is. Therefore, each CPE should process data in X-dimension as much as possible.

Under a special condition, if the LDM of one CPE can hold the data of one XY-plane, the entire plane stored in continuous memory locations can be assigned to a CPE as a basic unit. X-dimensional FFTs can be executed firstly, and then that of the Y-dimension. Finally, the data can be written back into memory by DMA.

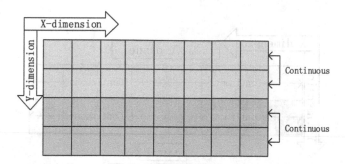

Fig. 1. X-dimensional data. Each CPE accesses continuous data

As for the cases where XY-plane data cannot be entirely loaded into LDM in one time, FFT in the Y-dimension will be executed in the following way. The stride between two adjacent elements in the Y-dimension is N_x, and slow non-continuous memory access occurs when a CPE tries to load the rows in the Y-dimension. Therefore, we try to assembly the longest data in the X-dimension that can be accessed continuously, all of which forms multiple columns in the Y dimension.

The whole XY-plane data is assigned to each CPE and form a with a basic workload unit. Firstly, M_y the number of maximum Y-dimensional FFTs that one CPE LDM can hold is calculated. The CPE loads M_y elements of each X-dimension for N_y times. The data is assembled into M_y entire Y-dimensional FFTs, and then the data are written back to memory after the calculation. The data access mode is shown in Fig. 2.

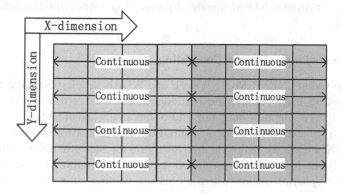

Fig. 2. Y-dimensional data assembling. Each CPE accesses data with same color

The implementation of Z-dimensional FFT is similar to that of the Y-dimension. The data of $N_x \times N_y$ Z-dimensional columns are assigned evenly to each CPE. Similarly, M_z the maximum number of Z-dimensional FFT that one CPE can bed hold is calculated. The continuous data in X-dimension are loaded into LDM by DMA for N_z times to form Z-dimensional FFTs. The access mode is shown in Fig. 3.

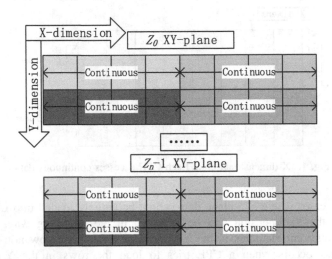

Fig. 3. Z-dimensional data assembling. Each CPE accesses data with same color

4 Optimizing the Hotspot Functions of VASP

4.1 Loop Parallelism Functions

The hotspot functions like ECCP, KINHAMIL, VHAMIL and so on perform calculations in SIMD (Single Instruction Multiple Data) mode, which are suitable to be accelerated for many-core CPU using loop parallelism. The basic idea is to divide vectors into 64 parts, so that each CPE is able to compute its own share. The CPE code of the hotspot functions can be accelerated by several to dozens of times faster than the MPE baseline.

4.2 The Piecewise Continuous Computing

The data involved in CREXP_MUL_WAVE and WORK_MUL_CREXP can be called piecewise continuously, because the pseudopotential data is distributed only in an atom-centric sphere. The distribution of grid points in the spherical region is shown in Fig. 4, which is exemplified by a simplified two-dimensional grid. The array NONLR_S%NLI holds the indices in the global grid for each grid point in the spherical region, namely the index of the wavefunctions and the Hamiltonion potential array.

Due to the spherical region where atoms are confined, the number of elements related to pseudopotential is small. If they are assigned to 64 CPEs evenly, the data of each CPE is too small in volume to be handled efficiently, and the continuous data may

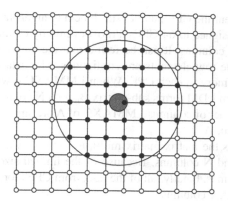

Fig. 4. Grid points in pseudopotential region.

be assigned to different CPEs. Therefore, fewer CPEs are used to compute for each phase factor array. Empirically it is a good choice to use 16 CPEs for each.

Firstly, array NLI is divided into sixteen parts evenly, and each CPE loads its own NLI data. If the difference between the value of the present element and the next element is 1, it indicates the wavefunctions or Hamiltonion data are stored continuously. Otherwise, it means the next element is not located continuously, and the present element is the tail of the current continuous data segment. CPE loads the data segment to LDM, and writes the result data back after computing. This algorithm can greatly improve the efficiency of DMA.

5 Optimizing DGEMM

It should be firstly noted that the matrix in the VASP is stored in the row-major order, not preferable for BLAS functions. Thus matrix operation parameters of the VASP should be modified in compliance with the actual operational logic. In this section, we describe the matrix operations in the row-order storage.

In the RMM and the DAV algorithm, DGEMM is called in two functions: RACC0MU and RRPOMU. The matrix scale of DGEMM in RACC0MU and RRPOMU is limited by the largest atomic angular quantum count (LMMAXC) in the system, NSIM and the maximal number of grid points in the pseudopotential spherical region (INDMAX). For this type of matrix-matrix multiplication, the use of a general DGEMM may lead to a less satisfactory performance; and thus a special DGEMM kernel is developed.

The matrix A of DGEMM in RACC0MU is an array named TMP, which is generated by the predecessor code. Data is stored in the row major order with a number of rows M whose maximal value is 2 * NSIM, and that of columns to be LMMAXC. The matrix B is NONLR_S%RPROJ, with a maximum number of rows to be LMMAXC, and that of columns to be INDMAX. The output matrix C has M rows and INDMAX columns.

In order to implement the CPE parallelism, blocking algorithm is applied to matrix B. First, the data are assigned to 64 CPEs almost evenly by columns, each of which is responsible for several columns. It can be found that the column elements are stored non-continuously, while row elements are continuous. The data of N columns in one row is loaded from memory to each CPE. When LMMAXC rows are loaded to LDM for each CPE, the data in LDM forms sub-matrix B_n with N columns. Since the number of rows M and the number of columns LMMAXC of A are small, each CPE can hold a complete copy of matrix A.

Each CPE performs the matrix-matrix multiplication of A and B_n and produces a matrix with M rows and N columns. Because of the limited size of LDM, each CPE should execute many times. Finally, all of the data from CPEs form the resultant matrix of M rows and INDMAX columns.

The matrix A of DGEMM in RPROMU is an array named WORK, which is generated by the predecessor code, with the maximal row number of M to be 2 * NSIM and the maximal column number INDMAX. Matrix B is NONLR_S% RPROJ, with a maximal number of rows to be INDMAX, and that of columns of to be LMMAXC. The output matrix has M rows and LMMAXC columns.

The matrix A and B are divided into blocks. They are evenly assigned to 64 CPEs. Each CPE loads data of several columns of all rows into LDM, and when two small blocks are formed, the matrix-matrix multiplication is performed.

Each CPE will produce a matrix of M rows and LMMAXC columns. The final data are formed by summing up the matrix elements from all the 64 CPEs.

6   Experimental Results

The RELAX case contains 32 Ge atoms, one Ru atom. The relax operation is performed. The result of SW26010 MPE and SW26010 CPE are in consistent with that of the X86 platform.

The comparison between the performance of MPE VASP and CPE VASP is listed in Tables 2 and 3.

ZGEMM is a computing intensive calculation with good acceleration result as high as more than 20 times. The speedup of DGEMM is limited by the matrix scale.

For FFT, the acceleration result of the X-dimension is the best due to the continuity of the data layout in the X-dimension. The Y-dimension and Z-dimension FFT data are discontinuous, and the acceleration is relatively less.

For the loop parallelism functions, the acceleration is enough to decrease the percentage of the execution time to an acceptable extent.

Two functions CREXP_MUL_WAVE and WORK_MUL_CREXP have a poor speedup due to the piecewise continuous access of the memory.

Finally, the two algorithms RMM-DIIS and DAV of RELAX have an overall acceleration as high as 2.90 times and 4.48 times, respectively.

Table 2. Performance comparison of RMM

Function	MPE time(s)	CPE time(s)	Speedup
ZGEMM	310.08	14.50	21.38
RPRO.DGEMM	29.03	7.60	3.82
RACC0MU.DGEMM	18.77	4.76	3.94
FFT.X	366.95	59.17	6.20
FFT.Y	364.91	73.65	4.95
FFT.Z	393.79	78.47	5.02
ECCP.LOCAL	110.87	10.67	10.39
ECCP.KIN	14.08	1.84	7.65
VHMAIL	56.28	7.74	7.27
KINHAMIL	6.70	1.23	5.45
PW_CHARGE	12.69	2.48	5.12
CREXP_MUL_WAVE	7.17	2.09	3.43
WORK_MUL_CREXP	7.33	2.50	2.93
VASP	2350.14	810.37	2.90

Table 3. Performance comparison of DAV

Function	MPE time(s)	CPE time(s)	Speedup
ZGEMM	1490.84	55.57	26.83
RPRO.DGEMM	2.32	0.61	3.81
RACC.DGEMM	45.82	13.57	3.38
FFT.X	468.87	76.51	6.13
FFT.Y	464.49	95.12	4.88
FFT.Z	490.81	102.78	4.78
ECCP.LOCAL	28.38	2.70	10.51
ECCP.KIN	3.57	0.47	7.60
VHMAIL	72.35	8.79	8.23
KINHAMIL	3.57	1.43	2.50
PW_CHARGE	11.54	2.26	5.11
CREXP_MUL_WAVE	0.57	0.16	3.56
WORK_MUL_CREXP	15.47	12.99	1.19
VASP	4088.97	913.39	4.48

7 Conclusions

VASP is a first-principle quantum mechanical software that is widely used. The porting and optimization of it on Sunway TaihuLight supercomputer is very important. According to the features of the SW26010 many-core architecture, the hotspot functions have been ported and optimized for the CPE mesh, and a significant speedup is obtained.

The completed optimizations in this paper aim at accelerating the intra-process computations, without the concern for the inter-process operations. In the future, we will further optimize the aspect of data communication among multiple processes and CGs on the Sunway TaihuLight supercomputer.

References

1. Fu, H., Liao, J., Yang, J., et al.: The Sunway TaihuLight supercomputer: system and applications. Sci. China: Inf. Sci. **59**(7), 1–16 (2016)
2. Yang, C., Xue, W., Fu, H., et al.: 10 m-core scalable fully-implicit solver for non hydrostatic atmospheric dynamics. In: Proceedings of SC16. ACM, Salt Lake City (2016)
3. Fu, H., He, C., Chen, B., et al.: 18.9-pops nonlinear earthquake simulation on Sunway TaihuLight: enabling depiction of 18-Hz and 8-meter scenarios. In: Proceedings of SC17, Denver, CO, USA (2017)
4. About VASP. http://www.vasp.at/index.php/about-vasp/59-about-vasp. Accessed 23 May 2018
5. Maintz, S., Eck, B., Dronskowski, R.: Speeding up plane-wave electronic-structure calculations using graphics-processing units. Comput. Phys. Commun. **182**, 1421–1427 (2011)
6. Hutchinson, M., Widom, M.: VASP on a GPU: application to exact-exchange calculations of the stability of elemental boron. Comput. Phys. Commun. **183**, 1422–1426 (2012)
7. Hacene, M., Anciaux-Sedrakian, A., Rozanska, X., et al.: Accelerating VASP electronic structure calculations using graphic processing units. J. Comput. Chem. **33**, 2581–2589 (2012)
8. Zhao, Z.J., Marsman, M., Wende, F., Kim, J.: Performance of hybrid MPI/OpenMP VASP on cray XC40 based on intel knights landing many integrated core architecture. In: CUG Conference Proceedings (2017)
9. Algorithms used in VASP calculate electronic groundstate. https://cms.mpi.univie.ac.at/vasp/vasp/Algorithms_used_in_VASP_calculate_electronic_groundstate.html. Accessed 23 May 2018
10. Kresse, G., Furthmuller, J.: Efficiency of ab-initio total energy calculations for metals and semiconductors using a plane-wave basis set. Comput. Mater. Sci. **6**, 15–50 (1996)
11. Wende, F., Marsman, M., Zhao, Z., et al.: Porting VASP from MPI to MPI+OpenMP [SIMD]. In: de Supinski, B., Olivier, S., Terboven, C., Chapman, B., Müller, M. (eds.) IWOMP 2017. LNCS, vol. 10468, pp. 107–122. Springer, Heidelberg (2017). https://doi.org/10.1007/978-3-319-65578-9_8
12. Tuning VASP: Fast Fourier Transforms. https://www.nsc.liu.se/~pla/blog/2013/01/10/tuning-ffts/. Accessed 23 May 2018

A Data Reuse Method for Fast Search Motion Estimation

Hongjie Li[1], Yanhui Ding[1], Weizhi Xu[1], Hui Yu[2], and Li Sun[3(✉)]

[1] School of Information Science and Engineering,
Shandong Normal University, Jinan 250358, China
[2] School of Management Science and Engineering,
Shandong Normal University, Jinan 250014, China
[3] Financial Department, Shandong Normal University, Jinan 250358, China
sunli_sdnu@126.com

Abstract. In motion estimation, the search regions of two adjacent current blocks have overlapping data. In view of this, the paper proposes a data reuse method for fast search motion estimation. The method reuses the overlapping data between the search areas of two adjacent blocks. The overlapping data are further divided into two parts, a definite data reuse area and a possible data reuse area. With this method, the memory access time of the algorithm is reduced, and the performance of the algorithm is further improved. And the proposed reuse method can effectively reduce the loading of redundant data. A typical fast search algorithm, diamond search, is used as a case study to verify the effectiveness of the method. The method is implemented on GPU platform. The experimental results show that the data reuse method can reduce the running time by 40%–60% compared with the algorithm of no use data reuse.

Keywords: Motion estimation · Data reuse · Diamond search
CUDA

1 Introduction

Motion Estimation (ME) is an important part of video applications such as video coding and frame rate up-conversion. ME requires very high computational complexity, and it usually takes up most of the running time for these video applications. For example, in video coding, motion estimation is closely related to the complexity of the coding. The complexity of motion estimation and disparity estimation for multiview video coding (MVC) is 99% of the total MVC [1]. Therefore, it is necessary to optimize the performance to reduce the running time of motion estimation. This is very important for real-time video applications.

Motion estimation is the process of finding the matching block. The motion estimation algorithm includes the full search algorithm and the fast search algorithm. Full search motion estimation algorithm [2] is an accurate motion estimation algorithm, but the search time consumption can be several times as fast search motion estimation algorithm. Fast search algorithms include new three step search algorithm [3], four step search algorithm [4], hexagon search algorithm [5], etc.

© Springer Nature Switzerland AG 2018
T. Hu et al. (Eds.): ICA3PP 2018 Workshops, LNCS 11338, pp. 27–33, 2018.
https://doi.org/10.1007/978-3-030-05234-8_4

In previous studies, the data reuse method has been widely used in full search algorithm, but it was seldom considered for fast search motion estimation algorithm. Although the fast search algorithm is faster than the full search algorithm, it still takes a lot of time [6]. The main reason is the irregular memory access of the fast search algorithm, which increases the off-chip memory traffic.

In this paper, a new data reuse method for fast search motion estimation is proposed. The method reuses the overlapping data between the search areas of two adjacent blocks. The overlapping data are further divided into two parts, a definite data reuse area and a possible data reuse area. And the experimental results on GPU platform show that the running time of the algorithm can be reduced by 40% to 60% after using the proposed method of data reuse.

The rest of this paper is organized as follows. Section 2 introduces the related work of data reuses of motion estimation algorithm. And Sect. 3 proposes the method of data reuses in search area. Then Sect. 4 implements the reuse method of the search area in memory. The experimental data are in Sect. 5, and finally conclude in Sect. 6.

2 Data Reuse of Motion Estimation Algorithm

Data reuse is an effective method to optimize the performance of motion estimation [7]. Shim et al. proposed the search area selective reuse algorithm to reuse the data of the existing frame in memory, which reduces the memory access time effectively [8]. Tuan et al. studied the data reuse attributes of full-search, analyzed the memory bandwidth in ME, and explored the problem of data reuse [9]. Four levels (A, B, C and D) were defined according to the reuse degree of the previous frame access.

The data reuse method has a beneficial effect on the full search motion estimation, but there is little research on the fast search motion estimation. For fast search motion estimation, Kim et al. proposed the sub-region partitioning method, and using the optimized order to improve the reuse of each sub-region partitioning in the sub-region, effectively reducing redundant data loading [10].

This paper mainly studies the data reuse method of fast search motion estimation, and puts forward the method of search area reuse. The method discovers overlapping data of adjacent search areas for reuse. At the same time, the overlapping data are further divided into two parts: a definite data reuse area and a possible data reuse area.

3 Data Reuse Method for Fast Search Motion Estimation Algorithm

3.1 Data Reuse Between the Search Areas

Data reuse of the fast search motion estimation algorithm can be achieved by reusing the overlapping data between the search areas of the current adjacent blocks. Taking the diamond search algorithm as an example (Fig. 1), the block size is 16×16 and the search area size is 32×32. As shown in Fig. 1, the smaller blocks are two adjacent blocks, the small circle represents the diamond search strategy for each search point, and the large blocks are the search areas of the two adjacent blocks. The search area of the left block contains half the search area on the right, which is the overlapping area between the two search areas. By reusing the data of the overlapping area, searching for two adjacent blocks can read the data from the off-chip memory to the on-chip memory only once instead of twice, thereby reducing the number of off-chip memory accesses.

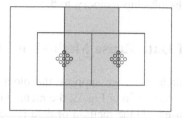

Fig. 1. Search areas of two adjacent current blocks

3.2 Definite+Possible Data Reuse Area

Unlike the full search motion estimation, the fast search motion estimation has uncertain search steps. Because the first step of the fast search motion estimation algorithm is fixed (take the corresponding location of the current block as the search center), there is a definite data reuse area between the search areas of the two current blocks (Fig. 2). However, the search center or search direction of the second step is uncertain. When the fast search algorithm performs the second step, the search center is determined by the result of the first step. Therefore, there is also a possible data reuse area. This paper divides the reusable data of the fast search motion estimation algorithm into the definite reuse data and possible reuse data according to the algorithm's search process to improve the performance of the algorithm.

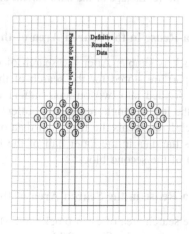

Fig. 2. Definite data reuse area and possible data reuse area

Figure 2 gives the search points or search areas of two current blocks. Numbers in the small circles are the search steps of diamond search. There must be a definite reuse data area wherever the search direction of the adjacent current block is, because the search center of the first step is fixed. If the second step of the two current blocks goes as in Fig. 2, there will be a possible reuse data area. When the on-chip memory size is large enough, we can put both definite reuse data and possible data reuse data on chip, which will further reduce the off-chip memory traffic.

4   Implementation of Data Reuse Method in Memory

In the case of diamond search (DS), we suppose the block size is 16×16 and the search area size is 32×32. As shown in Fig. 3, the method of data reuse in the search area is divided into three cases: (1) the method of data reuse in the search area of the first block, (2) the method of data reuse in the search area of the even block, (3) the method of data reuse in the search area of the odd block (except the first block).

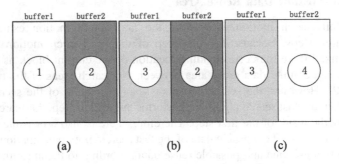

Fig. 3. (a) Storage of the first current block's search area in SM. (b) Storage of the second current block's search area in SM. (c) Storage of the third current block's search area in SM.

4.1   The Method of Data Reuse in the Search Area of the First Block

The storage of the first block is simple. After the search of the first block ends, the reusable data in the latter part are stored for the search of the second block. Shared Memory (SM) on GPU is divided into two buffers, buffer1 and buffer2. Figure 3(a) represents the whole SM, the left rectangle represents buffer1, and the right rectangle represents buffer2. The circle1 represents the front half data of the first block's search area. The circle2 represents the data in the latter half of the first block's search area, which is also reusable data of the second block.

4.2   The Method of Data Reuse in the Search Area of the Even Block

To explain how to store the search area of even blocks in SM, we can take the search area of the second block as an example. Figure 3(b) represents the entire SM. Circle2 represents reusable data which are already in buffer2 and not needed to be loaded from off-chip memory. Circle3 represents the data that need to be loaded from off-chip memory to make up another half of the second block's search area. Data in buffer1 and buffer2 combine to form the complete search area of the second block.

4.3 The Method of Data Reuse in the Search Area of the Odd Block

To explain how to store the search area of odd blocks in SM, we can take the search area of the third current block as an example. Figure 3(c) shows the whole SM. Circle3 in buffer1 shows the stored reusable data of the second block's search area, and circle4 in buffer2 shows the data that need to be loaded from off-chip memory. Buffer1 and buffer2 combine to form the complete search area of the third block.

The process of definite+possible reuse data area reuse method is similar to the process of search area reuse method, which also uses the shared memory to store both the definite reuse data and the possible reuse data. The introduction of possible reuse data can further improve the performance of the algorithm.

5 Experimental Results

The experimental environment is the Windows 10 operating system. The CPU is Intel G530, and GPU is NVIDIA GeForce GTX 750 Ti with CUDA 8.0. The program is run and debugged in Visual Studio 2013. The diamond search is used as an example in the experiment. The block size is 64×64 and the search area size is 128×128.

The experimental results are shown in Table 1. Six test sequences of Football, Foreman, News, Mobisode2, Johnny, and SlideShow were tested. In Table 1, Sequence represents different tested sequences. Size represents image size of the test sequence. No data reuse (s) represents the running time in seconds when no data reuse is adopted. Definite data reuse(s) is the data reuse method of search area, means that only definite reusable data is considered and reused in shared memory. The percentage of time improvements over No data reuse is also given for Definite data reuse and Definite +Possible data reuse respectively in Table 1.

Table 1. Comparison of data reuse in DS

Sequence	Size	No data reuse(s)	Definite data reuse (s)		Definite+Possible data reuse(s)	
Football	176×144	0.073053	0.061476	15.84%	0.060625	17.01%
Foreman	352×288	0.254124	0.149723	41.08%	0.146758	42.24%
News	352×288	0.253877	0.149040	41.29%	0.146849	42.15%
Mobisode2	416×240	0.231372	0.139689	39.62%	0.138105	40.31%
Johnny	1280×720	2.514633	1.012222	59.74%	0.977472	61.12%
SlideShow	1280×720	2.518903	1.015279	59.69%	0.991458	60.63%

Experimental results show that the proposed data reuse methods (Definite data reuse and Definite+Possible data reuse) effectively improve the performance compared with No data reuse. Improvements of most test sequences are up to 40%, and some sequences even reach 61.12%. For all the sequences, the method of Definite+Possible data reuse need less running time. This indicates that it is effective to put possible reuse data in the shared memory besides definite reuse data. As the resolution of the test sequence becomes larger, the running time reduction ratio of fast motion estimation with the proposed data reuse method also becomes larger. For example, News (352 × 288) decreases by 42.15%, while Johnny (1280 × 720) decreases by 61.12%.

6 Conclusion

In this paper, a novel data reuse method for fast search motion estimation is proposed. The overlapping data between the search areas of two adjacent current blocks are reused. The overlapping area is further divided into two parts, a definite data reuse area and a possible data reuse area. The proposed reuse method can effectively reduce off-chip memory traffic. And experimental results on GPU/CUDA platform show that the running time of the algorithm can be reduced by over 60% after using the proposed method of data reuse.

Acknowledgment. The work is supported by Primary Research & Development Plan of Shandong Province (2017GGX10112), and the Shandong Natural Science Foundation (No. ZR2015 FQ009) and NNSF of China (No. 61520106005, No. 61602285, and No. 61602284).

References

1. Jiang, C., Nooshabadi, S.: GPU accelerated motion and disparity estimations for multiview coding. In: IEEE International Conference on Image Processing, pp. 2106–2110. IEEE (2014)
2. Kim, J.-N., Byun, S.-C., Kim, Y.-H., Ahn, B.-H.: Fast full search motion estimation algorithm using early detection of impossible candidate vectors. IEEE Trans. Signal Process. **50**(9), 2355–2365 (2002)
3. Park, D., Jang, Y., Lee, J.: A new fast three step search motion estimation algorithm in H.264. In: 2007 International Forum on Strategic Technology, pp. 541–544 (2007)
4. Gaikwad, M.M.: Implementation of four step search algorithm of motion estimation using FPGA. Int. J. Adv. Res. Comput. Sci. Electron. Eng. **1**(3), 68 (2012)
5. Ali, I., Raja, G., Muzammil, M., Khan, A.K.: Adaptive modified hexagon based search motion estimation algorithm. In: IEEE Fourth International Conference on Consumer Electronics, pp. 147–148. IEEE, Berlin (2014)
6. Fan, R., Zhang, Y., Li, B.: Motion classification-based fast motion estimation for high-efficiency video coding. IEEE Trans. Multimed. **19**(5), 893–907 (2017)
7. Xu, W., Yin, S., Liu, L., Liu, Z., Wei, S.: High-performance motion estimation for image sensors with video compression. Sensors **15**(8), 20752–20778 (2015)
8. Shim, H., Kang, K., Kyung, C.-M.: Search area selective reuse algorithm in motion estimation. In: 2007 IEEE International Conference on Multimedia and Expo, pp. 1611–1614 (2007)

9. Tuan, J.-C., Chang, T.-S., Jen, C.-W.: On the data reuse and memory bandwidth analysis for full-search block-matching VLSI architecture. IEEE Trans. Circuits Syst. Video Technol. **12** (1), 61–72 (2002)

10. Kim, T.S., SunWoo, M.H.: Data reusable search scan methods for low power motion estimation. J. Inst. Electron. Eng. Korea **50**(9), 85–91 (2013)

I-Center Loss for Deep Neural Networks

Senlin Cheng$^{(\boxtimes)}$ and Liutong Xu

School of Computer Science,
Beijing University of Posts and Telecommunications, Beijing, China
972705994@qq.com, xliutong@bupt.edu.cn

Abstract. Convolutional Neural Network (CNN) have been widely used for image classification and computer vision tasks such as face recognition, target detection. Softmax loss is one of the most commonly used components to train CNN, which only penalizes the classification loss. So we consider how to train intra-class compactness and inter-class separability better. In this paper, we proposed an I-Center Loss to make inter-class having a better separability, which means that I-Center Loss penalizes the difference between each center of classes. With I-Center Loss, we trained a robust CNN to achieve a better performance. Extensive experiments on MNIST, CIFAR10, LFW (face datasets for face recognition) demonstrate the effectiveness of the I-center loss. We have tried different models, visualized the experimental results and showed the effectiveness of our proposed I-center loss.

Keywords: Softmax loss · I-center loss · Inter-class · Center of classes
CNN

1 Introduction

Image classification and recognition are still difficult problem in machine learning and computer vision tasks. Recent years, the deep convolutional neural network(CNN) have a state-of-art performance in many image classification tasks such as hand-written digit recognition [1], visual object classification [2–6], object recognition [4], and face recognition such as DeepFace [7], FaceNet [8], Deep-Id [9–11], OpenFace [12]. In order to train a CNN model, there are some tricks when training CNN such as Regularization [13], Dropout [2], new activations [5], different CNN network structure [4], different pooling methods [5, 14] and so on. On the other hand, some researchers also optimize the task from loss function by using softmax in the last layer to classify images to different classes. It can penalize the classification loss, but it is limited due to its lack of encouraging the discriminability of features and not consider the intra-class compactness and inter-class separability.

Recently, some researchers begin to design different loss functions which could learn discriminative features so that it can have a better performance. A deep convolutional neural network can learn a good feature if its intra-class compactness and inter-class separability are well maximized. So contrastive loss [10], triplet loss [8], were proposed to have better intra-class compactness and inter-class separability. However, we need to select some training pairs and triplets when using contrastive loss and triplet

© Springer Nature Switzerland AG 2018
T. Hu et al. (Eds.): ICA3PP 2018 Workshops, LNCS 11338, pp. 34–44, 2018.
https://doi.org/10.1007/978-3-030-05234-8_5

loss although they do really improve the performance and extract more discriminative features. The selection of samples is important for the training result, if all training samples are selected, the complexity can go up to $O(N^2)$ where N is the total number of training samples. The L-softmax loss [15] will enhance the angle margin between different classes. But the angle margin is hard to train. A-softmax [16] was developed to explicitly enforce the angle margin with two limitations based on the L-softmax. The center loss [17] learns different centers of different classes, it was combined with the sofmax loss and the intra-class compactness, but center loss did not consider the inter-class separability.

In this paper, we propose the I-center loss, which penalize the inter-class separability and align the center of each class to have a general representation for all classes. I-center loss considers the difference between the L2 norm of each center of classes and the mean L2 norm of all centers. When training, we combine multiple losses (softmax loss, center loss, and I-center loss) so that we can train a more robust CNN to have a better representation for all classes. It means that this not only consider the intra-class, but also consider the inter-class.

Experiments and visualizations show the effectiveness of our method. The experiments on MNIST, CIFAR10, LFW (face datasets for face recognition) and compare different CNN models, our method have a better performance.

2   Related Work

In order to learn better discriminative feature, there are two ways to improve the performance. One way is to improve the deep CNN structures, another way is to design better loss functions.

CNN Structures: VGGNet explored the relationship between the depth of the convolutional neural network and its performance through stacking 3 * 3 small convolutional kernals and 2 * 2 maximum pooling layer. GooleNet controls the amount of computation and the number of parameters, and its classification performance is very good. ResNet Solves the missing information problem in information transmission of traditional CNN, the entire network only need to learn the differences between the input and output, simplifies the learning difficulty and goal. The R-CNN resorted to a recurrent CNN for visual classification by incorporating recurrent connections into each convolutional layer. Although existing CNN structures have achieved promising results for classification, they still have limitation because of softmax-loss.

Loss Functions: Recent years, There are many related works about loss functions such as contrastive loss, triplet loss, center loss, L-softmax loss and A-softmax loss. Expected for the contrastive loss and triplet loss, they need pre-selected sample pairs or triples, the aim of other loss functions not only consider the intra-class compactness, but also the inter-class separability. Our work combined the center loss with softmax loss to learn discriminative features. The softmax loss differ from softmax which is widely used in CNN and it can be written as:

$$L_{Soft\,max} = \frac{1}{N}\sum_i L_i = \frac{1}{N}\sum_i - \log \frac{e^{f_{y_i}}}{\sum_j e^{f_j}} \qquad (1)$$

where x_i denotes the deep feature of the i-th training sample. y_i is its corresponding label. f_j represents the j-th element of the class output vector f of the final full connection layer, and N is the number of training samples. f is the output of the final connection layer, so f_{y_i} can be expressed as $f_{y_i} = W_{y_i}^T x_i$.

3 Proposed Method

In this section, we introduce center loss and indicate its weakness. We introduce the I-center loss, present the formulation of the I-center loss, which considers the intra-class compactness and inter-class separability. And we will show how to optimize the I-center loss with stochastic gradients descent.

3.1 Center Loss

As shown in Fig. 1(a), the features extracted from the deep neural network trained based on softmax loss are distinguishable, but the discriminant ability is not enough because of the characteristics of the class changes, the distance between intra-class is greater than the distance between inter-class. So the center loss is developed to improve the ability of the features extracted from deep neural networks. As shown in Fig. 1(b), this loss can minimize the intra-class variations while keeping the features of different classes separable. The loss function can be expressed as:

$$L_c = \frac{1}{2}\sum_{i=1}^{m}\left\|x_i - c_{y_i}\right\|_2^2 \qquad (2)$$

where m denotes the number of training samples, x_i denotes the ith training sample. y_i is its corresponding label. L_c denotes its center loss. c_{y_i} denotes the y_ith class center of deep features. Then the author combined softmax loss and center loss to train the network, it can be expressed as:

$$L = L_{soft\,max} + \lambda L_c \qquad (3)$$

Where λ is a scalar to balance the center loss and softmax loss, $L_{softmax}$ denotes the softmax loss, L_c denotes the center loss and L denotes the sum of the two losses.

The Weakness of Center Loss: We believe that a good design loss function should simultaneously consider the intra-class compactness and inter-class separability. the center loss consider the intra-class and have a large margin. However, this loss does not consider the inter-class. This phenomenon makes the distance of different classes not far enough so that the feature learn from deep neural network will be not more discriminative.

3.2   I-Center Loss

We introduce the I-center loss. We assume there are m classes, the kth class has n_k samples. the ith sample of the feature is x_i. c_k is the kth class center, it can be expressed as:

$$c_k = \frac{1}{n_k} \sum_{i=1}^{n_k} x_i \tag{4}$$

The I-center loss can be expressed as:

$$L_I = \left(s\frac{1}{m} \sum_{k=1}^{m} \|c_k\|_2^2 - \|c_y\|_2^2 \right)^2 \tag{5}$$

This loss function aims to make different classes centers a large margin. Where $\frac{1}{m}\sum_{k=1}^{m} \|c_k\|_2^2$ is the mean value of all classes centers Euclidean norm. s is a parameter to control the far or near that we penalize the centers. Given the ith sample, the loss generates the cost from the distant center to the mean value of all centers. As can be seen in Fig. 1(c), This distant center can push the centers close to the distant center so that consider the inter-class separability. our I-center loss can improve the power of the deep features extracted from deep neural networks. Here we add softmax loss and center loss to jointly supervise the training of the CNN model. Total loss can be written as:

$$L = L_{soft\,max} + \lambda L_c + \gamma L_I$$
$$= -\log\left(\frac{e^{w_y^T x_i + b_y}}{\sum_{j=1}^{m} e^{w_j^T x_i + b_j}} \right) + \frac{\lambda}{2}\|x_i - c_y\|^2 \tag{6}$$

$$+ \gamma \left(s\frac{1}{m} \sum_{k=1}^{m} \|c_k\|_2^2 - \|c_y\|_2^2 \right)^2 \tag{7}$$

Where γ denotes the scalar used for balancing the three loss functions and λ is the same scalar to balance the three loss functions. When γ and λ are both 0, this total loss becomes original softmax loss.

3.3   Loss Optimization

In this section, we optimize the total loss function and show the details of the backward propagation using stochastic gradient descent (SGD). In total loss, w_j and b_j are the same ways to optimize with the original softmax loss. c_k is the center of the class, it should be random initialized and updated based on the mini-batch, so what we consider about the optimization is x_i. The gradient x of the total loss function can be written as:

$$\frac{\partial L}{\partial x_i} = \frac{\partial L_{soft\,max}}{\partial x_i} + \lambda \frac{\partial L_c}{\partial x_i} + \gamma \frac{\partial L_I}{\partial x_i} \tag{8}$$

According to the chain rule, the first item $\frac{\partial L_{soft\,max}}{\partial x_i}$ can be written as:

$$\frac{\partial L_{soft\,max}}{\partial x_i} = \frac{\partial L_{soft\,max}}{\partial y(x_i)} \frac{\partial y(x_i)}{\partial x_i} \tag{9}$$

Where $y(x_i)$ can be written as

$$y(x_i) = \frac{e^{w_y^T x_i + b_y}}{\sum\limits_{j=1}^{m} e^{w_j^T x_i + b_j}} \tag{10}$$

The Eq. (9) becomes:

$$
\begin{aligned}
\frac{\partial L_{soft\,max}}{\partial x_i} &= \frac{1}{y(x_i)} \left(\frac{e^{w_y^T x_i + b_y} \cdot w_y}{\sum_{j=1}^{m} e^{w_j^T x_i + b_j}} - \frac{e^{w_y^T x_i + b_y}}{\left(\sum_{j=1}^{m} e^{w_j^T x_i + b_j} \right)^2} e^{w_y^T x_i + b_y} \cdot w_y \right) \\
&= \frac{1}{y(x_i)} \left(y(x_i)w_y - (y(x_i))^2 w_y \right) \\
&= (1 - y(x_i))w_y
\end{aligned}
\tag{11}
$$

The next item $\lambda \frac{\partial L_c}{\partial x_i}$ can be written as:

$$\lambda \frac{\partial L_c}{\partial x_i} = \lambda (x_i - c_y) \tag{12}$$

Then optimize the proposed I-center loss. Firstly, we assume:

$$\tau = \frac{1}{m} \sum_{k=1}^{m} \|c_k\|_2^2 \tag{13}$$

Taking Eq. (13) into Eq. (5), we get:

$$L_I = \gamma \left(s \cdot \tau - \|c_y\|_2^2 \right)^2 \tag{14}$$

With the chain rule, we can compute the $\gamma \frac{\partial L_I}{\partial x_i}$ as:

$$\gamma \frac{\partial L_I}{\partial x_i} = \gamma \frac{\partial L_I}{\partial c_y} \cdot \frac{\partial c_y}{\partial x_i} \tag{15}$$

$\frac{\partial L_I}{\partial c_y}$ can be computed as:

$$\frac{\partial L_I}{\partial c_y} = 2\left(s \cdot \tau - \|c_y\|_2^2\right)\left(\frac{2s}{m}c_y - 2c_y\right)$$

$$= \left(s \cdot \tau - \|c_y\|_2^2\right)\left(\frac{4s}{m} - 4\right)c_y \qquad (16)$$

$\frac{\partial c_y}{\partial x_i}$ can be computed as:

$$\frac{\partial c_y}{\partial x_i} = \frac{1}{n_y}$$

We can get the result of $\gamma\frac{\partial L_I}{\partial x_i}$:

$$\gamma\frac{\partial L_I}{\partial x_i} = \gamma\frac{1}{n_y}\left(s \cdot \tau - \|c_y\|_2^2\right)\left(\frac{4s}{m} - 4\right)c_y \qquad (17)$$

From Eq. (17), we can see that $s \cdot \tau - \|c_y\|_2^2 > 0$, where s is an integer. It makes the $\frac{\partial L_I}{\partial x_i}$ have the direction of outside. The gradients of the total loss can be expressed as:

$$\frac{\partial L}{\partial x_i} = (1 - y(x_i))w_y + \gamma\frac{1}{n_y}\left(s \cdot \tau - \|c_y\|_2^2\right)\left(\frac{4s}{m} - 4\right)c_y$$
$$+ \lambda\left(x_i - c_y\right) \qquad (18)$$

Then the above parameters can be computed with backward propagation algorithm, we can optimize the CNN model with stochastic gradient descent (SGD).

4 Experiments

In this section, we evaluate the experiments on two typical visual tasks: visual classification and face recognition. The experiments demonstrate our proposed I-center loss is robust on different datasets, can not only improve the accuracy on visual classification, but also boost the performance on visual recognition. In visual classification, we used dataset (MNIST [18] and CIFAR10 [19]). In face recognition, we use the usual face datasets LFW [20]. We implement the I-center loss and do experiments using Tensorflow.

4.1 Experiments on MNIST and Visualization

Firstly, we introduce the MNIST dataset, contains 60,000 training images and 10,000 testing images in total. The images all hand-written digits 0–9 in 10 classes which are 28 * 28 in size.

We use the network LeNets++ in the experiments, the LeNets++ is based on LeNet and it is more deeper and wider. In order to visualize the datasets, we reduce the last hidden layer dimension to 2, although this dimension losts a lot of information, also can reflect the relationship of original features. The details of the network architecture are given in Table 1.

Table 1. The CNNs architecture we use for MNIST, called LeNets++. $(5, 32)_{/1,2}$ * 2 denotes 2 cascaded convolution layers with 32 filters of size 5 * 5, the stride and padding are 1 and 2. $2_{/2,0}$ denotes the max-pooling layers with grid of 2 * 2, where the stride and padding are 2 and 0. we use Parametric Rectified Linear Unit (PRelu) as the nonlinear activation function.

	stage1	stage2	stage3	stage4
layer	conv + pool	conv + pool	conv + pool	FC
LeNets	$(5, 20)_{/1,0} + 2_{/2,0}$	$(5, 50)_{/1,0} + 2_{/2,0}$		500
LeNets ++	$(5, 32)_{/1,2}$ * 2 + $_{/1,2}$	$(5, 64)_{/1,2}$ * 2 + $2_{/2,0}$	$(5, 128)_{/1,2}$ * 2 + $2_{/2,0}$	2

When training and testing the MNIST, we use only all original training images and testing images without any data augmentation. The result is shown in Table 2. I-center loss boosts accuracy of 0.39% compared to the softmax loss and 0.25% compared to the center loss.

Table 2. Classification accuracy (%) on MNIST dataset

Method	Accuracy (%)
Softmax	98.8
Center loss	98.94
Our I-center loss	**99.19**

We use all testing images and visualize the deep features of the last hidden layer in Fig. 1. We can observe that:

(1) with sofmax loss only, we can train a deep neural network to make the features separable, but not consider the intra-class compactness.
(2) the center loss considers the intra-class compactness and have a better performance compared to the softmax loss, but the inter-class separability is not good enough. It is close to each other and some times the performance will be limited.
(3) what we proposed I-center loss can consider a large margin of the inter-class separability. This can achieve a better performance than center loss. Intuitively, the distance between classes gets greater.

4.2   Experiments on CIFAR10

The CIFAR10 dataset includes 10 classes of natural images with 50,000 traing images and 10,000 testing images. Each image is RGB image of size 32 * 32.

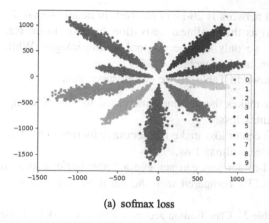

(a) sofmax loss

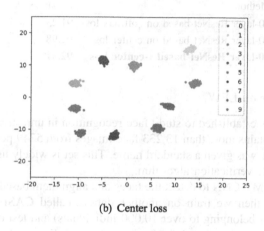

(b) Center loss

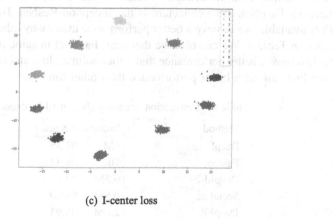

(c) I-center loss

Fig. 1. Visualization of MNIST. Note: The center loss can be observed that the distance between the classes is very small compared to softmax, and the I-center loss we proposed has a greater distance than the center loss. In our experiments, we select $\gamma = 0.0001$ and $s = 0.5$ to train the deep neural network.

The deep neural network is 20-layer ResNet. In detail, we use Parametric Rectified Linear Unit (PRelu) as the nonlinear activation function to do data augmentation in training. In testing, we only use the original testing images. While training, we use Batch Normalization, set loss weight $\lambda = 0.1$.

The result is shown in Table 3. We can observe that:

(1) the center loss makes the accuracy increased by 0.85% compared with the nets only used softmax loss.
(2) our proposed I-center loss make the accuracy increased by 1.18% compared with the net only used softmax loss.
(3) our proposed I-center loss can achieve a better performance and the accuracy is increased by 0.43% compared with the net used center loss.

Table 3. Classification accuracy (%) on CIFAR10 dataset

Method	Accuracy (%)
20-layer ResNet based on softmax loss	91.23
20-layer ResNet based on center loss	91.98
20-layer ResNet based I-center loss	**92.41**

4.3   Experiments on LFW

The LFW dataset is established to study face recognition in unrestricted environments. This collection contains more than 13,233 face images from 5749 persons (all from the Internet). Each face was given a standard name. This set is widely used to evaluate the performance of face verification algorithm.

Firstly, we use MT-CNN to detect the faces and align them based on 5 points (eyes, nose and mouth), then we train on another dataset called CASIA-WebFace (490k labeled face images belonging to over 10,000 individuals) and test on 6,000 face pairs on LFW. We train a single network for feature extraction. For good comparison, we use the network FaceNet, the architecture is the Inception-ResNet. Based on the network publicly available, we achieve a better performance than many other models. The result is shown in Table 4. We can observe that train FaceNet in same dataset and use the I-center loss have a better performance than other softmax loss and center loss. Secondly, I-center loss can get a better performance than other models.

Table 4. Verification accuracy (%) on LFW dataset

Method	Images	Accuracy (%)
DeepFace	4M	97.35
Fusion	10M	98.37
DeepId-2+	0.5M	98.70
SeetaFce	0.5M	98.60
DeepFR	2.6M	98.95
FaceNet(softmax)	260M	98.41
FaceNet(center loss)	260M	99.53
FaceNet(I-center loss)	**260M**	**99.67**

5   Conclusion

In this paper, we proposed an I-center loss for deep neural networks. With softmax loss and center loss joint training, we not only consider the intra-class compactness but also consider the inter-class separability. We train a robust CNN to learn discriminative features so that it can have a better performance. The extensive experiments and visualizations of different datasets demonstrated the effectiveness of the proposed approach.

References

1. Wan, L., Zeiler, M., Zhang, S.: Regularization of neural networks using dropconnect. In: ICML (2013)
2. Krizhevsky, A., Sutskever, I., Hinton, G.E.: Imagenet classification with deep convolutional neural networks. In: Advances in Neural Information Processing Systems, pp. 1097–1105 (2012)
3. Simonyan, K., Zisserman, A.: Very deep convolutional networks for large-scale image recognition, arXiv preprint arXiv:1409.1556 (2014)
4. Szegedy, C., et al.: Going deeper with convolutions. In: Proceedings of the IEEE Conference on Computer Vision and Pattern Recognition, pp. 1–9 (2015)
5. He, K., Zhang, X., Ren, S., Sun, J.: Delving deep into rectifiers: surpassing human-level performance on imagenet classification. In: Proceedings of the IEEE International Conference on Computer Vision, pp. 1026–1034 (2015)
6. He, K., Zhang, X., Ren, S., Sun, J.: Deep residual learning for image recognition, arXiv preprint arXiv:1512.03385 (2015)
7. Parkhi, O.M., Vedaldi, A., Zisserman, A.: Deep face recognition. In: British Machine Vision Conference, vol. 1, p. 6 (2015)
8. Schroff, F., Kalenichenko, D., Philbin, J.: Facenet: a unified embedding for face recognition and clustering. In: Proceedings of the IEEE Conference on Computer Vision and Pattern Recognition, pp. 815–823 (2015)
9. Sun, Y., Wang, X., Tang, X.: Deep learning face representation from predicting 10,000 classes. In: Proceedings of the IEEE Conference on Computer Vision and Pattern Recognition, pp. 1891–1898 (2014)
10. Sun, Y., Chen, Y., Wang, X., Tang, X.: Deep learning face representation by joint identification-verification. In: Advances in Neural Information Processing Systems, pp. 1988–1996 (2014)
11. Sun, Y., Wang, X., Tang, X.: Deeply learned face representations are sparse, selective, and robust. In: Proceedings of the IEEE Conference on Computer Vision and Pattern Recognition, pp. 2892–2900 (2015)
12. Liu, X., Kan, M., Wu, W., Shan, S., Chen, X.: VIPLFaceNet: an open source deep face recognition SDK, arXiv preprint arXiv:1609.03892 (2016)
13. Srivastava, N., Hinton, G.E., Krizhevsky, A.: Dropout: a simple way to prevent neural networks from overfitting. JMLR 15(1), 1929–1958 (2014)
14. Goodfellow, I.J., Warde-Farley, D., Mirza, M., Courville, A.C., Bengio, Y.: Maxout networks. In: ICML (3), vol. 28, pp. 1319–1327 (2013)
15. Liu, W., Wen, Y., Yu, Z.: Large-margin softmax loss for convolutional neural networks. In: ICML (2016)

16. Liu, W., Wen, Y., Yu, Z., Li, M., Raj, B., Song, L.: Sphereface: deep hypersphere embedding for face recognition. In: CVPR 2017
17. Wen, Y., Zhang, K., Li, Z., Qiao, Y.: A discriminative feature learning approach for deep face recognition. In: Leibe, B., Matas, J., Sebe, N., Welling, M. (eds.) ECCV 2016. LNCS, vol. 9911, pp. 499–515. Springer, Cham (2016). https://doi.org/10.1007/978-3-319-46478-7_31
18. LeCun, Y., Cortes, C., Burges, C.J.C.: The MNIST database of handwritten digits (1998)
19. Krizhevsky, A., Hinton, G.: Learning multiple layers of features from tiny images (2009)
20. Huang, G.B., Ramesh, M., Berg, T., Learned-Miller, E.: Labeled faces in the wild: a database for studying face recognition in unconstrained environments. Technical report, 07-49, University of Massachusetts, Amherst, October 2007

Nodes Deployment Optimization Algorithm of Underwater Wireless Sensor Networks

Min Cui[1(✉)], Fengtong Mei[1], Qiangyi Li[2(✉)], and Qiangnan Li[2]

[1] Zhengzhou University of Industrial Technology,
Zhengzhou 451150, Henan, China
cjjl98@yeah.net
[2] Henan University of Science and Technology, Luoyang 471023, Henan, China
cxl979@yeah.net

Abstract. Underwater wireless sensor networks nodes deployment optimization problem is studied and underwater wireless sensor nodes deployment determines its capability and lifetime. If no underwater wireless sensor node is available in the monitoring area of underwater wireless sensor networks due to used up energy or any other reasons, the monitoring area where is not detected by any underwater wireless sensor node forms coverage holes. In order to improve the coverage of the underwater wireless sensor networks and prolong the lifetime of the underwater wireless sensor networks, based on the perception model, establish nodes detection model, combining with the data fusion. Because the underwater wireless sensor networks nodes coverage holes appear when the initial randomly deployment, a nodes deployment algorithm based on perception model of underwater wireless sensor networks is designed in this article. The simulation results show that this algorithm can effectively reduce the number of deployment underwater wireless sensor networks nodes, improve the efficiency of underwater wireless sensor networks coverage, reduce the underwater wireless sensor networks nodes energy consumption, prolong the lifetime of the underwater wireless sensor networks.

Keywords: Nodes deployment · Optimization algorithm
Underwater wireless sensor networks

1 Introduction

Because the wireless sensor network nodes coverage holes appear when the initial randomly deployment, a nodes deployment algorithm based on perception model of wireless sensor network is designed in this article [1–5]. In order to improve the coverage of the wireless sensor network and prolong the lifetime of the wireless sensor network, based on the perception model, establish nodes detection model, combining with the data fusion [6–10]. This algorithm can effectively reduce the number of deployment wireless sensor network nodes, improve the efficiency of wireless sensor network coverage, reduce the wireless sensor network nodes energy consumption, and prolong the lifetime of the wireless sensor network [11–15].

T. Hu et al. (Eds.): ICA3PP 2018 Workshops, LNCS 11338, pp. 45–50, 2018.
https://doi.org/10.1007/978-3-030-05234-8_6

2 Assumption

To simplify the calculation, randomly deploy the quantity N_k of the k-th type mobile nodes in the monitoring region and mobile wireless sensor node s_j owns wireless sensor network ID number j.

The k-th type wireless sensor nodes in the network own the same sensing radius R_{sk}, the same communication radius R_{ck}, and $R_{ck} = 2\,R_{sk}$.

The wireless sensor nodes can obtain the location information of itself and its neighbor nodes.

The k-th type mobile node owns E_k energy and is sufficient to support the completion of the mobile node position migration process.

The k-th type mobile node sending 1 byte data consumes E_{sk} energy and receiving 1 byte data consumes E_{rk} energy.

The k-th type mobile node migration 1 m consumes E_{mk} energy.

3 Coverage Model

The monitored area owns A × B × C pixels which means that the size of each pixel is the $\Delta x \times \Delta y \times \Delta z$.

The perceived probability of the i-th pixel is perceived by the wireless sensor network is $P(p_i)$, when $P(p_i) \geq P_{th}$ (P_{th} is the minimum allowable perceived probability for the wireless sensor network), the pixels can be regarded as perceived by the wireless sensor network.

The i-th pixel is whether perceived by the wireless sensor node perceived to be used $P_{cov}(P_i)$ to measure, i.e.

$$P_{cov}(p_i) = \begin{cases} 0 & if \quad P(p_i) < P_{th} \\ 1 & if \quad P(p_i) < P_{th} \end{cases} \tag{1}$$

The coverage rate is the perceived area and the sum of monitoring area ratio is defined in this article, i.e.

$$R_{area} = \frac{P_{area}}{S_{area}} = \frac{\Delta x \times \Delta y \times \Delta z \times \sum\limits_{x=1}^{A}\sum\limits_{y=1}^{B}\sum\limits_{z=1}^{C} P_{cov}(p_i)}{\Delta x \times \Delta y \times \Delta z \times A \times B \times C} \tag{2}$$

Among them, P_{area} is the perceived area while S_{area} is the sum of monitoring area.

4 Perception Model

The event r_{ij} is defined that the i-th pixel p_i which is perceived by the ID number j wireless sensor nodes, the probability of occurrence of the event is $P(r_{ij})$ which is the perceived probability $P(p_i, s_j)$ that the pixel p_i is perceived by wireless sensor node s_j, i.e.

$$P(p_i, s_j) = \begin{cases} 1 & if & d(p_i, s_j) \leq R_{sk} - R_{ek} \\ \ln\{1 - \frac{e-1}{2R_{ek}}[d(p_i, s_j) - R_{sk} - R_{ek}]\} & if & R_{sk} - R_{ek} < d(p_i, s_j) < R_{sk} + R_{ek} \\ 0 & if & d(p_i, s_j) \geq R_{sk} + R_{ek} \end{cases}$$

$$(3)$$

Among them, the $d(p_i, s_j)$ is the distance between the i-th pixel p_i and the j-th wireless sensor node s_j, the sensing radius of the k-th type wireless sensor node is R_{sk}, the perceived error range of the k-th type wireless sensor node is R_{ek}.

This article used a number of wireless sensor nodes cooperative sensing monitoring method and the pixel p_i is perceived by all wireless sensor nodes collaborate perceived probability is

$$P(p_i) = 1 - \prod_{j=1}^{N} [1 - P(p_i, s_j)]$$

$$(4)$$

5 This Article Algorithm

The position of wireless sensor network node S_i is (x_i, y_i, z_i), the perception model is in the following:

$$P(S_i, T) = \begin{cases} 0 & d(S_i, T) \geq R + R_e, \\ \frac{E_{rem}}{E_{ini}} e^{-\gamma \alpha^{\beta}} & R - R_e < d(S_i, T) < R + R_e \\ 1 & d(S_i, T) < R - R_e \end{cases}$$

$$(10)$$

Among them, $P(S_i, T)$ is the perception probability of the wireless sensor network node S_i to target point T, $d(S_i, T)$ is the distance between sensor node S_i and the target point T, R_e is a uncertainty perception measure of wireless sensor node S_i, E_{ini} is the initial energy of the wireless sensor node S_i, E_{rem} is the remaining energy of the wireless sensor node S_i, α, β, γ are the perception of the wireless sensor node within the scope of monitoring quality coefficient.

6 Simulation Result

MATLAB software is used as simulation in this article. Assume that require p-reliability coverage in the monitoring area, among them p = 0.9, and do not consider the effect of target distribution and other environmental factors. According to the characteristics of the passive sonar and underwater sensor networks node and the related definitions, respectively the simulation random deployment algorithm and based on the "virtual force" deployment algorithm under monitoring area coverage performance and deployment algorithm based on perception model after monitoring area coverage performance and target node test results.

The simulation results are shown in Figs. 1, 2 and 3.

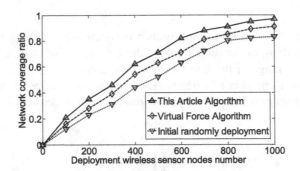

Fig. 1. Relations of network coverage and nodes number

Figure 1 is under the initial randomly deployment, virtual force algorithm and this article algorithm, in the same test area with an increase in the number of nodes. In contrast to initial randomly deployment and virtual force algorithm, this article algorithm has more effective coverage, a single node perception is more efficient, this is a direct result of the node deployment, compared virtual force algorithm and initial randomly deployment reduced the scope of sensor node overlapping sense perception, and because this article algorithm compared virtual force algorithm adopted data fusion algorithm, and reduced the perceived blind area, therefore, this article algorithm under the effective coverage of the sensor network greater than virtual force algorithm, virtual force algorithm is higher than the initial randomly deployment.

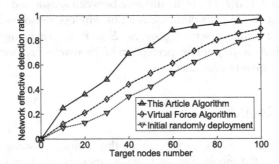

Fig. 2. Relations of network effective detection ratio and target nodes number

Figure 2 is under the initial randomly deployment, virtual force algorithm and this article algorithm, in the same detection area to deploy the same number of sensor node, respectively, with different number of effective detection rate of the target node contrast figure. By the graph, this article algorithm, the wireless sensor network for effective detection of the target node rate than initial randomly deployment and virtual force algorithm, this is because the this article algorithm deployment under the data fusion algorithm is adopted to perception results effective fusion of different sensors, improve the detection probability of the target node, increase the effective coverage.

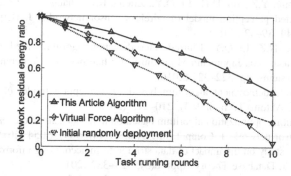

Fig. 3. Relations of network residual energy and task running rounds

Figure 3 is under the initial randomly deployment, virtual force algorithm and this article algorithm, at the same detection area under the same number, under the same coverage performance, the perception node residual energy contrast figure of sensor networks. Because the virtual force algorithm and this article algorithm in the initial stage of perceptual mobile node, and this article algorithm under the movement number is greater than the virtual force algorithm, so the energy consumption is larger, and the energy consumption is greater than the virtual force algorithm this article algorithm is presented. However due to both used the redundancy node dormancy mechanism, after complete the deployment, virtual force algorithm and this article algorithm energy per unit time is less than initial randomly deployment, due to the redundancy this article algorithm under network is greater than the virtual force algorithm, therefore, this article algorithm consumes energy is smaller than the virtual force algorithm. Therefore this article algorithm compared with other algorithm own the longer lifetime of the network.

7 Conclusion

This article aims at wireless sensor network nodes deployment algorithm based on perception model, in order to improve the coverage of the wireless sensor network and prolong the lifetime of the wireless sensor network, based on the perception model, establish nodes detection model, combining with the data fusion. This article algorithm can effectively reduce the number of deployment wireless sensor network nodes, improve the efficiency of wireless sensor network coverage, reduce the wireless sensor network nodes energy consumption, and prolong the lifetime of the wireless sensor network.

References

1. Song, X.L., Gong, Y.Z., Jin, D.H., Li, Q.Y., Jing, H.C.: Coverage hole recovery algorithm based on molecule model in heterogeneous WSNs. Int. J. Comput. Commun. Control **12**(4), 562–576 (2017)
2. Song, X.L., Gong, Y.Z., Jin, D.H., Li, Q.Y., Zheng, R.J., Zhang, M.C.: Nodes deployment based on directed perception model of wireless sensor networks. J. Beijing Univ. Posts Telecommun. **40**, 39–42 (2017)
3. Zhao, M.Z., Liu, N.Z., Li, Q.Y.: Blurred video detection algorithm based on support vector machine of Schistosoma Japonicum Miracidium. In: International Conference on Advanced Mechatronic Systems, pp. 322–327 (2016)
4. Jing, H.C.: Node deployment algorithm based on perception model of wireless sensor network. Int. J. Autom. Technol. **9**(3), 210–215 (2015)
5. Jing, H.C.: Routing optimization algorithm based on nodes density and energy consumption of wireless sensor network. J. Comput. Inf. Syst. **11**(14), 5047–5054 (2015)
6. Jing, H.C.: The study on the impact of data storage from accounting information processing procedure. Int. J. Database Theory Appl. **8**(3), 323–332 (2015)
7. Jing, H.C.: Improved ultrasonic CT imaging algorithm of concrete structures based on simulated annealing. Sens. Transducers **162**(1), 238–243 (2014)
8. Zhang, J.W., Li, S.W., Li, Q.Y., Liu, Y.C., Wu, N.N.: Coverage hole recovery algorithm based on perceived probability in heterogeneous wireless sensor network. J. Comput. Inf. Syst. **10**(7), 2983–2990 (2014)
9. Jing, H.C.: Coverage holes recovery algorithm based on nodes balance distance of underwater wireless sensor network. Int. J. Smart Sens. Intell. Syst. **7**(4), 1890–1907 (2014)
10. Wu, N.N., et al.: Mobile nodes deployment scheme design based on perceived probability model in heterogeneous wireless sensor network. J. Robot. Mechatron. **26**(5), 616–621 (2014)
11. Li, Q.Y., Ma, D.Q., Zhang, J.W.: Nodes deployment algorithm based on perceived probability of wireless sensor network. Comput. Meas. Control. **22**(2), 643–645 (2014)
12. Jing, H.C.: Improving SAFT imaging technology for ultrasonic detection of concrete structures. J. Appl. Sci. **13**(21), 4363–4370 (2013)
13. Li, S.W., Ma, D.Q., Li, Q.Y., Zhang, J.W., Zhang, X.: Nodes deployment algorithm based on perceived probability of heterogeneous wireless sensor network. In: International Conference on Advanced Mechatronic Systems, pp. 374–378 (2013)
14. Zhang, H.T., Bai, G., Liu, C.P.: Improved simulated annealing algorithm for broadcast routing of wireless sensor network. J. Comput. Inf. Syst. **9**(6), 2303–2310 (2013)
15. Li, Q.Y., Ma, D.Q., Zhang, J.W., Fu, F.Z.: Nodes deployment algorithm of wireless sensor network based on evidence theory. Comput. Meas. Control. **21**(6), 1715–1717 (2013)

A Novel Kernel Clustering Method for SVM Training Sample Reduction

Tong-Bo Wang[(⊠)]

College of Information Science & Technology, Hainan University,
Haikou 570228, China
tongbowang933@163.com

Abstract. This paper presents a new algorithm named Kernel Bisecting k-means and Sample Removal (KBK-SR) as a sampling preprocess for SVM training to improve the scalability. The novel top-down clustering approach Kernel Bisecting k-means in the KBK-SR tends to fast produce balanced clusters of similar sizes in the kernel feature space, which makes KBK-SR efficient and effective for reducing training samples for nonlinear SVMs. Theoretical analysis and experimental results on three UCI real data benchmarks both show that, with very short sampling time, our algorithm dramatically accelerates SVM training while maintaining high test accuracy.

Keywords: Support vector machines · Top-down hierarchical clustering
Kernel bisecting k-means

1 Introduction

In recent years, a number of algorithms based on "divide-and-conquer" have been proposed to improve the scalability of SVMs, i.e., accelerate SVM training with large-scale samples, such as chunking algorithm [1], decomposition algorithm [2], sequential minimal optimization (SMO) [3], and SVM^{light} [4]. These approaches decompose a large training task into a series of smaller sub-tasks so that the overall SVM training time can be reduced, but the time complexity still needs further improvement in practice.

While training samples close to decision boundaries have higher chances to be support vectors (SVs), samples far from decision boundaries have less effect when identifying SVs. Therefore, some algorithms have been proposed to sample a small portion of training data which are more likely to be SVs, such as active learning [5], random sampling [6], and clustering-based SVM [7]. All the methods above need to train SVMs and/or scan the whole training set for many times to get the current selection of data, so their efficiency is still limited by the training speed of SVMs and the scale of training sets.

Wang et al. [8] proposed an algorithm named sample reduction by data structure analysis (SR-DSA), which selects potential SVs based on structure information extracted from the training set by agglomerative hierarchical clustering (AHC). However, the AHC procedure in this approach has two drawbacks: (1) the distance between every two clusters must be calculated and stored, which means a space

© Springer Nature Switzerland AG 2018
T. Hu et al. (Eds.): ICA3PP 2018 Workshops, LNCS 11338, pp. 51–58, 2018.
https://doi.org/10.1007/978-3-030-05234-8_7

requirement proportional to N^2; (2) It is time-consuming to build the whole dendrogram to determine the appropriate number of clusters, i.e., merge distances corresponding to all possible numbers of clusters need to be computed and compared to find the knee point.

In view of the space and time inefficiency of the bottom-up AHC, this paper proposes a new sample reduction approach, which executes a top-down hierarchical clustering named as kernel bisecting k-means (KBK), to produce balanced clusters of similar sizes in the kernel feature space, followed by a sample removal (SR) procedure.

The remainder of this paper is organized as follows. In Sect. 2, we first provide a brief review of bisecting k-means, and then propose KBK. In Sect. 3, we describe our algorithm KBK-SR, elaborating the proposed KBK clustering procedure. Experiments are reported in Sect. 4, while we draw our conclusions in Sect. 5.

2 Kernel Bisecting k-Means

2.1 Bisecting k-Means Algorithm

The traditional k-means provides no guarantee of producing balanced clusters. Therefore, it is quite possible that a single cluster contains a large portion of the entire datasets, limiting the usefulness of this algorithm for improving scalability. Bisecting k-means [9] can be used to enforce balancing constraints, which is a vaiant of k-means and repeatedly bisects the largest remaining cluster into two subclusters at each step, until the desired value of k is reached. This algorithm starts with the whole data set as a single cluster, and typically converges to balanced clusters of similar sizes. Readers are referred to [9] for the steps in detail.

2.2 KBK—Kernel Bisecting k-Means

In comparison with k-means, the bisecting k-means algorithm is more efficient for large k and produces clusters with smaller entropy (i.e. purer clusters) [9]. However, like k-means, bisecting k-means yields piecewise linear borders among data, making the approach unsuitable for sample reduction preceding SVM training, because SVMs are developed mainly for nonlinear classification in applications. For this reason, we proposed kernel bisecting k-means (KBK) by integrating kernel methods with bisecting k-means. Kernel methods [10] are algorithms that, by replacing the inner product $<x, y>$ with an appropriate positive definite function $K(x, y)$, implicitly perform a nonlinear mapping $\Phi : X \rightarrow F$ from the input space X to a high dimensional feature space F endowed with an inner product defined as

$$K(x, y) = <\Phi(x), \Phi(y)> \tag{1}$$

To perform bisecting k-means in the feature space, referring to the algorithm listed in Sect. 2.1, we formally need to solve two problems. One is how to compute what we call the kernel squared Euclidian distance, i.e., the squared Euclidian distance in the feature space; the other is how to calculate the kernel mean vector of a cluster, i.e., the centroid in the feature space.

Using Eq. (1), we can compute the kernel squared Euclidian distance as

$$\|\Phi(x) - \Phi(y)\|^2 = K(x, x) - 2K(x, y) + K(y, y) \tag{2}$$

However, it is not so easy to solve the second problem. Let C be a cluster of l patterns (7), $C^{\Phi} = \{\Phi(x_j) | j = 1, \ldots, l\}$, and $\mu_{C^{\Phi}}$ be the mean vector of C^{Φ}. Then we have

$$\tau \mu_{C^{\Phi}} = \frac{1}{l} \sum_{j=1}^{l} \Phi(x_j) \tag{3}$$

Clearly $\mu_{C^{\Phi}}$ cannot be computed directly in the case of an unknown mapping Φ which is only performed implicitly by using kernel methods. Fortunately, there is no need to calculate $\mu_{C^{\Phi}}$, since it is not necessarily the case that $\mu_{C^{\Phi}}$ belongs to C_{Φ}. What we really need in practice is a pattern $m_1 \in C$, whose image $\Phi(m_1)$ is the closest element to $\mu_{C^{\Phi}}$ in C^{Φ}. From Eqs. (2)–(3), we have

$$\|\Phi(x_i) - \mu_{C^{\Phi}}\|^2 = K(x_i, x_i) - \frac{2}{l} \sum_{j=1}^{l} K(x_i, x_j) + \frac{1}{l^2} \sum_{i=1}^{l} \sum_{j=1}^{l} K(x_i, x_j) \tag{4}$$

where the final summation term is a constant. Let

$$r_i = K(x_i, x_i) - \frac{2}{l} \sum_{j=1}^{l} K(x_i, x_j) \tag{5}$$

then we can easily find i_1 subject to

$$r_{i_1} = \min_{1 \leq i \leq l} r_i, 1 \leq i_1 \leq l \tag{6}$$

It can be easily seen that

$$m_1 = x_{i_1} \tag{7}$$

Thus the bisecting k-means algorithm can be performed in the feature space, which is what we call KBK. The detailed algorithm is seen in the following.

3 KBK-SR for SVM Sample Reduction

3.1 The KBK-SR Algorithm

The kernel bisecting k-means and sample removing (KBK-SR) algorithm can be described as three steps, of which the first is KBK clustering procedure.

$S1$ Perform KBK clustering for positive class and negative class independently. For positive class P, given a certain threshold τ, the clustering $P = P1 \cup P2 \cup \ldots \cup P_{S_P}$ is achieved as follows:

$C_0 \leftarrow P, CS \leftarrow \{C_0\}$ (CS means set of clusters)

do

> select the largest remaining cluster C_j in CS bisecting step:
> use the method showed by Eqs. (5)–(7) to find m_1 in C_j;
> find m_2 in C_j, subject to $\|\Phi(m_2) - \Phi(m_1)\|^2 = \min\{\|\Phi(x) - \Phi(m_1)\|^2 x \in C_j\}$,
> where the kernel squared Euclidian distance is computed by Eq. (2);

> **do**

>> calculation step: for each data point of C_j, use Eq. (2) to compute the kernel squared Euclidean distance with m_1 and m_2, respectively, and assign the data point to its closest choice, forming two subclusters $C_{j_1} C_{j_2}$;
>> updates step; use the method showed by Eqs. (5)–(7) to update m_1 in C_{j1} and m_2 in C_{j_2}, respectively;

> **until** no change in m_1 and m_2

$$CS \leftarrow CS \cup \{C_{j_1}, C_{j_2}\}$$

until size of the largest cluster in CS is below τ.

For negative class N, the clustering $N = N_1 \cup N_2 \ldots \cup N_{S_N}$ is achieved in a similar way.

$S2$ Remove the interior samples in each relatively large cluster. For each cluster C, if $|C| \geq \tau_0$, calculate the kernel square Mahalanobis distance (the distance for short) from each data pattern in C to the cluster itself, sort the distances, and according to a given $\eta(0 < \eta < 1)$, pick out $\eta|C|$ patterns with the largest distances, and remove all other data points, where $|C|$ denotes the cardinal of C, and τ_0 is a certain small natural number (e.g. 5). Thus, the cluster C shrinks to C', which only contains $\eta|C|$ patterns.

$S3$ **For each relatively large cluster, remove exterior samples that are distant from the opposite class.** If $|C'| \geq \tau_0$ remove the points whose distances to the clusters in the opposite class are greater than the average distance, to get C''.

$S2$ and $S3$ composes the SR procedure, which aims at removing points that are impossible to have influence on the final decision boundary. The role of τ_0 is to skip very small clusters, which is different from the corresponding steps in SR-DSA [8].

3.2 A Toy Example

To visually demonstrate the process and the performance of our KBK-SR for SVM classification, we generate a two-dimensional synthetic dataset, displayed in Fig. 1(a), of 2048 points (1024 in each class). The original data are mapped by $\Phi: X \to F$: $(x, y)^T \in X, \Phi(x, y) = (x^2, y^2)$, and the image data are displayed in Fig. 1(b), which form 16 clusters (8 clusters for each class), each containing 128 points. Figure 1 (b) → (c) shows that KBK-SR successfully detected the clusters, and for each cluster effectively extracted the exterior points closer to the opposite class ($\eta = 0.15$). Training with the extracted points, we obtained the linear image decision boundary

$$4.91x + 9.66y - 170.05 = 0.$$

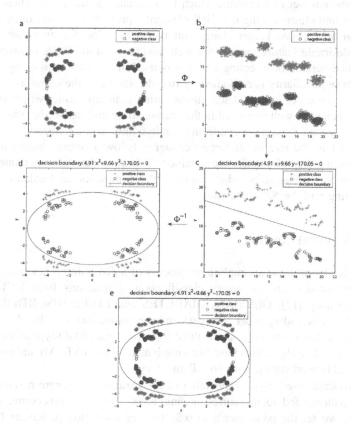

Fig. 1. Process and performance of KBK-SR for SVM classification on the toy dateset. (a) original dataset; (b) image dataset by mapping Φ; (c) extracted training points and the linear image decision boundary; (d) the corresponding elliptical decision boundary; (e) the classification result for the entire original dataset.

Using Φ^{-1}, this linear boundary is inversely mapped into an elliptical boundary (see Fig. 1(d))

$$4.91x^2 + 9.66y^2 - 170.05 = 0.$$

For the entire original dataset, the classification result is shown in Fig. 1(e).

3.3 Further Explanation

It seems to be a question whether there really exists a bisecting clustering structure for any dataset in the feature space, i.e., clusters of similar sizes, like the toy data in Sect. 3.2. Actually, it is impossible for a top-down clustering to fully detect the natural structure of data, unless the whole dendrogram is built. However, we define the size of a cluster as the number of its points, which is not related to distances. Therefore, it is reasonable to find clusters using the KBK clustering procedure. On the other hand, the choice of an appropriate kernel along with the right value for its parameters, i.e., choosing a desirable feature space, may well lead to a natural KBK clustering. Note that a modified version of bisecting k-means is used in the KBK clustering procedure (3.1 $S1$), whose peculiarity is embodied by two details. First, the initial assignment of m_1 and m_2 in the outer loop is deterministic rather than stochastic, which makes the initial two subclusters well separated in the feature space and fast leads to local optima of better quality than those produced from a random initialization. Second, the stopping criterion for $S1$ is, the size of the largest cluster is below a certain threshold τ, rather than a certain number of clusters are obtained. This provides safer guarantee of balanced clusters of similar sizes, which controls the computational burden of both the KBK clustering and the SR procedures.

4   Experimental Results

Our KBK-SR algorithm as a sampling preprocess of SVM training has been tested on three benchmark datasets for binary classification applications from UCI machine learning repository [12], GERMAN, DIABETES and LIVER-DISORDERS, whose sizes differ in a descending order. The performance comparison of KBK-SR, SR-DSA and no sampling has been made, all the three followed by an SMO-type algorithm with Gaussian kernel. The algorithms have been implemented in MATLAB and executed on a Xeon 2.7 GHz workstation with 16 GB memory.

We empirically used $2\sqrt{n}$ as the value of the parameter τ, where n stands for the number of patterns fed to the corresponding KBK clustering procedure. In all the experiments, we set the parameter η to 0.3. The regularization parameter C and the width parameter σ of Gaussian kernel were tuned using 5-fold cross-validation on the whole dataset.

For each dataset, we split it in half to training and test samples. Table 1 shows the time complexity and testing accuracies of the three methods, which are averaged over 30 random splits of the data to minimizing the possible misleading results. The results show that our KBK-SR dramatically outperforms SR-DSA in terms of the sampling time, and this advantage is more significant for a larger dataset. Also, our method greatly speeds up SVM training with very little loss of test accuracy when compared with SMO without sampling.

Table 1. Performance comparison of sampling methods

Dataset	Sampling	No. of sample	Sampling time (s)	Training time (s)	Test accuracy (%)
German	KBK-SR	156	0.65	6.41	78.54
	SR-DSA	134	9.80	3.27	71.36
	No sampling	500	0	89.63	78.67
Diabetes	KBK-SR	120	0.35	2.51	73.51
	SR-DSA	107	4.42	2.50	70.22
	No sampling	384	0	31.12	74.73
Liver-Dis	KBK-SR	59	0.78	1.28	75.02
	SR-DSA	53	1.46	1.17	73.63
	No sampling	173	0	5.19	76.28

5 Conclusion

In this paper, we present a novel clustering approach, Kernel Bisecting k-means, and further integrate it with a subsequent sample removal procedure to develop a new sample reduction algorithm named as KBK-SR, which effectively reduces training samples for SVMs. The main quality of Kernel Bisecting k-means consists in fast producing balanced clusters of similar sizes in the kernel feature space, which makes KBK-SR efficient and effective for reducing training samples for nonlinear SVMs. In comparison with SR-DSA, our algorithm significantly reduces the sampling time complexity while maintaining high test accuracy.

References

1. Boser, B.E., Guyon, I.M., Vapnik, V.N.: A training algorithm for optimal margin classifiers. In: Fifth Annual Workshop on Computational Learning Theory. ACM Press, Pittsburgh, pp. 144–152 (1992)
2. Osuna, E., Freund, R., Girosi, F.: An improved training algorithm for support vector machines. In: ICNNSP 1997, New York, pp. 276–285 (1997)
3. Platt, J.: Fast training of support vector machines using sequential minimal optimization. In: Schölkopf, B., Burges, C., Smola, A. (eds.) Advances in Kernel Methods - Support Vector Learning, pp. 185–208. MIT Press, Cambridge (1999)

4. Joachims, T.: Making large-scale SVM learning practical. In: Schölkopf, B., Burges, C., Smola, A. (eds.) Advances in Kernel Methods - Support Vector Learning, pp. 169–184. MIT Press, Cambridge (1999)
5. Schohn, G., Cohn, D.: Less is more: active learning with support vector machines. In: Proceedings of the 17th International Conference on Machine Learning (ICML 2000), pp. 839–846 (2000)
6. Lee, Y.J., Mangasarian, O.L.: RSVM: reduced support vector machines. In: Proceedings of the 1th SIAM International Conference on Data Mining, Chicago (2001)
7. Yu, H., Yang, J., Han, J.: Classifying large datasets using SVMs with hierarchical clusters. In: Proceedings of International Conference on Knowledge Discovery and Data Mining (KDD 2003), pp. 306–315 (2003)
8. Wang, D., Shi, L.: Selecting valuable training samples for SVMs via data structure analysis. Neurocomputing (2007). http://www.doi.org/10.1016/j.neucom.2007.09.008
9. Li, Y., Chung, S.M.: Parallel bisecting K-means with prediction clustering algorithm. J. Supercomput. **39**(1), 19–37 (2007)
10. Cristianini, N., Shawe-Taylor, J.: An Introduction to Support Vector Machines and Other Kernel-based Learning Methods. Cambridge University Press, Cambridge (2000)
11. Ruiz, A., López-de-Teruel, P.E.: Nonlinear kernel-based statistical pattern analysis. IEEE Trans. Neural Netw. **12**, 16–32 (2001)
12. http://www.ics.uci.edu/mlearn/MLRepository.html

Implementation of Beamforming for Large-Scale Circular Array Sonar Based on Parallel FIR Filter Structure in FPGA

Jun Wang[✉] and Junsheng Jiao

Science and Technology on Sonar Laboratory, Hangzhou Applied Acoustics
Research Institute, Hangzhou, China
king429001@163.com, 1985811474@qq.com

Abstract. In this paper, the directivity of the circular array is analyzed, real-time beamforming algorithm of circular array in frequency domain similar to parallel FIR filter structure is proposed by using the characteristic of the same directivity in different directions and the characteristic of steer vector symmetry. The coefficients of parallel FIR (Finite Impulse Response) filters are constant, while the steer vector of each frequency in the beamforming algorithm is variable, so the coefficients (steer vector) of the beamforming parallel filter need to be dynamically changed according to the frequency points. For frequency domain beamforming of high frequency large-scale circular array sonar, this algorithm only needs two shift registers, complex multipliers which is half the number of elements used in beamforming and a few logic resources to calculate steer vector in FPGA (Field Programmable Gate Array), and the algorithm can run at a higher working frequency. The lake-trial result shows that this parallel algorithm satisfies the real-time requirements of high-frequency large-scale circular array sonar, and the sonar has good azimuth resolution and detection performance.

Keywords: Circular array · Directivity · Beamforming · Parallel structure
FPGA

1 Introduction

Circular array is widely used in underwater sonar system, the greatest advantage of circular array compared to linear array and plane array is that it has the same detection ability in the range of 360°. High frequency circular array sonar is mainly used in underwater moving small target detection and imaging [1], Small target detection sonar has the following characteristics: the frequency of working center is mainly between 60 kHz–100 kHz, and the bandwidth is between 3 kHz–40 kHz, and the azimuth resolution is between 1.5° and 3.3°. The improvement of azimuth resolution requires more preformed beams, real-time broadband beamforming with high accuracy and wide dynamic range is a problem to be solved for small target detection sonar.

Based on the characteristics of circular array with the same directivity and steer vector symmetry, a real-time beamforming algorithm which has parallel FIR filter

© Springer Nature Switzerland AG 2018
T. Hu et al. (Eds.): ICA3PP 2018 Workshops, LNCS 11338, pp. 59–65, 2018.
https://doi.org/10.1007/978-3-030-05234-8_8

structure with dynamic change of filter coefficients is proposed, which has the advantages of high computational efficiency and less logical resources in FPGA.

The rest of the paper is organized as follows. Section 2 analyzes the directivity of the circular array and the characteristics of the beamforming. Section 3 introduces the structure of the FIR filter. Section 4 introduces steer vector calculation based on the CORDIC algorithm. Section 5 is real-time implementation of beamforming based on dynamic parallel FIR filter. Section 5 is the analysis of the lake-trial data. Section 6 concludes this paper.

2　Circular Array Directivity and Beamforming

Beamforming can be regarded as a spatial filter, which enhances the signal of interest and weakens the signal in other directions, beamforming in time domain has large amount of calculation and difficult to process in real time, so beamforming in frequency domain is usually used to reduce the computation.

2.1　Circular Array Directivity

Figure 1 shows schematic diagram of a planar discrete circular array uniformly distributed on the circumference, the radius of the discrete circular array is r, the array is numbered clockwise by $H_1, H_2, \ldots, H_N$, the direction of the center of the circle though H_1 is defined as $0°$, the angle of the adjacent array element is $\alpha = 2\pi/N$.

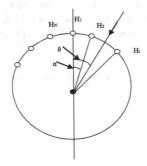

Fig. 1. Schematic diagram of a discrete circular array with uniform distribution

In calculating the directivity of the circular array, the reference point of time is selected on the center O, and the signal comes from the direction θ, the signal that reaches the O point is assumed to be $A\cos 2\pi ft$, the signal received by the array element H_i is

$$s_i(t) = A\cos[2\pi f(t + \tau_i(\theta))] \tag{1}$$

$\tau_i(\theta)$ is the delay of H_i relative to O,

$$\tau_i(\theta) = r\cos[\theta - (i-1)\alpha]/c \quad i = 1, 2, \ldots, N \tag{2}$$

c is the speed of sound in water, in order to form a beam in the direction of θ_0, the signal of H_i should be delayed by $\tau_i(\theta_0)$, and the signal after delay is

$$\begin{aligned} s_i(t - \tau_i(\theta_0)) &= A\cos[2\pi f(t + \tau_i(\theta) - \tau_i(\theta_0))] \\ &= A\cos[2\pi f(t + \Delta_i(\theta))] \end{aligned} \tag{3}$$

The expression of the directivity function is:

$$\begin{aligned} D(\theta) &= \left[E(s^2(t))\right]^{1/2}/N \\ &= \left[(\sum_{i=0}^{N}\cos 2\pi f\Delta_i(\theta))^2 + (\sum_{i=0}^{N}\sin 2\pi f\Delta_i(\theta))^2\right]/2 \end{aligned} \tag{4}$$

When $N \geq 4\pi r/(c/f)+2$, $D(\theta) \approx |J_0((4\pi r/\lambda)\sin((\theta - \theta_0)2))|$, Where $J_0(\cdot)$ is zero-order Bessel function.

$D(\theta)$ is only a function of $\theta - \theta_0$, therefore, the directivity of the circular array in all directions is the same, which is a superiority of the circular array over the linear array, When the beamforming algorithm calculates the steer vector, the steer vector in any pre-beam direction is the same.

2.2 Circular Array Beamforming

The circular array is usually installed in the ship bow, because the noise of the propeller comes from the ship stern, so it is not necessary to include the noise of the ship when the directivity of the forward direction is formed, usually part of the array elements are used in beamforming. For example, when pre-forming a beam of 0° direction, the array elements used are M elements of $H_{N-M/2+1} \sim H_N$ and $H_1 \sim H_{M/2}$, pre-forming a beam with $\alpha = 2\pi/N$ direction, the M elements used are $H_{N-M/2+2} \sim H_N$ and $H_1 \sim H_{M/2+1}$, that is, one array element is cyclically moved, and so on, one beam is pre-formed and one element is cyclically moved (Fig. 2).

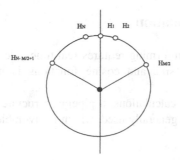

Fig. 2. Schematic diagram of circular array working sector

The formula of circular array wideband beamforming is

$$Y_l(k) = \sum_{i=0}^{M/2-1} X_{(i+l)\text{mod}N}(k)H_i(k) + \sum_{i=0}^{M/2-1} X_{(i-M/2+N+l)\text{mod}N}H_i(k) \qquad (5)$$

Where $H_i(k) = \exp(-j \cdot (2\pi r f_k/c) \cdot \cos[(i+0.5) \cdot (2\pi/N)])$, because the directivity of each direction of the circular array is the same, the steer vector is symmetrical, only the steer vector at $i = 0, 1, \ldots M/2 - 1$ need to be calculated, this characteristics of circular array can be used to link frequency domain beamforming with time domain FIR filter.

3 FIR Filter

FIR filter in time domain can be expressed as convolution

$$y(n) = x(n) * h(n) = \sum_{k=0}^{M-1} h(k)x(n-k) \qquad (6)$$

In Eq. (6), $h(n)$ is the filter coefficient, M is the order of the filter, and M filter coefficients are multiplied by M corresponding data, which can be implemented using different architectures (serial, semi-parallel or full-parallel).

The FIR filter can be implemented in parallel using multiple multipliers and adders. The parallel filter can complete filtering in one clock cycle, but it takes a lot of multipliers and accumulators to increase the filter speed.

As can be seen from the comparisons of Eqs. (5) and (6), the circular array frequency domain beamforming and the time domain FIR filtering have similar convolution operations. The M coefficients are multiplied by the M corresponding data, both the FIR filter coefficients and the beamforming steer vectors are symmetric, so a parallel filter structure can be used to calculate the multiplication in the circular array beamforming. The difference is that the steer vector of the circular array beamforming is a function of the frequency f_k, it is dynamic.

4 Steer Vector Calculation

The frequency domain beamforming requires real-time calculation of the steer vector $H_i(k)$, The calculation of sine and cosine functions is mainly achieved through CORDIC algorithm.

In high-speed real-time calculations, a pipeline structure composed of multi-level CORDIC operation units is generally used, which is favorable for high-speed and real-time operations.

5   Real-Time Implementation of Beamforming in FPGA

Taking a certain type of circular array sonar wideband frequency domain beamforming, the number of array elements is 360, the number of frequency point is 2730 and pre-forming number is 360, the wideband frequency domain beamforming of this sonar requires 360 * 2730 * 64 complex multiplications in 34.1 ms, due to the limited number of DSP multipliers, it is difficult to meet the real-time requirements with DSP.

Pre-forming one beam and one frequency point requires the use of one frequency point data of 128 array elements, forming 360 beams and one frequency point requiring one frequency point data of 487 array elements. In order to input data continuously in the FPGA, it is necessary to expand one frequency point data of 360 array elements into 487 array elements (360 + 64 + 63 = 487).

Beamforming based on FIR parallel filter is shown in Fig. 3, when the shift register of frequency point data is full of 128, the data of 64 points of the current clock after the addition of the symmetrical position are registered, and then parallel multiplication is performed with the 64 steer vector registered, finally 64 parallel multiplication results are added, output one pre-formed beamforming result at one frequency point, one clock completes 64 multiplication and addition operations.

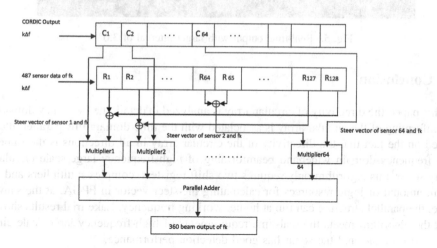

Fig. 3. Diagram of beamforming implementation based on FIR parallel filter

When one data is input into the shift register, the shift register performs a shift operation to complete one data update, at the same time, this algorithm completes 64 multiply-accumulate operations for one frequency point, and outputs a pre-formed beam result simultaneously. When the 487th data is input to the shift register, 360 pre-formed beams of the current frequency point are also completed at the same time. After 487 points of one frequency data have been output, 487 points of the next frequency data are input, and the steer vectors of 64 element of this frequency point are updated at the same time.

6   Lake-Trial Data Processing

In the lake-trial, the sonar array is 11 m in water and two diameter 100×100 mm stainless steel cylinders are suspended at the distance of 15 m from the sonar array as the target, the target is also 11 m in water. Sonar transmits LFM wideband pulse signal and moves one target until sonar can't distinguish two targets, then record the target azimuth. Figure 4 is a real-time system screenshot of two target intervals of 3.25°, two targets can be clearly distinguish. Figure 5 is real-time system screenshot of two target intervals of 3.0°, and two targets can't be correctly identified.

Fig. 4. Real-time output with target interval of 3.25°

Fig. 5. Real-time output with target interval of 3.0°

7   Conclusion

In this paper, the directivity of circular array is analyzed in detail, the frequency domain beamforming of the circular array is associated with the time-domain FIR parallel filter based on the fact that the directivity of the circular array in all directions is the same. For frequency-domain wideband beamforming of high-frequency large-scale circular array sonar, this algorithm only requires two shift registers, complex multipliers and a small amount of logic resources for calculating the steer vector in FPGA, at the same time, the parallel structure can run at higher working frequency. Lake-trial results show that the algorithm meets the real-time requirements of high-frequency large-scale circular array sonar, and the sonar has good detection performance.

References

1. Yeqiang, H., Tian, X., Zhou, F.: A real-time 3-D underwater acoustical imaging system. IEEE J. Oceanic Eng. **39**(4), 620–629 (2014)
2. Liua, Y., Maa, P., Cuia, H.: Design and development of FPGA-based high-performance radar data stream mining system. Procedia Comput. Sci. **55**, 876–885 (2015)
3. Wang, W., Liang, D., Wang, Z., Yu, H., Liu, Q.: Design and implementation of a FPGA and DSP based MIMO radar imaging system. Radioengineering **24**(2), 518–526 (2015)
4. Gutierrez, R., Valls, J.: Low-power FPGA-implementation of atan(Y/X) using look-up table methods for communication applications. J. Sign. Process. Syst. **56**, 25–33 (2009)
5. Cruza, J.F., Camacho, J., Brizuela, J., Moreno, J.M., Fritsch, C.: Modular architecture for ultrasound beamforming with FPGAs. In: International Congress on Ultrasonics AIP Conference Proceedings, vol. 1433, pp. 181–184 (2012)

A Practical and Aggressive Loop Fission Technique

Bo Zhao[1,2(✉)], Yingying Li[2], Lin Han[2], Jie Zhao[2,3], Wei Gao[2], Rongcai Zhao[2], and Ramin Yahyapour[1]

[1] Gesellschaft für wissenschaftliche Datenverarbeitung mbH Göttingen, 37077 Göttingen, Germany
bo.zhao@gwdg.de
[2] State Key Laboratory of Mathematical Engineering and Advanced Computing, Zhengzhou 450001, China
[3] French Institute for Research in Computer Science and Automation, Rocquencourt, France

Abstract. Loop fission is an effective loop optimization for exploiting fine-grained parallelism. Currently, loop fission is widely used in existing parallelizing compilers. To fully exploit the optimization, we proposed and implemented a practical and aggressive loop fission technique. First, we present an aggressive dependence graph pruning method to eliminate pseudo dependences caused by the conservativeness of compilers. Second, we introduce a topological sort based loop fission algorithm to distribute loops correctly. Finally, to enhance the performance of the generated programs which have potential of loop fission, we propose an advanced loop fission strategy. We evaluate these techniques and algorithms in the experimental section.

Keywords: Loop fission · Automatic vectorization
Compiling optimization

1 Introduction

Many efforts have been devoted to solving the memory-based dependence testing issues at the very beginning of the parallelizing compiler research until the introduction of the Ω test and the compiler community transferred their attention to loop optimizations [3–5]. Therefore, from the beginning of 1990s, the designers of parallel compilers have been focusing on the research of program structure optimization [2,10]. Loop nests are essential and have been continuously exploited, enhancing both parallelism and data locality in programs. The technique of loop optimization is able to achieve better parallel performance by changing the execution order through changing or reconfiguring the program structure [5,6]. Recently, loop optimization plays a more and more important role in the fields such as high-level hardware synthesis and generation of self-adaptive libraries to further improve the performance of parallel compilers.

© Springer Nature Switzerland AG 2018
T. Hu et al. (Eds.): ICA3PP 2018 Workshops, LNCS 11338, pp. 66–75, 2018.
https://doi.org/10.1007/978-3-030-05234-8_9

Loop optimizations improve the data locality through the transformation and scheduling of iteration space [6]. Currently, loop optimization methods utilized in parallelizing compilers include but not limit to loop interchange, loop fusion and loop fission, etc. [5,7,8]. When exploiting coarse-grained parallelism, we need parallelize the outermost loops. On the contrary, fine-grained parallelism exploitation goes into the opposite direction. As a method to minimize the volume of communications and synchronizations, loop fission is designed to improve the data locality and reuse.

Open64 is an advanced product-level source to source compiler and it is mainly designed to realize compilation optimizations. It is extensible, portable and compatible with gcc/g++. Based on open64-5.0 [9] compiler, our research group designed and realized an automatically vectorization tool SW-VEC oriented to domestic high performance processors. When utilizing SW-VEC compiler to optimize loops in programs, some of the generated parallel code enjoy very limited performance improvement using loop fission. Consequently, in order to carry out loop fission more effectively with SW-VEC compiler, a practical and aggressive loop fission technique is proposed. With the algorithm proposed in this paper, loop fission can be applied correctly for program parallelization optimization and the performance is further improved comparing to the original programs. The main contributions of this paper are as following.

(1) An aggressive array dependency graph pruning technique is proposed to eliminate the pseudo dependencies caused by conservative analysis of the compiler. This is the foundation for further loop optimization.
(2) Based on the aggressive array dependency graph pruning technique and dependency graph vertex topological sort, a loop fission algorithm is proposed to generate correct parallel code executing on the domestic high performance computing system.
(3) On the basis of the code generated after loop fission, an optimized loop fission strategy is designed and implemented. Comparing with the original loop fission method, the method proposed in this paper can automatically realize the optimization of loop fission completely and improve its performance.

2   Related Work

Loop optimizations are significant in automatic parallelization for maximizing parallelism and loop fission plays an important role in it. High-level loop transformations are a key instrument in mapping computational kernels to effectively exploit resources in modern processor architectures [12]. Polyhedral model [12,13] is currently a popular mathematical abstraction for program transformations. The model abstracts the iteration space of loops and access space of array into the convex polyhedron on the multidimensional space, performing loop transformations by changing the schedule of programs. Then it implements loop exchanges and optimization by transforming the convex polyhedron on the multi-dimensional space. Although the polyhedral model provides a simple and effective method to take into all loop optimization methods into consideration generally, the polyhedral space cost needed by the affine transformation from loop iteration space to array access space is very large and the related transformation across multi-dimensional spaces is also a very complex problem. Therefore, extending the polyhedral model into practical is still on the way. Some classical compiler tools, such as Graphite designed by GCC 4.5 and WRaP-IT designed by Open64 [15, 16] considered the theory research but had no practical implementation in released versions.

3   Aggressive Array Dependency Graph Pruning Technique

3.1   A Fast Look at Loop Fission in SW-VEC

When realizing the loop fission algorithm, four kinds of dependency graphs are mainly taken into consideration. They are adg (array dependency graph), sdg (statement dependency graph), dep_g_p (strong connectivity dependency graph) and ac_g (strong connectivity condensation dependency graph). Array dependency graph is the foundation, in which each vertex represents an array reference and each edge indicates a dependency between the two array reference nodes.

Two vertexes are reachable when dependency circle exists between them in the statement dependency graph. Vertexes in the dependency graph will be divided into several strongly connected components and all the vertexes in each component are reachable to each other. On the basis of the statement dependency graph, compilers will first construct the vertexes of each strong connectivity dependency graph and each statement itself is a strong connectivity. Then we can add dependency edges in the strong connectivity dependency graph according to the statement dependency graph. At the moment, the number of vertex in the strong connectivity dependency graph may reduce and then we can cohere each strongly connected component consisting of several vertexes into one vertex to get the strong connectivity condensation dependency graph of loops.

Example 1:

```
for(i=1;i<LEN-1;i++)
S1 a[i] = i;
S2 b[i] = c[i-1];
S3 c[i] = b[i-1];
```

Taking example 1 into consideration, we can get array dependency graph, statement dependency graph, strong connectivity dependency graph and strong connectivity condensation dependency graph of the loop, as shown in Fig. 1(a)–(d) respectively. For the strong connectivity condensation dependency graph, statements in one node must be distributed to the same loop to keep the original dependencies.

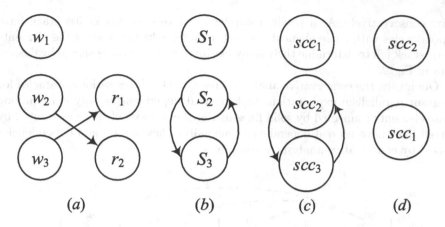

Fig. 1. Four kinds of dependency graphs in example 1.

Aggressive loop fission algorithm distributes different strongly connected component nodes according to the final strong connectivity condensation dependency graph and add related loops before distributed statement sets. On the basis, we can get the final distributed code. From the analysis process, it is obvious to see that array dependency graph is the foundation and strong connectivity condensation dependency graph is the basis for loop fission.

3.2   Removing Pseudo Dependencies

When building array dependency graph, compilers add dependency edges between dependent vertexes according to the beginning address of array reference. There are two steps to build array dependency graph in SW-VEC compiler. The first step is to compute the beginning address of the array reference in current nest loops. In this step the compiler maintains a stack for each array beginning address. If the beginning address of an array is exactly the same with the one related to the stack, items related to this array in symbol table will be pushed into the stack, as shown in Fig. 2. When the compiler cannot get the starting address of an array, the default beginning address is 0 and the array will be pulled into the 0# stack. Afterwards, for each pair of array reference, if one of the two arrays is pulled into 0# stack, one dependency edge is added between them, which is defaulted in the compiler. When the two arrays are both not in 0# stack and if they are in the same stack, one dependency edge is added between the vertexes related to these two reference nodes in the array dependency graph.

We assume there are n beginning addresses having related stacks and use $e_i(0 <= i <= n - 1)$ to represent the elements in each stack, where the ith Ω has k_i elements. For compilers, keeping the accuracy of one program is more important than improving its performance. Consequently, optimizing compilers usually choose conservative analysis strategy, i.e., when the dependency information is unknown, we should believe there exist dependencies in array reference pairs conservatively. As a result, compilers believe elements in 0# stack have dependencies with those elements in each other stacks because all the elements in 0# stack fail to determine their array beginning addresses, as shown by dashed lines in Fig. 2.

Obviously, the conservative analysis strategy introduces serious obstacles for program parallelism exploitation. In fact, real dependencies only exist among those elements connected by solid lines in Fig. 2 and most of those connected by dotted lines have no real dependencies actually. They are pseudo dependencies caused by conservative analysis of compilers.

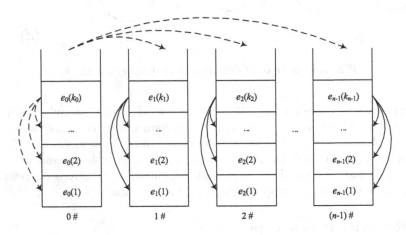

Fig. 2. Corresponding stacks of initial array access address when building array dependency graph.

In order to eliminate pseudo dependencies, we should continue to analyze the properties of the elements connected by dashed lines. As shown in Fig. 2, at least one element connected by the dashed lines is in 0# stack and elements in 0# stack are arrays whose beginning addresses are unknown. One important reason for unknown array beginning address in 0# stack is side-effect, such as array alias, caused by procedure calls. However, inter-procedural analysis is quite difficult for parallel compiling and there is still no complete solution currently. Consequently, we need to apply some aggressive methods to eliminate pseudo dependencies and then improve the parallel program performance.

4   Optimized Loop Fission Algorithm

4.1   Loop Fission Algorithm Based on Topological Sorting

The execution results before and after loop fission are consistent because there is no dependency between the two strong connectivity in Fig. 1(d) and we can execute the program in arbitrary sequence without leading to fault results. Nevertheless, the execution result after loop fission is inconsistent with the original result.

The topological sorting of a directed acyclic graph DAG is to sort all the nodes in DAG into a linear sequence. On the basis, for every pair of nodes u and v, if an edge exists from u to v, node u will be located before node v in the linear sequence. Therefore, we take a topological sorting for the nodes in the strong connectivity condensation dependency graph and the edges in the graph indicate the dependencies among strong connectivity. At this moment, we can distribute the loops based on the queues after topological sorting and the former nodes in the topological sorting queue will be located more forward after distribution, which means the dependencies in the original program are maintained. The algorithm of topological sorting for nodes in the strong connectivity condensation dependency graph is shown in Algorithm 1, where ac_g means the strong connectivity condensation dependency graph and all the functions related to this dependency graph have been already realized. Calling such function, the queue keeps the node numbers of the strong connectivity condensation dependency graph after topological sorting.

Algorithm 1. Optimized Loop Fission Algorithm

1: **Input:** queue[] before topological sorting
2: **Output:** queue[] after topological sorting
3: **Algorithm:**
4: $tmp\_loop \leftarrow loop$
5: **function** TOPOLOGICAL_SORT(QUEUE[])
6:     $g \leftarrow ac\_g$
7:     $index \leftarrow 0$
8:     $i \leftarrow 1$
9:     **while**$(i < g- > vertex\_count\_num + 1)$
10:         **if**$(!vertex[i]- > Get\_In\_Edge())$
11:             $queue[index + +] \leftarrow i$
12:         **else**
13:             **return**
14:     **for**$(i = 0; i < head; i + +)$
15:         $j \leftarrow queue[i]$
16:         $e \leftarrow g- > Get\_out\_Edge(j)$
17:         **while**$(e)\{$
18:             $e1 \leftarrow e$
19:             $e \leftarrow g- > Get\_Next\_Out\_Edge(e)$
20:             $sink \leftarrow g- > Get\_Sink(e1)$
21:             $g- > Delete\_Edge(e1)$
22:             **if**$(!vertex[i]- > Get\_In\_Edge())$
23:                 $queue[index + +] \leftarrow sink$
24:     **return** $queue[]$

4.2   Optimized Loop Fission Scheme

In order to realize loop fission automatically in SW-VEC compiler, we delete the recognition process for compiling pragma in our loop fission algorithm. SW-VEC compiler will recognize whether there is compiling pragma before loop nests when the compiler is in the stage of loop nest optimization process. If so, the identifier needing fission will be set true. Our method sets the identifier needing fission true if only the compiling option $-LNO : fission = 1$ is adopted. However, this setting may lead to new problems, that is, the loops needing no fission will also be distributed under this compiling option. Considering example 2, its dependency graphs are shown in Fig. 3.

Example 2:

```
for(i=1;i<LEN-1;i++)
S1 a[i] = i;
S2 b[i] = LEN-i;
S3 c[i] = d[i-1];
S4 d[i] = c[i-1];
```

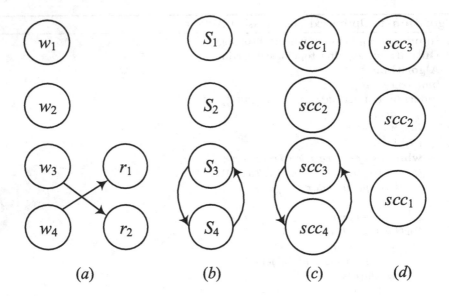

Fig. 3. Four types dependency graphs of example 2.

Considering the examples above, we need to distribute the nodes containing dependency circle formed by some statements in the strong connectivity condensation dependency graph. These statements form a strong connectivity and correspond to a node in the dependency graph, which means such a node contains several statements. If a node related to a strong connectivity only has one statement, the node need not to be distributed outside. According to this principle, we obtain the optimized loop fission strategy. We get the node numbers of the strong connectivity condensation dependency graph related to the queue gained by topological sorting described in Sect. 4.1. If the strong connectivity corresponding to a node contains only one statement, it will be kept original. Otherwise, it will be distributed. The algorithm is shown in Algorithm 2, where ac_g means the strong connectivity condensation dependency graph of the loop. All the functions related to the dependency graph are realized in SW-VEC compiler.

Algorithm 2. Optimized Loop Fission Algorithm

1: **Input:** Nest Loop to be Distributed
2: **Output:** Distributed Nest Loop
3: **Algorithm:**
4: $tmp\_loop \leftarrow loop$
5: **function** OPT_FISSION(LOOP)
6:      $loop\_count \leftarrow ac\_g-> Get\_Vertex\_Count()$
7:      **for** $(i = 0; i < loop\_count; i + +)\{$ **do**
8:          $size \leftarrow ac\_g-> Get\_Vertex\_Count()$
9:          **if** $size == 1$ **then**
10:             $stmt \leftarrow stmt-> next$
11:             **Continue**
12:         $tmp\_loop2 \leftarrow$ **null**
13:         $Separate(tmp\_loop, stmt-> prev, tmp\_loop2)$
14:         $tmp\_loop1 \leftarrow tmp\_loop2$
15:         **for** $(j = 0; j < size; j + +)$ **do**
16:             $stmt \leftarrow stmt-> next$
17:     **return** $queue[]$

---

5   Evaluation

The experimental platform is SunWay system, with Redhat Enterprise 5 OS, 2.0 GHz CPU, 2 GB memory, 32 KB L1 cache, 256 KB cache, 8 KB page size and 256 bits vector register which can deal with 4 floating type or 8 integer operation.

The benchmark is SPEC2006 which is a very popular version of system evaluation benchmarks proposed by Standard Performance Evaluation Corporation. The benchmark contains 12 different integer benchmark tests and 17 different float benchmark tests.

5.1   Efficiency Verification of Pruning Technique

A pruning technique of dependency graph was proposed in this paper to eliminate the pseudo dependencies caused by the conservative analysis of compilers.

This pruning technique is aggressive and therefore we need to verify its accuracy when compiling practical applications and programs.

We use SW-VEC to compile the test cases without using our pruning technique of dependency graph at first and then we compile the benchmark once again using the compiling option -ado. The results indicate that our algorithm has no influence on the accuracy of the test cases and can keep the result consistency.

For the test cases, we can eliminate pseudo dependencies under the compiling option -ado and choose the following 4 programs for analysis, namely 401.bzip2, 437.leslie3d, 456.hmmer and 470.lbm. We calculate the number of dependency edges before and after using -ado option. (Only calculate the dependency edge number of the loops related to the eliminated edge while not that of the whole program.) The experimental results are shown in Fig. 4, indicating the efficiency of our algorithm.

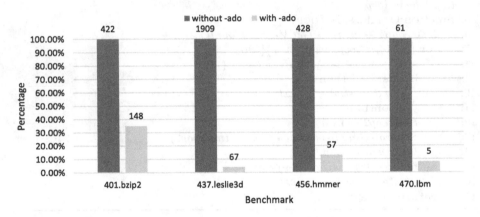

Fig. 4. Comparison of dependency edges of 4 kernel loops before and after using compiling option $-ado$.

5.2   Accuracy Verification of Loop Fission Algorithm

We verified the accuracy of our aggressive pruning technique of array dependency graph. On the basis, we test the accuracy of our loop fission algorithm. The experimental results demonstrate that our technique can keep the semantic consistency of the tested benchmarks.

6   Conclusion

Loop fission is an effective loop optimization technique for fine-grained parallelism. Aiming at solving the problems of loop fission algorithms in current parallel compilers, an aggressive pruning technique of array dependency graph is proposed in this paper at first. This pruning technique can efficiently eliminate the pseudo dependencies due to the conservative analysis of compilers, which forms the foundation of loop fission and other loop optimizations for the compilers. Then a loop fission algorithm based on topological sorting is introduced to guarantee the accuracy of the distributed codes. Finally, an optimized loop fission strategy is proposed on the basis of accurate distributed codes. Compared with the complete loop fission scheme, our strategy can efficiently improve the performance for the testing benchmarks. The experimental results and evaluation indicate the accuracy and efficiency of our method proposed in this paper.

References

1. Culler, D.E., Singh, J.P., Gupta, A.: Parallel Computer Architecture: A Hardware/software Approach. Gulf Professional Publishing, Houston (1999)
2. Kirk, D.B., Wen-Mei, W.H.: Programming Massively Parallel Processors: A Hands-on Approach. Morgan Kaufmann, Burlington (2016)
3. Kumar, V., et al.: Introduction to Parallel Computing: Design and Analysis of Algorithms, vol. 400. Benjamin/Cummings, Redwood City (1994)
4. Pugh, W.: The Omega test: a fast and practical integer programming algorithm for dependence analysis. In: Proceedings of the 1991 ACM/IEEE Conference on Supercomputing. ACM (1991)
5. Luporini, F., et al.: Cross-loop optimization of arithmetic intensity for finite element local assembly. ACM Trans. Archit. Code Optim. (TACO) 11(4), 57 (2015)
6. Kennedy, K., McKinley, K.S.: Optimizing for parallelism and data locality. In: ACM International Conference on Supercomputing 25th Anniversary Volume. ACM (2014)
7. Allen, J.R., Kennedy, K.: Automatic loop interchange. ACM Sigplan Notices 19(6), 233–246 (1984)
8. Banerjee, U.: Loop Parallelization. Springer, Heidelberg (2013)
9. open64-5.0 compiler source code. http://sourceforge.net/projects/open64/files/open64/Open64-5.0
10. McFarling, S.: Program optimization for instruction caches. ACM SIGARCH Comput. Archit. News 17(2), 183–191 (1989)
11. Allen, R., Kennedy, K.: Optimizing Compilers for Modern Architectures: a Dependence-Based Approach, vol. 1. Morgan Kaufmann, San Francisco (2002)
12. Pouchet, L.-N., et al.: Loop transformations: convexity, pruning and optimization. ACM SIGPLAN Notices 46(1), 549–562 (2011)
13. Kong, M., et al.: When polyhedral transformations meet SIMD code generation. ACM Sigplan Notices. 48(6), 127–138 (2013)
14. Maleki, S., et al.: An evaluation of vectorizing compilers. In: 2011 International Conference on Parallel Architectures and Compilation Techniques (PACT). IEEE (2011)
15. Bastoul, C., Cohen, A., Girbal, S., Sharma, S., Temam, O.: Putting polyhedral loop transformations to work. In: Rauchwerger, L. (ed.) LCPC 2003. LNCS, vol. 2958, pp. 209–225. Springer, Heidelberg (2004). https://doi.org/10.1007/978-3-540-24644-2_14
16. Hoefler, T., Lumsdaine, A., Dongarra, J.: Towards efficient mapreduce using MPI. In: Ropo, M., Westerholm, J., Dongarra, J. (eds.) EuroPVM/MPI 2009. LNCS, vol. 5759, pp. 240–249. Springer, Heidelberg (2009). https://doi.org/10.1007/978-3-642-03770-2_30

Super-Sampling by Learning-Based Super-Resolution

Ping Du, Jinhuan Zhang, and Jun Long$^{(\boxtimes)}$

School of Information Science and Engineering, Central South University,
Changsha 410083, Hunan, China
jlong@csu.edu.cn

Abstract. In this paper, we present a novel problem of intelligent image processing, which is how to infer a finer image in terms of intensity levels for a given image. We explain the motivation for this effort and present a simple technique that makes it possible to apply the existing learning-based super-resolution methods to this new problem. As a result of the adoption of the intelligent methods, the proposed algorithm needs notably little human assistance. We also verify our algorithm experimentally in the paper.

Keywords: Texture synthesis · Super-resolution · Image manifold

1 Introduction

While it seems to be an outdated task determining more intensity levels for an image, because our ability to handle visual signals has been improved considerably from the early age, when each single bit counts, an entry level DSLR has up to 4,096 intensity levels. However, in practical photography, a camera often cannot cover the entire dynamic range for a scene with high contrast and thus yields a partially over- or pre-exposed image. Occasionally, the photographer sacrifices exposure for a safe shutter time. In each case, there are areas in the image where the visual signal is only sampled with limited precision, thereby increasing the need for estimating richer intensity levels.

Let us take a image as the result of sampling a continuous 2-D visual signal in limited spatial positions and with limited precision. We refer to supersampling as the technique for improving the sampling precision of an image in contrast to the term super-resolution referring to enriching the spatial positions where the signal is sampled. Traditional low-level image processing techniques are not adequate for this problem because they involve adding information, which is impossible without proper modeled prior knowledge. However, it is not trivial to design a model representing the relations between signals sampled with low precision and their high-precision correspondence. This idea comes from the following two facts:

We can trade spatial domain precision for intensity domain precision, e.g., by averaging the value at neighboring pixels. Learning-based super-resolution techniques have been developed. Based on these facts, we propose a technique for image supersampling. In our framework, the user chooses a training image with similar content to the image to be super-sampled but in a larger size. Next, we apply super-resolution to

T. Hu et al. (Eds.): ICA3PP 2018 Workshops, LNCS 11338, pp. 76–83, 2018.
https://doi.org/10.1007/978-3-030-05234-8_10

convert the input image into a larger size, which is followed by smoothing and down-sampling. The resulting image is of the same size as the input image but with enriched intensity levels.

2 Related Work

The term "super-sampling" was originally used as an antialiasing technique in the computer graphics community [1]. In recent years, there are many smart image processing methods that have been proposed to improve image quality or enhance the information an image conveys. Convolutional neural networks are deep learning architectures and suitable for image classification [2], fingerprint detection [3] and facial recognition [4]. Generative adversarial networks provide an attractive means of generating natural images [5]. Image fusion is a proven, helpful approach to achieve robust and accurate facial recognition [6]. Local representation plays an important role in discovering the structures in images from a database and applying the prior knowledge to recover target images [7]. Useful features have been proposed to represent infrared facial images and help recognition [8]. Furthermore, structural knowledge can be leveraged to extract useful information from low resolution images [9]. Our spatial super-resolution method is directly based on previous work [10], in which the author take patches from the images as samples from manifolds and uses the geometric structure of the manifold to model the relations between the low-resolution and high-resolution images. The geometric structure of a manifold is represented by its locally linear embedding coefficients [11, 12]. Antialiasing is a set of low-level image processing techniques, which are to eliminate the sudden changes of pixel values at the edges of an image. These changes are not welcomed because the pixels are usually square-shaped and are of uniform color with each individual pixel. When an edge in an image, e.g., the border of an object, passes pixels, they make the edge look jagged (aliasing). By performing antialiasing to an image, we enrich the pixel levels in the transiting area of an edge, which make the image more visually appealing.

Different from the traditional antialiasing technique, in this paper we address the problem of designing a smart scheme to enrich the pixel levels in the whole image, and in contrast, we maintain the sharpness of the image during processing. Our work is also related to the low-level vision task of image hallucination, about which there are numerous studies available [10], which is the most related work to ours in this area. In their paper, the authors cut patches from a training image as training samples and use the LLE to represent the geometry of a manifold. However, the authors imagine the high frequency of an image for super-resolution, while we imagine the chromatic channel of an image for colorization.

3 Super-Sampling from Super-Resolution

3.1 Problem Analysis

An ideal *image* is a 2-D scalar field $I : R^2 \rightarrow R$, and each channel of an image is treated equally; therefore, we take the illuminant channel as example in our discussion. Next, a digital image $I_D : Z^2 \rightarrow Z$ is generated by sampling the original image I at nodes of a discrete grid in the image spatial domain and then ranking the value of I at each node into discrete intensity levels. This process can be seen as choosing the closest points in a 3-D grid to represent the surface of I. The problem of enriching the intensities in a digital image is to use a sampling grid with denser points in the intensity direction. However, information theory tells us that this is impossible without prior information about the image. Therefore, we adopt a learning-based framework for the following purpose: the user first gives the system an image of the similar subject/scene as the input image; then, the system extracts the prior knowledge from the training image and infuses the information into the input image to enrich its intensity levels. The learning-based superresolution methods address the similar problem as ours, but the other methods work on the sampling grid in the spatial domain. Inspired by them, we build models describing the relations between digital images generated from the same I and with different sampling densities in the intensity domain. Provided a training image, we may adjust our model parameters and use it for the inference. However, instead of *simulating* the way the super-resolution works, we can *use* those algorithms directly. This approach is based on the simple observation that we can trade spatial resolution for intensity resolution by simply averaging. This approach directly brings the following two advantages: one is obviously the repository of existing super-resolution tools and the other is that when one wants to super-sample an image to more than 256 intensity levels, it is considerably easier to find a larger training image than to find a training image with more than 256 intensity levels. On the other hand, however, the sampling grid for an image has two spatial dimensions and only one intensity dimension. This intuitively means that if we have "spare" spatial precision, we can trade it for the evaluation precision with efficiency. For example, by simply averaging the 2×2 pixels in an image, we can increase the intensity levels of the image on the order of 4. We design our learning-based super-sampling framework based on the above knowledge that the ability to do spatial super-resolution can be used to enrich the intensity levels. We adopt existing learning-based super-resolution technique to enlarge the input image. Next, the resulting big image is blurred and down-sampled to generate an image with the original size but enriched intensities.

3.2   Problem Analysis

We briefly introduce the spatial super-resolution method adopted in previous research [10]. Given a low resolution image and training low and high resolution image pairs, all of the images are cut into overlapping patches. The image manifold assumption identifies that the pixel values in a patch are controlled by only a few factors; thus, they are distributed in a generally non-linear, low-dimensional manifold. We agree on another natural assumption that the manifold of the low resolution patches and the manifold of the high resolution patches are similar [10]. Given a low-resolution input patch, the spatial super-resolution algorithm first finds its neighborhood in the low-resolution manifold in the training data. Next, the algorithm estimates the high-resolution patch with the corresponding high-resolution neighborhood, and with the coefficients computed from approximation, it determines the input with low resolution neighbors.

3.3 Problem Analysis

In our description, "x/X" is for the low-resolution patches and images, and "y/Y" is for the high-resolution patches and images. "s" is for the training data, and "t" is for the input and objective. Given an input image $\mathbf{X}_t$ with l_0 intensity levels and a training image $\mathbf{Y}_s$ we hallucinate image X_t^1 with l_1 intensity levels from $\mathbf{X}_t$ with the help of $\mathbf{Y}_s$, where $l_1 > l_0$:

1. Generate low-resolution training input image $\mathbf{X}_s$.
2. Cut images into patches as follows: $X_t := \{x_t^q\}_{q=1}^{N_t}$, $X_s := \{x_s^p\}_{p=1}^{N_s}$ and $Y_s := \{y_s^p\}_{p=1}^{N_s}$; N_t and N_s are the number of patches in the input image and training images, respectively.
3. Do super-resolution for each patch $x_t^q \in X_t$
   a. Find K nearest neighbors $\mathbf{N}_q$ for X_t^q.
   b. Linearly combine the neighbors $\{x_s^r\}_{r \in N^q}$ with coefficient vector $\mathbf{w}_q$ to approximate X_t^q.
   c. Synthesize the high-resolution patch Y_t^q by combining the corresponding neighbors $\{y_s^r\}_{r \in N^q}$ in $\mathbf{Y}_s$.
4. Mosaic the high-resolution image $\mathbf{Y}_t$ by collecting all $\{y_t\}$.
5. Filter the resulting image $\mathbf{Y}_t$ with a low-pass filter and down-sample to generate X_t^1 with the same size of $\mathbf{X}_t$ and enriched intensity levels.

In step 1, we down-sample to $\mathbf{Y}_s$ at a ratio r, such that the increase of the sampling grid number from $\mathbf{X}_s$ to $\mathbf{Y}_s$, which is r_2, equals that from $\mathbf{X}_t$ to X_t^1, which is $l_1 = l_0$. Therefore, we use ratio $r = \sqrt{l_1/l_0}$ to down-sample and generate $\mathbf{Y}_s$. The same analysis applies for designing the low-pass filter before down-sampling $\mathbf{Y}_t$ to generate X_t^1. For the details of step 3, the reader may refer to previous research [10]. Additionally, note that the nearest neighbors in step 3.1 are determined according to the Euclidean distance, and vector $\mathbf{w}$ found in step 3.2 is constrained to have 2-normal 1.

4 Experiment

4.1 Experimental Configuration

We use a publicly available data set (downloadable at "www.thedigital-pictures.com") for the both input and the training images. In all of our experiments, the input images include 16 gray scale images. The object is to convert the images into images with 256 gray scales. According to the analysis in the last section, the spatial super-resolution ratio r is chosen as 4. To save space and processing time, we use the original images of approximately 500×300 pixels; thus, the input image is approximately 120×75 pixels. In the spatial super-resolution stage, we represent the input patches with the same feature vectors as in previous research [10]. For the high-resolution feature vectors, we extract the high-frequency frequency components from the training patches. Different from the common spatial super-resolution tasks, we down-sample to the resulting image, shrink it back to the original size; therefore, we only count the estimated high-frequency component for the input image. For a pair of training images, $\mathbf{X}_t$ and $\mathbf{Y}_t$, we use cubic interpolation to enlarge $\mathbf{X}_t$, obtaining Y_t^L. Next, the high frequency component is extracted as

$$Y_t^H = Y_t - Y_t^L$$

From Y_t^H, we extract patches at the same position as $\{\mathbf{y}_t\}$ in $\mathbf{Y}_t$.

In our experiments, the low-resolution patches $\{\mathbf{x}_t\}$ and $\{\mathbf{x}_s\}$ are 6×6 pixels and the high-resolution patches are 24×24 pixels. Our algorithm is not sensitive to patch size. In our implementation, input patch sizes from 4×4 to 8×8 yield no significant differences. It is not sensitive to the neighbor number either. In all of our experiments, we set $K = 5$.

4.2   Experimental Result

Figure 1 shows the super-sampling result for a squirrel image.

Fig. 1. Super-sampling a 16-intensity-level image of a squirrel. (a) training; (b) input; (c) super-resolution; (d) high frequency; (e) blurred; (f) our super-sampled; (g) real 256-intensity image; (h) and (i) zoomed boxes in (g), from left to right: input, blurred, ours, real.

Figure 1(a) is the input image with only 16 intensity levels. Figure 1(b) is the training image. Figure 1(c) is the super-resolution result of the input image. Figure 1(d) is the high frequency component synthesized through learning; it is the difference between the simple enlarged image and the image generated by the super-resolution algorithm. The image in Fig. 1(e) is generated by simply blurring the input image with a 2×2 averaging low-pass filter. This naive method is to directly trade the spatial resolution for intensity resolution. Figure 1(f) is our super-sampling result. Figure 1(g) is the real 256-intensity-level image. Our super-sampling softens the image; meanwhile, it keeps crisp edges. For example, the eye of the squirrel in the box in (g) is zoomed in on (h). The four panels in (h) show (from left to right) the eye in the input, in the directly blurred image, in the super-sampled result, and in the ground-truth image, respectively. In panel (i), we can see that for the background area, our method smooths the image to the same extent as the blurring method.

Figure 2 shows the super-sampling result of a child image. The contents of each panel are explained in the footnote of the figure and as above. In Fig. 2(f), it shows that the eye in our resulting image is crisper than that in the blurred image. In Fig. 2(g), we can see that the texture of the skin is softer in our image. This superior quality is because the learned high-frequency information enables us to use a softer low-pass filter before we down-sampling without blurring the image excessively. In fact, the 2×2 filter for the direct blurring can only enrich the intensity levels by the order of 4 at extreme. A 3×3 filter will blur the image too much, leaving few details.

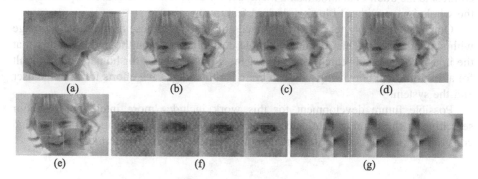

Fig. 2. Super-sampling a 16-intensity-level image of a child (a) training; (b) input; (c) blurred; (d) ours; (e) real; (f) and (g) zoomed boxes in (e)

In Fig. 3, we show the result of a deer image. In this experiment, (f) shows the zoomed area of the horn and head of the deer. It can be observed that the horn in our result is sharper and the head has higher contrast; however, the background in both our resulting image and the blurred image is softened without distinguishable difference. Additionally, we can see from (g) that our method softens the body of the deer as well as the background; however, it keeps more contrast than the blurred image.

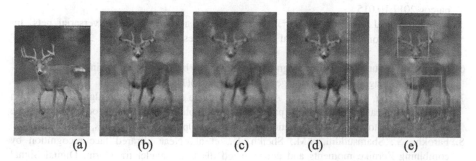

Fig. 3. Super-sampling a 16-intensity-level image of a deer (a) training; (b) input; (c) blurred; (d) ours; (e) real; (f) and (g) zoomed boxes in (e).

We do more examples in the experiment, in which our algorithm implements super-sampling while maintaining the image details. Note that the ratio of the sizes between the training and input images in all these experiments are 4:1. We use different ratios in drawing the figures to make them clear to read.

5   Conclusions

In this paper, we present an intelligent algorithm for the new problem of super-sampling an image. Our framework is novel because it finds the new application of interpolation in the intensity domain for learning-based super-resolution methods. In contrast to the traditional antialiasing methods, we complete intelligent interpolation for the whole image without blurring desired features.

Our method is easy to use. It only needs the user to choose a high quality image with similar content. This seemingly simple design is based on the understanding that the image content and search for a similar image is very easy for humans but difficult for a machine, and borrowing a human brain for this stage save efforts for both the user and the system.

Possible future development for this work includes more intelligent neighbor searching in the training data, such as adopting techniques of image primitives and constraining smoothness between neighboring patches with graphic modeling.

References

1. Freeman, H.: Computer processing of line-drawing images. ACM Comput. Surv. (CSUR) **6** (1), 57–97 (1974)
2. Krizhevsky, A., Sutskever, I., Hinton, G.E.: ImageNet classification with deep convolutional neural networks. In: International Conference on Neural Information Processing Systems. Curran Associates Inc., pp. 1097–1105 (2012)
3. Yuan, C., Li, X., Wu, Q.M.J., Li, J., Sun, X.: Fingerprint liveness detection from different fingerprint materials using convolutional neural network and principal component analysis. CMC Comput. Mater. Continua **53**(3), 357–371 (2017)
4. Li, Y., Wang, G., Nie, L., Wang, Q.: Distance metric optimization driven convolutional neural network for age invariant face recognition. Pattern Recogn. https://doi.org/10.1016/j.patcog.2017.10.015
5. Goodfellow, I.J., Pouget-Abadie, J., Mirza, M., et al.: Generative adversarial nets. In: International Conference on Neural Information Processing Systems, pp. 2672–2680. MIT Press (2014)
6. Narang, N., Bourlai, T.: Face recognition in the SWIR band when using single sensor multi-wavelength imaging systems. Image Vis. Comput. **33**(1), 26–43 (2015)
7. Feng, K., Zhou, T., Cui, J., et al.: An example image super-resolution algorithm based on modified k-means with hybrid particle swarm optimization. In: Proceedings of the SPIE/COS Photonics Asia. International Society for Optics and Photonics, pp. 1–11 (2014)
8. Farokhi, S., Shamsuddin, S.M., Sheikh, U., et al.: Near infrared face recognition by combining Zernike moments and undecimated discrete wavelet transform. Digital Signal Process. **31**(1), 13–27 (2014)

9. Biswas, S., Aggarwal, G., Flynn, P.J., et al.: Pose-robust recognition of low-resolution face images. IEEE Trans. Pattern Anal. Mach. Intell. **35**(12), 3037–3049 (2013)
10. Chang, H., Yeung, D.-Y., Xiong, Y.: Super-resolution through neighbor embedding. In: 2004 CVPR 2004 Proceedings of the 2004 IEEE Computer Society Conference on Proceedings of the Computer Vision and Pattern Recognition, pp. 1–8. IEEE (2004)
11. Roweis, S.T., Saul, L.K.: Nonlinear dimensionality reduction by locally linear embedding. Science **290**(5500), 2323–2326 (2000)
12. Wang, N., Tao, D., Gao, X., et al.: A comprehensive survey to face hallucination. Int. J. Comput. Vis. **106**(1), 9–30 (2014)

Nodes Deployment Optimization Algorithm Based on Improved Evidence Theory

Xiaoli Song[1,2], Yunzhan Gong[1], Dahai Jin[1], Qiangyi Li[2(✉)], and Hengchang Jing[2]

[1] State Key Laboratory of Networking and Switching Technology, Beijing University of Posts and Telecommunications, Beijing 100876, China
[2] Henan University of Science and Technology, Henan 471023, Luoyang, China
cjjl98@yeah.net

Abstract. Underwater wireless sensor networks (UWSNs) applications for ocean monitoring, deep sea surveillance, and locating natural resources are gaining popularity. To monitor the underwater environment or any object of interest, these applications are required to deploy underwater connected node sensors for obtaining useful data. For thriving UWSNs, it is essential that an efficient and secure node deployment mechanism is in place. In this article, we are presenting a novel nodes deployment scheme which is based on evidence theory approach and cater-for 3D-UWSNs. This scheme implements sonar probability perception and an enhanced data fusion model to improve prior probability deployment algorithm of D-S evidence theory. The viability of our algorithm is verified by performing multiple simulation experiments. The simulation results reveal that as compared to other schemes, our algorithm deploys fewer nodes with enhanced network judgment criteria and expanded detection capabilities for a relatively large area.

Keywords: Evidence theory · Nodes deployment algorithm
Underwater wireless sensor networks · Data fusion · Coverage

1 Introduction

Consequently, underwater wireless sensor networks (UWSNs) is emerging technological development for underwater explorations [1–3]. UWSNs refers to a network comprised of autonomous and low powered wireless sensor nodes which are deployed in a designated area in order to sense the underwater properties such as quality, temperature, and pressure [4–6]. These underwater connected sensors are supposed to be unattended and continue to work for a long time [7–9]. One of the objectives of UWSNs to obtain data which may be of diverse nature such as marine time, environmental protection, military purposes, early warning system [10–12]. Keeping in view the application prospects, it can be deduced that UWSNs which is a subfield of wireless sensor networks (WSNs) is an important field of study and it is gradually becoming a hot spot for research in coming days [13–15].

© Springer Nature Switzerland AG 2018
T. Hu et al. (Eds.): ICA3PP 2018 Workshops, LNCS 11338, pp. 84–89, 2018.
https://doi.org/10.1007/978-3-030-05234-8_11

2 Probability Perception Model of Passive Sonar Node

Considering the assumption that H0 and H1 are binary assumptions, H0 indicates that there is no target and H1 represents the target. Assuming that the sonar works in passive mode, the output of the receiver obeys the Gaussian distribution. This assumption is mainly applicable to the typical passive sonar receiver, such as the square integral processor. The probability density function of the receiver output can be written as:

When H0,

$$P_N(x) = \frac{1}{\sigma_N\sqrt{2\pi}}\exp\left[-\frac{(x - M_N)^2}{2\sigma_N^2}\right] \tag{1}$$

Among them, M_N, σ_N^2 are for the mean and variance of the output noise

When H1,

$$P_{S+N}(x) = \frac{1}{\sigma_{S+N}\sqrt{2\pi}}\exp\left[-\frac{(x - M_{S+N})^2}{2\sigma_{S+N}^2}\right] \tag{2}$$

Among them, M_{S+N}, σ_{S+N}^2 are the mean and variance of the signal plus noise. Assuming that the detection threshold of the receiver is V_T, and let

$$y_1 = (V_T - M_N)/\sigma_N, y_2 = -(V_T - M_{S+N})/\sigma_{S+N} \tag{3}$$

The false alarm detection probability of the first sonar are given

$$P_{F_i} = \int_{V_T}^{\infty} P_N(x)dx = 1 - \Phi(y_1) \tag{4}$$

$$P_{D_i} = \int_{V_T}^{\infty} P_{S+N}(x)dx = \Phi(y_2) \tag{5}$$

The output probability signal-to-noise ratio $d_i = (M_{S+N} - M_N)^2/\sigma_N^2$ is usually defined for the normal signal processing system. The mean of the noise is $M_N = 0$. In the case of long-distance detection, it can be considered that the mean variance of the signal is much less than that of the noise $\sigma_{S+N} \approx \sigma_N$

$$y_2 = \sqrt{d_i} - V_T/\sigma_N = \sqrt{d_i} - y_1 \tag{6}$$

Assuming that the target sound source is SL, the center frequency is f, the ambient noise is NL. All sonar bases can be the same i.e. receiving directivity index is DI; the integral gain of energy detection is $51g\,BT$. The propagation loss of sound signal in the ocean adopts the following model:

$$TL(R_i) = 20\lg R_i + \lambda R_i \tag{7}$$

Among them, R_i = distance between the target and the i sonar receiver is the absorption coefficient.

The passive sonar equation is

$$DT = SL - TL(R_i) - NL + DL \tag{8}$$

Among them, $DT = 5\lg d_i - 5\lg BT$ is for detection threshold.

3 Data Fusion Model Based on Improved D-S Evidence Theory

In order to obtain more reliable monitoring results in UWSNs environment, the improved D-S fusion criterion and passive sonar equation is represented by equation:

$$\Gamma(U) = \theta_1 u_1 + \theta_2 u_2 + \cdots \theta_i u_i \cdots + \theta_n u_n = \sum_{i=1}^{n} \theta_n u_n \tag{9}$$

Among them, $\Gamma(U)$ is defined as "for a given vector U fusion node determine target reliability". θ_i represents the first evidence received from a sonar node which has an inverse correlation with $TL(R_i)$ which is the acoustic signal propagation loss in the ocean. The larger $TL(R_i)$ value will lead to a smaller value of θ_i, which implies that the credibility of the evidence will be low. At this time, as per Eq. (9) and relevant knowledge of evidence theory, the improved d-s judgment criterion is represented by Eq. (10):

$$\kappa(U) = P(u_0 = 1|U) = \begin{cases} 1, \Gamma(U) \geq t \\ 0, \Gamma(U) < t \end{cases} \tag{10}$$

Among them, $\kappa(U)$ is the result of the target-occurrence which is obtained from the fusion node for the given vector U and t is the threshold determined by the fusion node.

4 Analysis of Simulation Results

According to the parameters this section analysis of our algorithm, non-uniform deployment algorithm and uniform deployment algorithm are presented. The reliability of the detection results of the target nodes under the same number of sensor conditions maximum detection area and same sensor node detection was observed for all three algorithms. Where $H = 1000\,m$ and the results are shown in Figs. 1, 2 and 3:

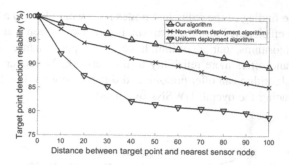

Fig. 1. The reliability of the detection results of the target node.

Figure 1 is a comparison diagram of the reliability of the detection results of the target nodes under the same number of sensor conditions in our algorithm, non-uniform deployment algorithm and uniform deployment algorithm. our algorithm, non-uniform deployment algorithm two algorithm considering the prior probability of target distribution and target probability of large area node deployment density also increases accordingly, uniform deployment algorithm, and compared the results of testing reliability is higher. It can be seen from the figure that the data fusion algorithm improves the detection reliability of the test results. In the same condition, the detection result of our algorithm is higher than that of non-uniform deployment algorithm.

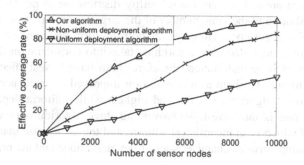

Fig. 2. Comparison of effective confidence coverage with changes in the number of sensor nodes.

Figure 2 is a comparison diagram of the effective reliability coverage rate of the same test area with the increase of the number of sensor nodes in our algorithm, non-uniform deployment algorithm, and uniform deployment algorithm. From the figure, it can be seen that for the same test area, along with the increasing perception of the node, the effective coverage detection area was also increasing. However, the uniform deployment algorithm has a linear growth, while the growth of our algorithm and non-uniform deployment algorithm is fast after a slow first half (particularly for our algorithm). This is because when after effective coverage of more than 60% of the detection area, the finding of the redundant nodes rises which lead to a gradual decline in node coverage efficiency. From the analysis, it can also be seen that as compared to the other two algorithms, our algorithm have better performance. It has superior redundancy rate and offers more reliability to the network. Moreover, due to the less node usage, our algorithm can offer prolong and durable network life. Similarly, it can also result in reducing the overall UWSNs overhead.

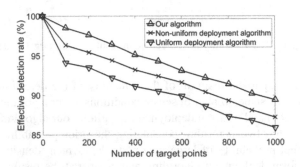

Fig. 3. Contrast diagram of effective detection rate.

Figure 3 depicts the effective detection rate comparison of our algorithm, non-uniform deployment algorithm, and uniform deployment algorithm algorithms under the same detection areas. It covers the reliability distribution as per target node prior probability distribution of the same number of the target node. All three algorithms can detect most of the target node. However, as both uniform deployment algorithm and non-uniform deployment algorithm algorithms take into consideration the prior probability of the target node distribution, therefore, both have lowest effective detection rates compared to our algorithm as it is based on improved d-s evidence theory. Non-uniform deployment algorithm has the 2nd highest while uniform deployment algorithm detection rate is the lowest. Moreover, all three algorithms produce effective detection rate of which is an inconsistent pattern, and this is because that there exists a variable relationship between characteristics of the target node and the prior probability distribution.

5 Conclusion and Future Work

UWSNs offers a promising solution to ever demanding applications. However, unpredictable conditions of water environment create serious constraints in the design and deployment of such networks. In this paper, we proposed a 3D node deployment algorithm for underwater sensor networks. Our work uses to improve the D-S evidence theory approach. A passive sonar probability perception model and enhanced data fusion model are used while taking into consideration the prior probability of underwater sensor network node deployment algorithm. Our algorithm empowers us to achieve an expanded coverage detection area while deploying fewer nodes which is less resource intensive at the time.

Acknowledgements. This work was partially supported by the National Natural Science Foundation of China (NSFC) under Grant No. U1736110 and the Soft Scientific Research Projects in Henan Province, China under Grant No. 172400410013. The authors also gratefully acknowledge the helpful comments and suggestions of the editors and reviewers, which have improved the presentation.

References

1. Song, X.L., Gong, Y.Z., Jin, D.H., Li, Q.Y., Jing, H.C.: Coverage hole recovery algorithm based on molecule model in heterogeneous WSNs. Int. J. Comput. Commun. Control **12**(4), 562–576 (2017)
2. Song, X.L., Gong, Y.Z., Jin, D.H., Li, Q.Y., Zheng, R.J., Zhang, M.C.: Nodes deployment based on directed perception model of wireless sensor networks. J. Beijing Univ. Posts Telecommun. **40**, 39–42 (2017)
3. Zhao, M.Z., Liu, N.Z., Li, Q.Y.: Blurred video detection algorithm based on support vector machine of schistosoma japonicum miracidium. In: International Conference on Advanced Mechatronic Systems, pp. 322–327 (2016)
4. Jing, H.C.: Node deployment algorithm based on perception model of wireless sensor network. Int. J. Autom. Technol. **9**(3), 210–215 (2015)
5. Jing, H.C.: Routing optimization algorithm based on nodes density and energy consumption of wireless sensor network. J. Comput. Inf. Syst. **11**(14), 5047–5054 (2015)
6. Jing, H.C.: The study on the impact of data storage from accounting information processing procedure. Int. J. Database Theory Appl. **8**(3), 323–332 (2015)
7. Jing, H.C.: Improved ultrasonic CT imaging algorithm of concrete structures based on simulated annealing. Sens. Transducers **162**(1), 238–243 (2014)
8. Zhang, J.W., Li, S.W., Li, Q.Y., Liu, Y.C., Wu, N.N.: Coverage hole recovery algorithm based on perceived probability in heterogeneous wireless sensor network. J. Comput. Inf. Syst. **10**(7), 2983–2990 (2014)
9. Jing, H.C.: Coverage holes recovery algorithm based on nodes balance distance of underwater wireless sensor network. Int. J. Smart Sens. Intell. Syst. **7**(4), 1890–1907 (2014)
10. Wu, N.N., et al.: Mobile nodes deployment scheme design based on perceived probability model in heterogeneous wireless sensor network. J. Robot. Mechatron. **26**(5), 616–621 (2014)
11. Li, Q.Y., Ma, D.Q., Zhang, J.W.: Nodes deployment algorithm based on perceived probability of wireless sensor network. Comput. Meas. Control. **22**(2), 643–645 (2014)
12. Jing, H.C.: Improving SAFT imaging technology for ultrasonic detection of concrete structures. J. Appl. Sci. **13**(21), 4363–4370 (2013)
13. Shi-Wei, L., Dong-Qian, M., Qiang-Yi, L., Ju-Wei, Z., Xue, Z.: Nodes deployment algorithm based on perceived probability of heterogeneous wireless sensor network. In: International Conference on Advanced Mechatronic Systems, pp. 374–378 (2013)
14. Zhang, H.T., Bai, G., Liu, C.P.: Improved simulated annealing algorithm for broadcast routing of wireless sensor network. J. Comput. Inf. Syst. **9**(6), 2303–2310 (2013)
15. Li, Q.Y., Ma, D.Q., Zhang, J.W., Fu, F.Z.: Nodes deployment algorithm of wireless sensor network based on evidence theory. Comput. Meas. Control. **21**(6), 1715–1717 (2013)

The Research and Implementation of a Distributed Crawler System Based on Apache Flink

Feng Ye[1,3(✉)], Zongfei Jing[2], Qian Huang[1], Cheng Hu[1],
and Yong Chen[3]

[1] Hohai University, Nanjing, Jiangsu 211100, People's Republic of China
yefeng1022@hhu.edu.cn
[2] University of Chinese Academy of Sciences,
Beijing 100049, People's Republic of China
[3] Nanjing Longyuan Micro-Electronic Company, Nanjing, Jiangsu 211106,
People's Republic of China

Abstract. Web information is growing at an explosive rate. The crawling ability of the single-machine crawler becomes the bottleneck, so distributed web crawling techniques become the focus of research. However, the existing distributed web crawler systems have some shortcomings. Thread management for solving thread synchronization and resource competition is usually designed by using pure multi-thread asynchronous methods. But the execution of this mechanism observably reduces the performance. Moreover, the deduplication algorithms lead to low efficiency in dealing with large data sets or the problem of occupying large storage space. Therefore, we propose and implement a distributed web crawler system based on Apache Flink, which combines and integrates the Mesos/Marathon framework. It can make full use of the computing resources of the cluster and significantly improve the efficiency of the web crawler system. Taking the data of Netease news pages as an example, the experimental results show that the distributed crawler proposed has higher execution efficiency and reliability.

Keywords: The distributed crawler · Apache Flink · URL filter
The distributed crawling management

1 Introduction

With the explosive growth of web pages, how to acquire the valuable information from the web quickly and reliably has become a research hotspot in the era of big data. Web crawler systems based on single-machine come to the bottlenecks in terms of scalability and performance. Moreover, web content and form become richer, more flexible and diverse, the inverted index for text data of the traditional crawler system is difficult to organize and classify the information. Therefore, with the rapid development of distributed computing and stream data processing technologies, we need to study a novel solution for the problems above.

T. Hu et al. (Eds.): ICA3PP 2018 Workshops, LNCS 11338, pp. 90–98, 2018.
https://doi.org/10.1007/978-3-030-05234-8_12

The so-called distributed crawler is the combination of traditional crawler and distributed processing framework. Based on computers cluster, a distributed crawler can perform crawling tasks in parallel using some task allocation mechanisms, and the crawler program on each computer can execute the task independently. Compared with traditional single-machine crawlers, distributed crawler systems often have higher throughput, lower latencies and better expansibility. Therefore, this paper proposes and implements a distributed crawler system based on Apache Flink, which combines and integrates Mesos/Marathon framework. It adopts the incremental crawling, and then extracts the text information from web pages that are crawled. Distributed crawler management can schedule the crawlers in the cluster, so as to make full use of the cluster's computing resource.

The remainder of the paper is organized as follows. Section 2 introduces some works related to this article. In Sect. 3, the architecture of the distributed crawler system proposed is explained. In Sect. 4, the key mechanisms of our distributed crawler are introduced in detail. Section 5 analyzes the performance and reliability of the distributed crawler system. Section 6 provides a summary of the research.

2 Related Work

Distributed crawler systems have been studied and applied widely [1–7]. The authors in [1] put forth several distributed web crawler architectures, and presented a classification method of evaluation criteria for the first time. Their research laid a foundation for the subsequent research of distributed crawler. UbiCrawler [2] was a cross-platform, linear scalability and fault-tolerance distributed crawler. Cambazoglu et al. [3] utilized grid computing to combine servers, storage and network together to implement a distributed crawler. Apoidea [4] was a distributed web crawler which was fully based on distributed P2P architecture. In [5], the researchers studied different crawling strategies to judge and weigh the problems of communication overhead, crawling throughput and load balancing, and then proposed a distributed web crawler based on distributed hash table. Mercator [6] was developed by Compaq and used by the Altavista search engine. Google Crawler was a distributed web crawler system using Google File System (GFS) and MapReduce [7]. Recently, some advances have been made in distributed crawling systems and some prototype systems have also been implemented [8–11].

However, the existing distributed crawler systems still have some shortcomings: (1) With regard to thread synchronization and resource competition, Thread management for solving thread synchronization and resource competition is usually designed by using pure multi-thread asynchronous methods. The execution of this mechanism observably reduces the performance. (2) When dealing with large-scale data sets, the deduplication algorithm has the problem of low efficiency or occupying large storage space. (3) The research on different distributed platforms is not sufficient, and MapReduce or Hadoop makes the distributed crawler inefficient in many scenarios.

Therefore, this paper presents a novel distributed crawler system, which is composed of two parts: a distributed crawler management and a crawler which supports distributed processing. Based on distributed framework of Marathon, Mesos and Zookeeper, the distributed crawler management can schedule the crawlers. Meanwhile,

Apache Flink [12, 13] is used as the underlying platform support for distributed crawlers. Various resources of host computers are used more efficiently, and multi-container technology is used to replace multi-threading technology. Flink supports the running of each crawler. The Bloom Filter algorithm [14] is combined with Redis to solve the deduplication problem in web crawlers, which making the crawler system more efficient.

3   The Architecture Proposed

The architecture of the distributed crawler system proposed is shown in Fig. 1. The overall architecture is hierarchical with four layers from bottom to top: infrastructure layer, platform layer, business logic layer and UI layer.

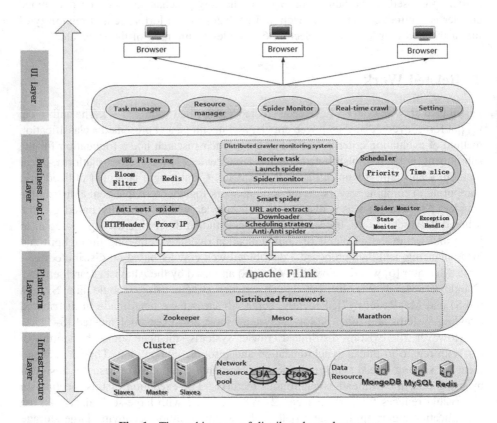

Fig. 1. The architecture of distributed crawler system

The infrastructure layer is mainly composed of a cluster of servers running Ubuntu, which provides the infrastructure resource and supporting capability for distributed crawler system. On the cluster, Redis and other databases are deployed to store the web pages that are crawled.

At the platform layer, a distributed processing framework based on Mesos, Marathon and Zookeeper is used to ensure the crawler system to run stably and efficiently. Zookeeper can maintain the communication between masters and is responsible for electing a leader. Mesos manages individual master and slave nodes, and is responsible for the allocation of cluster resources. Marathon is a job scheduler for issuing tasks in bulk, creating the containers and starting the crawlers. Running on top of the distributed framework is Apache Flink. Apache Flink is considered to be the latest generation of big data processing engine, which is an open source and unified platform for stream and batch data processing. Apache Flink is chosen as a distributed platform because we can abstract the process of grasping web pages and automatically structuring them into a large-scale streaming data processing. In this way, we can make full use of the advantages of stream processing capability to speed up the crawling and web data processing.

The business logic layer is the core of the whole system, which is divided into two sub-systems, namely the distributed crawling management and the distributed crawlers. Five main functions are implemented: (1) crawling the news blog pages; (2) automatically structuring the content of web pages; (3) formulating and implementing the scheduling strategies according to the priority and time slice of crawling tasks; (4) the corresponding Anti-Anti-Spider mechanism; (5) the efficient URL deduplication strategy.

UI layer provides a user interface or connection. It shows each crawler's running status, the basic infrastructure resources and the information or analysis results of various kinds of websites. Through the UI layer, users can submit crawling tasks to the distributed crawler management through the browser. Then the system stores the tasks to the core database. At this point, the distributed crawler can get crawling tasks from the core database, obtain data from the corresponding website, store the crawled content to the corresponding database, and store the request by increment to Redis to implement incremental web crawling.

4 Key Mechanisms

4.1 The Design of Distributed Framework

This system implements a distributed framework based on open source software: Zookeeper, Mesos, Marathon and Apache Flink. The task processing process of Apache Flink is shown in Fig. 2.

JobManager acts as a manager and is mainly responsible for allocating resources to each task and scheduling the execution sequence of tasks. In order to eliminate single point of failure of JobManager as much as possible, we adopted Zookeeper which can provide a consistent service for distributed applications, including configuration maintenance, name service, distributed synchronization, group service and so on. Mesos is a resource management framework, which can run a variety of distributed system types on machines of the cluster to share resources dynamically and efficiently. It provides failure detection, task tracking, task monitoring, low-level resource management and fine-grained resource sharing. Marathon is a lightweight, extensible

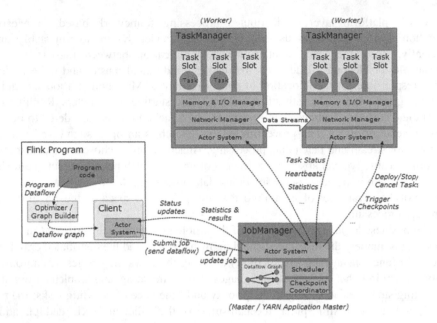

Fig. 2. Apache Flink's task processing process

container layout framework for Mesos. It supports running long services and any Linux binary distribution as it is in the cluster for multi-process management.

4.2 Spider Component

The crawling tasks submitted to the distributed crawler management are handed over to the crawler. The crawler gets the task from core database, initializes corresponding setting according to task information, generates crawler file and then executes the task on Apache Flink.

The distributed crawler system proposed is developed in Python. Scrapy is selected as an application framework for crawling website pages and extracting structural data. As an open source and collaborative framework for extracting the data you need from websites, Scrapy has a lot of advantages such as replacing regular, powerful statistics and log system with a more readable Xpath and running on different URLs simultaneously. Therefore, the distributed crawler is implemented based on Scrapy framework. Meanwhile, to support distributed processing of files, the system further integrates the Scrapy-Redis plugin to achieve distributed crawling. Scrapy-Redis puts the access of requests into the Redis queue, so that more than one server can implement crawling and items processing at the same time, which greatly improves the efficiency of data crawling and processing.

4.3 The Deduplication of URL

Due to the complex relationship among different links of websites, it is very common to find the same URL that needs downloading in the crawling process. Therefore, there is a need to implement duplicating detection for URL. Only the un-crawled URL will be submitted to the downloader middleware of Scrapy to download. In the Scrapy-Redis framework, the fingerprint of a request is calculated firstly, which is equivalent to a tag unique to the request. Then, the fingerprint is put into a set which performs the deduplication and this set is included in the Redis database. The aim of duplicating detection of the repeated requests and URL can be realized.

However, as web page data increases, the memory space occupied will rise dramatically, resulting in a dramatic drop in the performance of distributed crawler systems. If a persistence method which store URL in the database is employed, frequent database access operations are inevitable, which is extremely inefficient. To solve the two problems above, Bloom Filter is chosen to complete duplicate detection of URL.

After implementing the Bloom Filter algorithm, the crawlers work in an improved Scrapy-Redis framework. Compared with the original one, it can effectively reduce the memory usage and decrease the consumption of resources in the Redis database. In the case of limited hardware resources, especially the shortage of memory resources, it can effectively improve the stability of crawling.

5 Experiment and Analysis

The system is deployed in a cluster and the hardware environment includes: CPU is Intel® Xeon® Processor E5-2650; memory is Kingston 16 GB; GPU is GTX1060. Software tools include CentOS release 6.5 (Final), Apache Flink 1.3.0, Zookeeper 3.4.12, Mesos 1.6.0 and Marathon 1.6.322. These experiments are conducted on Netease News page (http://news.163.com/).

5.1 Comparison Between Single-Machine and Proposed Crawler System

Two kinds of crawlers are deployed into the host and distributed cluster respectively. The purpose of this experiment is to analyze and compare the result according to the number of pages crawled per unit time, as well as the utilization ratio of the hosts' CPU, memory and other aspects.

By observing situation every two hours in 7 h separately, the experiment evaluates the crawling efficiency, that is, evaluates the total number of pages the same crawler get in a distributed cluster and a single-machine environment. Since the distributed cluster has 4 host computers, the number of pages crawled in single computer environment times four for comparison. The experimental results are shown in Fig. 3. It is clear that the number of pages that are crawled is linear and our distributed crawlers are more efficient than four stand-alone crawlers.

As shown in Fig. 4, the better crawling efficiency is achieved for fetching web pages in the cluster, rather than in single-machine environment. In addition, the usage of host computers' CPU and memory can be monitored as analyzed. Figure 4 gives a

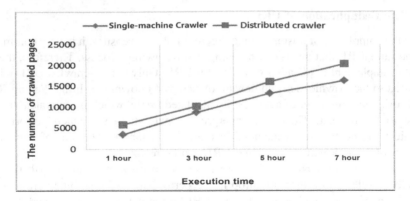

Fig. 3. Comparison of crawling ability between single-machine crawler and our distributed crawler

comparison result on CPU utilization ratio. Obviously, our distributed crawler has lower CPU utilization ratio and less memory than single-machine crawler. With the use of Redis, our distributed crawler has a faster growth rate in memory usage.

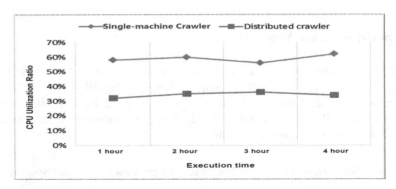

Fig. 4. Comparison of CPU utilization ratio between single-machine crawler and our distributed crawler

5.2 Comparison of Improved URL Deduplication

The system uses the Redis-based Bloom filter algorithm to deduplicate URL. This experiment compares the common deduplication data structures, namely BloomFilter, LinkList, HashMap and TreeMap. The data processed simulates URL with random characters (6 bits) and corresponding data structure in statistics deals with the time of text (ms) to measure the performance of the algorithm. The experimental results are shown in Fig. 5. We can see that the Bloom filter algorithm is superior to other algorithms in this scenario.

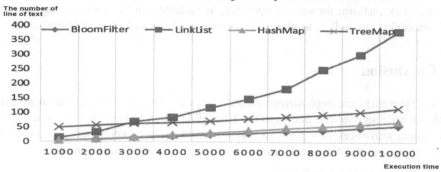

Fig. 5. Comparison of text deduplication efficiency

5.3 Reliability Analysis

In order to verify the stability and reliability for adopting Mesos/Marathon framework, we test the crawler based on Flink only and our proposed solution based Flink and Mesos/Marathon. The specific experimental method is to stop one node at the 5th hour and the 7th hour respectively and continue to count the numbers of pages at the five time points. From Fig. 6, we can see that when a master node is powered off at the 7th hour, the distributed crawler based on Flink falls into a stagnant state, while the distributed crawler based on Flink and Mesos/Marathon continues to work.

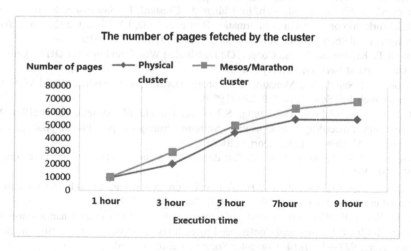

Fig. 6. Reliability comparison between two implementations with or without Mesos/Marathon framework

Obviously, adopting the Mesos/Marathon as the framework of distributed crawler system, Flink platform for stream processing is suitable. And it enhances the stability and availability, as well as to make full use of the distributed computing resource.

6 Conclusion

We have presented and implemented a distributed web crawler system based on Apache Flink, which combines and integrates the Mesos/Marathon framework. We believe that this system introduces new ideas in parallel crawling, and preliminary experimental results show that the distributed crawler proposed has higher execution efficiency and reliability.

Our distributed crawler system is an ongoing project, and our current goal is to test the crawler on larger and larger portions of the web.

References

1. Cho, J., Garcia-Molina, H.: Parallel crawlers. In: 11th International Conference Proceedings on World Wide Web, pp. 124–135. Association for Computing Machinery, Honolulu (2002)
2. Boldi, P., Codenotti, B., Santini, M., Vigna, S.: UbiCrawler: a scalable fully distributed web crawler. Softw.-Pract. Exp. **34**(8), 711–726 (2004)
3. Cambazoglu, B.B., Karaca, E., Kucukyilmaz, T., Turk, A., Aykanat, C.: Architecture of a grid-enabled web search engine. Inf. Process. Manag. **43**(3), 609–623 (2007)
4. Singh, A., Srivatsa, M., Liu, L., Miller, T.: Apoidea: a decentralized peer-to-peer architecture for crawling the world wide web. In: Callan, J., Crestani, F., Sanderson, M. (eds.) SIGIR 2003 Workshop on Distributed Information Retrieval 2003, LNCS, vol. 2924, pp. 126–142. Springer, Heidelberg (2004). https://doi.org/10.1007/978-3-540-24610-7_10
5. Loo, B.T., Krishnamurthy, S., Cooper, O.: Distributed Web Crawling over DHTs. University of California at Berkely, Berkely (2004)
6. Heydon, A., Najork, M.: Mercator: a scalable, extensible web crawler. World Wide Web-Internet Web Inf. Syst. **2**(4), 219–229 (1999)
7. Ghemawat, S., Gobioff, H., Leung, S.T.: The Google file system. In: the19th ACM Symposium Proceedings on Operating Systems Principles, pp. 29–43. Association for Computing Machinery, Lake George (2003)
8. Achsan, H.T.Y., Wibowo, W.C.: A fast distributed focused-web crawling. Proc. Eng. **69**, 492–499 (2014)
9. Huang, Q., Li, Q., Yan, Z., Fu, H.: A novel incremental parallel web crawler based on focused crawling. J. Comput. Inf. Syst. **9**(6), 2461–2469 (2013)
10. Su, L., Wang, F.: Web crawler model of fetching data speedily based on hadoop distributed system. In: IEEE International Conference Proceedings on Software Engineering and Service Science, pp. 927–931. IEEE Computer Society, Beijing (2016)
11. Yang, Y., Yang, J.: Design and implementation of a multi-area distributed crawler based on Skipnet-YL network. In: Pacific-Asia Conference Proceedings on Circuits Communications and System, pp. 4–6. IEEE Computer Society, Wuhan (2011)
12. Friedman, E., Tzoumas, K.: Introduction to Apache Flink: Stream Processing for Real Time and Beyond. O'Reilly Media, Sebastopol (2016)
13. Deshpande, T.: Learning Apache Flink. Packt Publishing, Birmingham (2017)
14. Gen, L.: Research and Optimization of Web Crawler System under Distributed Environment. Beijing University of Posts and Telecommunications, Beijing (2014)

ICA3PP 2018 Workshop on Security and Privacy in Data Processing

A Security Reinforcement Technology
of Telematics Box Based on Secure Element

Sun Yanan[1], Shen Jie[1(✉)], and Yang Zhou[2]

[1] University of Electronic Science and Technology of China,
Chengdu 611731, China
zeropoint17@hotmail.com
[2] DJI Technology Inc., Shenzhen 518057, China

Abstract. The telematics box is a vehicle communication terminal in the Internet of Vehicles, used to collect data from electronic control units and transfer data between users and application server. With the rapid development of Internet of Vehicles, T-Box provides users personalized service and abundant entertainment. However, it also becomes easy to cause security problems, such as disclosure of private information of owners, illegal control of vehicles and so on. Therefore, it is very important to reinforce the security of T-Box. To reinforce the security of T-Box, this paper will present a security reinforcement technology, which uses a secure element and traditional security measures to implements secure boot based on TrustZone and security service. This paper designs a software hierarchical model of security service based on the research of AUTOSAR and make innovative improvements to Transport Layer Security. Besides, to validate the feasibility of the solution, this paper also implements a security reinforcement technology and verifies the validity of it.

Keywords: T-Box · Secure element · AUTOSAR

1 Introduction

With the rapid development of Internet of Vehicles (IOV), the information security problems of T-Box have become even more prominent. At present, the security threat faced by T-Box can be divided into the following three aspects. First, the user's private information is not properly protected. Second, the lack of authentication and integrity check mechanisms makes the hardware easily tampered with. Third, the integrity and correctness of data in the process of network communication are easily attacked. This paper designs a security reinforcement technology referring to the software hierarchy model of AUTOSAR based on secure element to reinforce the security of T-Box.

2 Related Work

The current mainstream IOV security standards include EVITA, OVERSEE, and PRESERVE [1]. EVITA studies Hardware Secure Module (HSM), which provides HSM as a cryptographic coprocessor, providing a variety of cryptographic functions,

T. Hu et al. (Eds.): ICA3PP 2018 Workshops, LNCS 11338, pp. 101–116, 2018.
https://doi.org/10.1007/978-3-030-05234-8_13

including random number security generation, data integrity checking, and symmetric/non-Symmetric key encryption and decryption and all other cryptographic applications. OVERSEE integrates hardware modules to provide a unified security interface for applications by standardizing the operating environment. PRESERVE implements an IOV security subsystem that provides services including secure communication, security information, security management, and security analysis from the perspective of closer application. In addition, AUTOSAR has also proposed a cryptographic service classic platform based on HSM for automotive applications [2].

For the security flaws existing in the OS kernel, existing solutions at home and abroad are following the Global Platform's Trusted Execution Environment (TEE) specification to improve the hardware layer combination of the terminal. The TrustZone proposed by ARM divides the hardware resources of SOC into common areas and trusted areas [3]. It can place sensitive hardware resources that need protection in a trusted area. Through this method, resources are isolated from the normal environment. However, TrustZone does not specify the encryption and decryption capabilities and functional interfaces that the hardware should provide.

3   Network System of IOV

The network security system of IOV is shown in Fig. 1. It includes two parts: the vehicles terminal and the application server. The T-Box, gateway, and ECUs constitute the gateway, and ECUs constitute the in-vehicle system. The T-Box communicates with the back-end service platform through the wireless network.

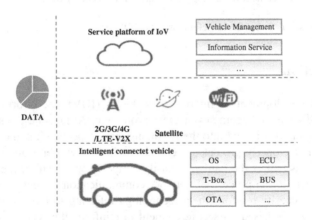

Fig. 1. The network security system of vehicle-mounted communication

The solution of security can be considered from two aspects. The first is to start with the T-Box itself, enhance its own security, and fundamentally block all kinds of attacks. Second, start from the communication framework and design a secure communication model to ensure secure communication and trusted authentication the T-Box and application servers.

The information security attributes of T-Box include confidentiality, integrity, availability, verifiability and auditability. Some threats against the confidentiality of vehicle terminals, collecting user data, leading to privacy leaks, some threats to destroy integrity, and some even undermine several attributes of information security at the same time. This paper categorizes the threats based on the destruction of these security attributes and introduces them one by one.

Cryptography plays a very important role in IOV. In addition, the key as the key data of cryptography technology, its secure storage has become the key to the security of IOV. At present, the commonly used methods include hardware protection and software protection. Hardware protection includes the SE hardware security module and other methods. Software protection requires that the user cannot store the key information in clear text in memory [6–8]. This paper uses SE for hardware protection and the white-box password algorithm for software protection.

4 White-Box AES Cryptography

4.1 Algorithm Components

This paper designs the components of white-box AES cryptographic algorithm as follows.

(a) T-boxes: In each round, AddRoundKey and SubBytes are combined to generate a look-up table of 16 8-bit inputs to 8-bit outputs, which we call T-boxes.

$$T_i^r(x) = S\big(x \oplus \hat{k}_{r-1}[i]\big) \qquad \text{for } i = 0, 1, \ldots, 15 \text{ and } r = 1, 2, \ldots, 9 \qquad (1)$$

$$T_i^{10}(x) = S\big(x \oplus \hat{k}_9[i]\big) \oplus k_{10}[i] \qquad \text{for } i = 0, 1, \ldots, 15$$

The T-boxes generation method is shown in Eq. 1. Round 10 requires round keys $\hat{k}_9$ and k_{10}, and it totally need to generate 160 T-boxes.

(b) Ty_i tables: In the encryption process of AES-128 rounds 1 to 9, after the matrix is linearly manipulated by ShiftRows, each byte is mapped by T-boxes. Finally, MixColumns operation with the MC matrix is required. This operation can also be expressed in the form of a lookup table and completed by looking up the table. Defining x_0, x_1, x_2, x_3 as the 4 bytes of a column of the state matrix, the Mix-Columns operation is shown in Eq. 2.

$$\begin{bmatrix} 02 & 03 & 01 & 01 \\ 01 & 02 & 03 & 01 \\ 01 & 01 & 02 & 03 \\ 03 & 01 & 01 & 02 \end{bmatrix} \begin{bmatrix} x_0 \\ x_1 \\ x_2 \\ x_3 \end{bmatrix} = x_0 \begin{bmatrix} 02 \\ 01 \\ 01 \\ 03 \end{bmatrix} \oplus x_1 \begin{bmatrix} 03 \\ 02 \\ 01 \\ 01 \end{bmatrix} \oplus x_2 \begin{bmatrix} 01 \\ 03 \\ 02 \\ 01 \end{bmatrix} \oplus x_3 \begin{bmatrix} 01 \\ 01 \\ 03 \\ 02 \end{bmatrix} \qquad (2)$$

Define the form of the XOR sum in the right side of Eq. 2 as $Ty_0 \oplus Ty_1 \oplus Ty_2 \oplus Ty_3$, Each 1-byte input x_i corresponds to the output Ty_i.

$$Ty_0(x) = x \cdot [02 \quad 01 \quad 01 \quad 03]^T \tag{3}$$

$$Ty_1(x) = x \cdot [03 \quad 02 \quad 01 \quad 01]^T$$

$$Ty_2(x) = x \cdot [01 \quad 03 \quad 02 \quad 01]^T$$

$$Ty_3(x) = x \cdot [01 \quad 01 \quad 03 \quad 02]^T$$

As shown in Eq. 3, Ty_i tables are 8-bit input and 32-bit output lookup tables. Using these lookup tables, it is not difficult to conclude that MixCloumns's operations on a 4-byte input of the status matrix is obtained by XORing the result of the lookup table. Since the AES input is 16 bytes per round and the Mix-Columns operation is performed in 1–9 rounds, the number of Ty_i tables required is: $16 \times 9 = 144$.

(c) XOR tables: The XOR operation in the cryptographic algorithm can also be represented by a lookup table. For example, Ty_i boxes need to be XORed when used in MixColumns operation. The XOR operation is also implemented using a lookup table, which is mainly used in combination with encoding and decoding of the white-box AES.

4.2 Design of Coding: Mixing Bijections

Using 4-bit serial input and output external coding can achieve the purpose of messing up the contents of the lookup table. However, in order to enhance the security of the lookup table, we need to adopt an internal encoding called linear transformation to achieve the purpose of spreading the content of the lookup table. So Mixing Bijections can be implemented with a reversible linear transformation.

Let M^n denote a set of $n \times n$ invertible matrices, M_v^n denote a set of $n \times n$ invertible matrices where the first row is a vector v, e_r denote a vector where the position r is 1 and the remaining position is 0, and the symbol "choose $\alpha \in_u S$" denote "select elements α from the set S based on uniform distribution".

The generation process of $n \times n$ invertible matric is as follows.

```
begin
    If n=1 then
        Let A₁,₁ =1;
        choose T₁,₁ ∈ᵤ F\{0};
    else
        choose v ∈ᵤ Fⁿ\{0ⁿ} such that v ≠ 0ⁿ;
        let r be the first nonzero coordinate of v;
        /* Assign Value to A:   */
            Let the first row of A = eᵣ;
        /* Assign Value to T:   */
            Let the rᵗʰ row of T=v;
            for all 1 ≤ i ≤ n, where i ≠ r, Tᵢ,ᵣ = 0;
        Gen(A[1,r],T[r,r],n-1).
    end
```

4.3   Lookup Table Program

The white-box AES lookup table program is mainly based on the implementation of the components, and then rely on the NTL math library to complete the white-box AES

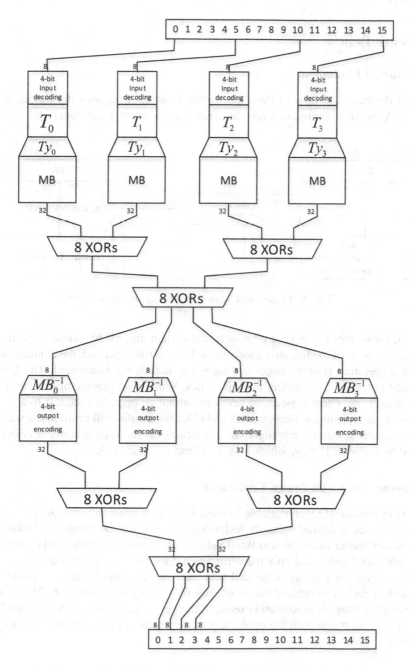

Fig. 2. Flow of white-box AES encryption

encoding, and finally use the file output to output the lookup table, issued to the lookup table program to complete the white-box AES algorithm encryption and decryption process. The white-box AES single round encryption process is shown in Fig. 2. Figure 2 can be used as a basis for the development of the white-box AES table lookup program.

5 Secure Boot

5.1 Current Limitation

Figure 3 describes the flow of the client application (CA) requests the trusted application (TA) service. There are a few disadvantages of current technology.

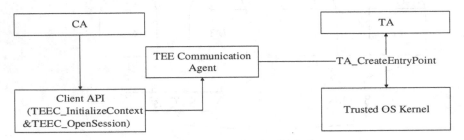

Fig. 3. Process of CA to request security service

First, the images in the boot process of the system may all be tampered with. The unverified process of loading may cause unpredictable risks. Second, the confidentiality of trusted operating system images and some key data is not guaranteed. Third, some CAs need to request TA services multiple times. With cryptographic operations as the representative, the client application needs to submit an operation request to a trusted application multiple times. Repeated TA and CA data transfer will result in the waste of system resources. Fourth, cryptographic operations in the TA's security services are assisted by software library, which may also lead to some risks.

5.2 Secure Boot with Image Verification

In the boot process of Open Portable Trusted Execution Environment (OP-TEE), each Bootloader uses a digital signature technology to generate a certificate. Before the previous Bootloader loads the next Bootloader, it needs to load and verify the certificate of the next Bootloader, and only the verification pass can load this Bootloader image.

The verification process is divided into two aspects. One is that the public key needs to be checked to prevent the public key from being tampered with. The other is that before the image is loaded and executed, the upper level needs to decrypt the head of the next level image with the public key to determine if the source of this image is legitimate.

Figure 4 shows the process of BL2 verification by BL1. The first step is to verify the public key. Compare the public key stored in the BL2 certificate with the public key embedded in the L-load program, if the two values are the same, check the certificate. After the certificate verification is passed, the next step is the inspection of the image. If the BL2 image hash with the certificate information are the same, the verification is completed and the BL2 image can be downloaded.

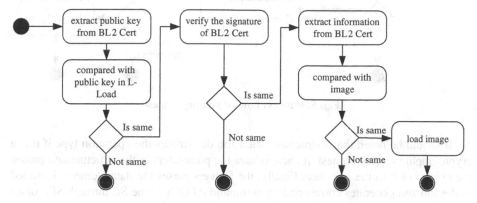

Fig. 4. Verification process of BL2

6 Security Service

6.1 Framework of Security Service

The T-Box needs to provide security services for applications on the premise that the security of the terminal operating environment is guaranteed. Through the study of the AUTOSAR software architecture and the hierarchical model of the crypto module proposed by ECU [4, 5], this paper proposes a modular hierarchical design of the security reinforcement technology for T-Box. The model, referring to the hierarchical structure of AUTOSAR crypto module "CSM → Interface → Drivers → SHE" is divided into four levels: security service layer, interface layer, driver layer, and hardware. This solution uses SE as security hardware to implement security-related functional support.

The service layer directly faces the vehicle applications and implements the encapsulation of secure communication, secure storage and cryptographic modules, providing interfaces that can be called by third-party applications. The lowermost layer is the hardware-driven layer responsible for information exchange with SE; There is also an interface layer between the layer and the driver layer, which encapsulates the SE-oriented interface of the driver layer into a hardware-independent interface that can be invoked directly by the service layer. SE as a security hardware implements a Vehicle-oriented security service application and can perform specific data security processing according to the instructions sent by the driver layer. The flow diagram is shown in Fig. 5.

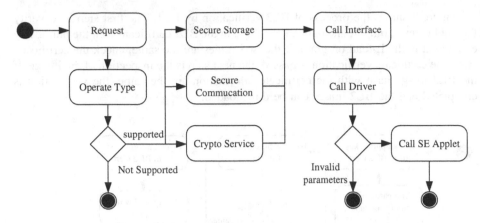

Fig. 5. Process flow of security request

It should be noted that a structure called Job determines the operation type if it is a cryptographic service request. It encapsulates the parameters in the structure and passes the pointer of it to the Interface. Finally, the Drivers parses the data elements included in the Job and generates corresponding command APDUs to the SE through SPI; other operation types have the same parameters in each layer, including operation type, data pointer to be processed, and data length. Table 1 defines data elements of Job structure.

Table 1. Definition of job structure

Name	Instructions
jobId	Identifier for the job structure
state	Determines the current job state
InputOutput	Structure containing input and output information depending on the job
keyId	Identifier of the Crypto Driver key

6.2   Optimization of TLS

HTTP and HTTPS are two commonly used network transmission protocols. When connecting to the server through HTTP, data is transmitted in plain text and the identity of data source is not verified. During the transmission, it is very easy for data to be hijacked, eavesdropped, tampered, etc. HTTPS can effectively solve this security problem. HTTPS can effectively protect user privacy by adding a reliable authentication mechanism, and prevent users from accessing forged server URLs to prevent website hijacking traffic.

When performing mutual authentication between a client and a server, both the certificate and its own private key are required. In order to ensure the reliability of the authentication process, the reliability of the private key storage is very important. Since the terminal does not have additional security measures, this paper proposes the HTTPS-SE for crypto operations.

This paper proposes to optimize the SSL/TLS handshake process and the optimized handshake process is shown in Fig. 6. Taking the server to send data and terminal to receive data as an example, the data transmission processes of the three protocols are shown in Fig. 7.

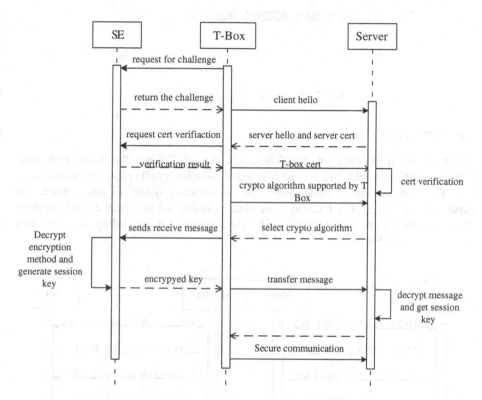

Fig. 6. Optimized TLS authentication flow diagram

TLS indicates the traditional TLS handshake, and TLS-SE indicates the TLS handshake with SE. Encryption indicates that the server encrypts data before sending it. TCP means Transmission Control Protocol used to establish the connection between the server and terminal. Decryption indicates that the received data is decrypted by terminal, and Decryption-SE means that the decryption is handled by SE.

As shown in Fig. 7, HTTP establishes a TCP connection to transmit data. HTTPS first performs a TLS handshake and determines whether to continue data transmission with TCP connection based on the handshake result. Compared with HTTP, HTTPS increases TLS handshake time and the time to process data for TLS, that is, the sender encrypts data and the receiver decrypts data. The HTTPS-SE process is the same as HTTPS, but limited by the computing power of SE, the time for TLS to handshake and process data in client increase.

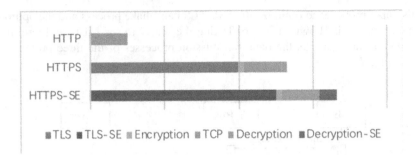

Fig. 7. Process flow of security request

6.3 SPI Driver

The communication between the T-Box and the SE follows the Serial Peripheral Interface (SPI) protocol. SPI is a high-speed full-duplex synchronous communication bus. The communication mode adopts the master-slave mode. In this scheme, the master device (hereinafter referred to as Master) is defined as terminal, and the slave device (referred to below as Slave) is SE. The process of downloading and uploading data is shown in Fig. 8.

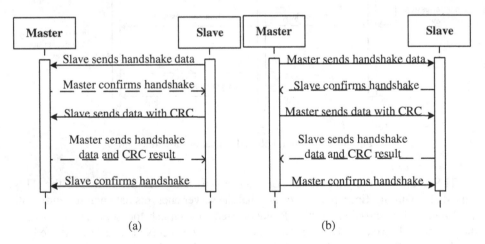

Fig. 8. Communication process with SPI. (a) Downloading; (b) Uploading

The download process is described as follows:

(a) Master first sends three bytes(A5, 5A and m) to handshake, where m is the length of the data to be sent by Master, which takes 1 byte, so the data length is 0–255.
(b) After Slave receives the handshake message, it returns "5A A5" to confirm the handshake.

(c) After Master sends the data, it will wait until the Slave sends the handshake of 5A A5. Which res is the result after the check, flag data is received and sent successfully.

(d) After receiving the handshake information from Slave, Master returns A5 5A as handshake confirmation. If res is correct, then the data is downloaded; otherwise, the handshake starts from the beginning.

The upload process is described as follows:

(a) Slave first sends "5A A5 m" to handshake, where m also represents the length of data to be sent.

(b) After Master receives the handshake message, it returns to A5 5A to confirm the handshake.

(c) Slave started to send data, also including header, data and crc three parts.

(d) Based on the m received before, Master reads m + 2 + 1 bytes of data from the SPI after sending "A5 5A" as handshaking confirmation.

(e) After Master receives the data, it sends the handshake information of "A5 5A" as res, which includes the result of the data check.

(f) After Slave receives the handshake information from the Master, it returns "5A A5" for confirmation. Afterwards, the confirmation is judged. If it is correct, the data upload is completed; otherwise, it is re-uploaded from the handshake.

7 An Easy Example: Vehicle Applications Update System

7.1 Prototype

In order to show the feasibility of the security reinforcement technology proposed above, an example of vehicle application update on the air will be briefly described. It is shown in Fig. 9.

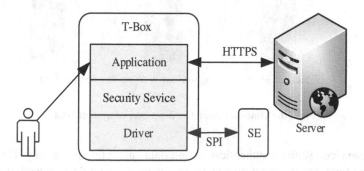

Fig. 9. Process flow of security request

When an application can be updated, the server will push update message to user. And if user agrees to update the application, the terminal will check the integrity of configure information that is stores in SE, and then request the server to establish an HTTPS connection and verifies the validity of the server certificate. While the two-way authentication between T-Box and the server is successful, the server will use its own key to calculate the signature for the software update package, send it to the application together with the update package using the session key encryption. When the terminal receives the encrypted message, it will use the crypto service to decrypt the message and use the server certificate to verify the signature to ensure that the information source is reliable and data has not been tampered with.

7.2   Performance Evaluation

Secure Boot. This paper uses SHA-256 to measure the integrity of each stage and uses RSA for digital signature and integrity recovery, which will result in additional time overhead.

In the verification environment of this paper, the boot process without any modification requires 29 s. Based on digital signature technology alone, loading the system kernel image from the EMMC instead of loading the BL32 image from the security unit requires 30.5 s for secure boot and increases the time-consuming ratio of 5.1%. With the security element added, it takes 33.9 s to finish secure boot and the time-consuming proportion is 10%. Among them, the system kernel image size is about 430 KB, the transmission time through the SPI is 3.4 s, as shown in Fig. 10.

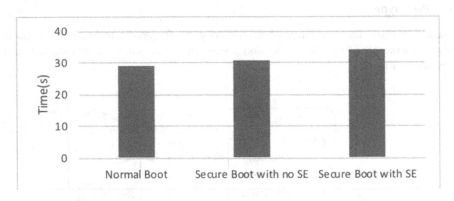

Fig. 10. Time-consuming comparison of system boot

Security Service. With no authentication and data encryption processing, HTTP takes the shortest time, but it cannot guarantee the security during data transmission. In the case of ensuring the security of terminal key, HTTPS improves the security of data but causing time-consuming increased. The HTTPS-SE proposed in this paper is a good guarantee for secure storage of terminal key, which can effectively prevent malicious software from attacking secure data. However, limited by the computing power of the

SE, it takes the longest time to transmit data. The following uses the 1 MB data as an example. The performance test results are shown in Fig. 11.

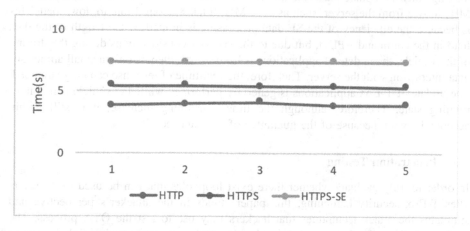

Fig. 11. Time-consuming comparison of data transmission

The security reinforcement technology is tested based on this example. The terminal and the server communicate with LTE-TDD, and the test cases are shown in Table 2.

Table 2. Descriptions of test results.

No.	Test	Expected	Actual	Average time
1	The server sends a certificate not signed by CA to the T-Box	Handshake failed	Passed	540 ms
2	The server sends a legal certificate to the T-Box	Handshake succeeded	Passed	614 ms
3	The server sends a data segment (5 KB) whose signature has been tampered with	Data validation failed.	Passed	136 ms
4	The server sends a data segment (5 KB) with a legal signature	Data is received successfully	Passed	128 ms
5	The server sends a package (5.2 MB) to the T-Box	Download finished, and the validity of the software package passed	Passed	84 s
6	The server sends a package (30.4 MB) to the T-Box	Download finished, and the validity of the software package passed	Passed	483 s

According to Table 2, it can be seen that in the communication between the terminal and the server, the reliability of the server's identity and the validity of the transmitted data can be effectively guaranteed, so the function can satisfy the demand. In terms of performance, if the amount of data volume is small, such as 5 KB, the request processing time is in milliseconds, which is negligible for users. However, when downloading software update packages that are generally between several MBs and tens of MBs in size from the server, such as 30.4 MB, It takes about 8 min to download. This is because the efficiency of the SE data processing is limited by the length of the data field in the command APDU, but due to the security considerations during the driving of the vehicle, the update of applications is limited, and there is only a small amount of data interaction with the server. Therefore, the real-time of response can be guaranteed. The update of T-Box applications is generally performed while the vehicle is in a non-running state. Therefore, although the time consuming increase, it is still within acceptable range because of the guarantee of the data security.

7.3   Penetration Testing

In order to truly evaluate whether there exist loopholes that can be used by attackers after T-Box security hardening, this paper stands in the attacker's perspective and simulates the attack techniques that hackers may use to test the OTA process. The methods include the following: general vulnerability scanning; using SolarWinds to search for network devices; using Ethereal to capture packets for analysis; and using tools such as X-Scan for password guessing. Test results are shown in Table 3.

Table 3. Descriptions of test results.

No.	Vulnerability	If found
1	Command injection	No
2	Code injection	No
3	File inclusion	No
4	Path traversal	No
5	HTTP response splitting	No
6	SOAP injection	No
7	XPath injection	No
8	LDAP injection	No
9	SMTP injection	No
10	Dangerous HTTP methods	No
11	Malicious file execution	No

Because of many open ports of the OTA server, malicious users can easily detect the type of service the port is running and attack the system based on possible vulnerabilities in the service. However, there are no security holes that can be exploited by attackers in the security-reinforced T-Box.

7.4 Security Analysis

This paper designs and implements a security reinforcement technology of T-Box and by guaranteeing the platform's own security, the reliability of communication between T-Box and the back-end servers and the security of data storage are realized. There are several common attack methods.

(a) Counterfeit identity

The communication between T-Box and the application server adopts the HTTPS. During the establishment of the connection, the identities of the two communicating parties are first authenticated with the X.509 certificate. The session key is negotiated according to the random number generated during the authentication process. Before transmitting the session key, the key is encrypted with the asymmetric encryption algorithm, so the plaintext will not be exposed during the entire transmission process. Therefore, the authentication process between T-Box and the server is reliable.

Assume that during data transmission, an attacker intercepted information. Because of the guarantee of the bidirectional authentication mechanism and the protection of the key in the encryption process, the attacker cannot obtain the key and respond correctly to the request sent by the server, ensuring that the reliability of T-Box identity.

(b) Stealing terminal data

During the use of T-Box, attackers may steal private data through malicious software. This paper designs a secure data storage mechanism that encrypts and stores information such as terminal configuration files and private data in the SE's memory. Once the data is encrypted and stored in the SE, the SE will internally update the operation record of the data, and at the same time, the signature of the operation record is sent to the application for verification of the next data request, ensuring that the request instruction can only get response if the data verification is successful. Based on the authentication mechanism provided by the SE itself, if no SE key, these data will not be easily stolen. If the attacker uses a brute force method, the SE will automatically change to the LOCKED state after multiple attempts, and thus cannot be used. Since the SE internal application runs in the Java Card OS, JCVM ensures that the data on the SE will not be attacked by other applications on the card. Therefore, using SE can effectively improve the storage security of T-Box, thereby ensuring the terminal configuration information.

At the same time, through the secure storage of the key and the existence of the key internal counter, brute force cracking can be prevented, and the reliability of the authentication mechanism when accessing the data is ensured.

(c) Attack keys

There are generally three ways to attack a key: The first is to export the secret key from the key saved entity. This paper encrypts and stores the key in SE to guarantee the security of key. Even if the SE application is entered illegally, the attacker can only get cipher text of key data. The second is brute force hacking, which guesses the key in an exhaustive way, depending on the security of the algorithm. The third is eavesdropping through the Internet. Since all data is transmitted in the form of cipher text in the network, and the session key expires, it is difficult for attackers to crack the key within an effective time.

8 Conclusions

Above all, a brand new security reinforcement technology is presented in this paper. It provides a complete security service for T-Box. From the perspective of active defense, it enhances the security of the terminal itself and at the same time satisfies the real-time requirements. In addition, the hierarchical design of T-Box software implements the hardware independence of the technology and increases the scalability of the technology.

The future studies will continue to concentrate on the application of actual scenarios. And the research on the security reinforcement of T-Box will be continued, making it more practical.

References

1. CAR 2 CAR: CAR 2 CAR Related Projects, Organizations and Task Forces (2015). https://www.car-2-car.org/index.php?id=6
2. AUTOSAR: Automotive Open System Architecture (2017). http://www.autosar.org/
3. TrustZone Technology: Electron. Eng. Prod. World 9, 5–8 (2013)
4. AUTOSAR: AUTOSAR-Layered Software Architecture (2016)
5. AUTOSAR: AUTOSAR-Specification of Crypto Service Manager (2017). http://www.autosar.org/
6. Park, J.Y., Yi, O., Choi, J.S.: Methods for practical white-box cryptography. In: 2010 International Conference on Information and Communication Technology Convergence (ICTC), pp. 474–479. IEEE (2010)
7. Karroumi, M.: Protecting white-box AES with dual ciphers. In: Rhee, K.-H., Nyang, D. (eds.) ICISC 2010. LNCS, vol. 6829, pp. 278–291. Springer, Heidelberg (2011). https://doi.org/10.1007/978-3-642-24209-0_19
8. Luo, R., Lai, X., You, R.: A new attempt of white-box AES implementation. In: 2014 International Conference on Security, Pattern Analysis, and Cybernetics (SPAC), 423–429. IEEE (2014)

Detecting Fake Reviews Based on Review-Rating Consistency and Multi-dimensional Time Series

Fang Youli[1], Wang Hong[1(✉)], Di Ruitong[1], Wang Lutong[1], and Jin Li[2]

[1] School of Information Science and Engineering, Shandong Normal University, Jinan 250014, China
1456029328@qq.com
[2] School of Computer Science and Educational Software, Guangzhou University, Guangzhou 510006, China

Abstract. Online reviews can help people get more information about stores and products. The potential customers tend to make decisions according to them. However, driven by profit, spammers post fake reviews to mislead the customers by promoting or demoting target store. Previous studies mainly utilize the rating as an indicator for detection. However, these studies ignore an important problem that the rating cannot represent the sentiment accurately. In this paper, we propose a method of identifying fake reviews based on rating- review consistency and multi-dimensional time series. We first incorporate the sentiment analysis techniques into fake review detection. Then, we further discuss the relationship between ratings and fake reviews. In the end, this paper establishes an effective time series to detect fake reviews. Experimental results show that our proposed methods have good detection result and outperform state-of-art methods.

Keywords: Fake review · Time series · Emotional polarity · Logic regression

1 Introduction

Online shopping caters to today's fast pace of life and brings convenience to people's lives. However, the existence of fake reviews has brought great challenges to create a fair online shopping environment. Driven by the interests, merchants sometimes employ a large number of reviewers to imitate ordinary customers to forge reviews. On the one hand, they praise their products, and on the other hand, they maliciously distort competitors. Therefore, how to effectively find these fake reviews has become an urgent problem to be solved.

The main contributions of this paper are as follows.

(1) We propose a new criterion for evaluating the difference between a review and its corresponding score, and further, present a fake review detecting model by using the rating and the review. Specifically, we analyze the emotional polarity and judge the consistency with its rating.

T. Hu et al. (Eds.): ICA3PP 2018 Workshops, LNCS 11338, pp. 117–123, 2018.
https://doi.org/10.1007/978-3-030-05234-8_14

(2) We study the characteristics of fake reviews in time dimension and fuse it in a multi-modal statistical detection method for fake reviews and ratings.

2 Related Work

In recent years, a lot of works focus on identifying spam [1] and malicious web pages [2], and achieve wonderful results. But the research works regarding the fake review detection are relatively few. So it is becoming a research hot spot. Ren [3] analyzed the influence of positive and negative sentiment polarity on reviews by language processing techniques. Chang [4] constructed a model with the most important attributes of language structure, such as words, concrete quantifiers and noun verb ratio. Li [5] detected fake reviews with integrated unsupervised learning.

By summary, the prior works detect fake reviews in a static manner and from the rating aspect or the review one respectively, without fusing two aspects together. So, in this paper, a dynamic multi-dimensional model for detecting fake reviews is presented, which integrates emotional sentiment analysis, rating and review consistency, and time series.

3 Methods and Models

The goal of this article is to effectively and efficiently detect fake reviews use emotional analysis technology and multi-dimensional time series.

3.1 Emotion Polarity of Review Text

In analyzing the emotion polarity of reviews, we consider three factors, that are, the influence of sentiment intensity, its weight on fake reviews, and the consistency between the sentiment intensity and the rating. Therefore, we propose a multi-modal detecting algorithm for fake reviews by integrating all these factors, especially the consistency between the emotional polarity and the score.

Equation 1 describes the difference between the semantic sentiment score and the rating, where $o(d)$ represents the semantic sentiment score, and $m(d)$ is the rating. If the product of $m(d)$ and $o(d)$ is greater than 0, then they are regarded as consistent. Otherwise, they are not.

$$f(d) = \begin{cases} 1, & m(d) * o(d) > 0 \\ 0, & else \end{cases} \tag{1}$$

Based on this, we can define the concept of emotional intensity $s(f)$. It refers to the influence of emotional words through distance on features, as shown in Eq. 2

$$s(f) = (-1)^{c_N} \sum_{w_j \in f} \frac{o(w_j)}{dis(w_j, f)} \qquad (2)$$

Where, $dis(w_i, f)$ represents the distance between the emotional words and features, $o(w_j)$ denotes the emotional polarity of a vocabulary. When a word is a positive vocabulary, its emotion polarity is represented by "+1". Conversely, when it is a negative vocabulary, its emotion polarity is represented by "−1". c_N denotes the number of characteristic negative words.

Then, we define the impact of features. It refers to the accuracy of judging fake reviews using different features, as show in Eq. 3. Where, $o(d)$ represents the emotional score of each review, $wh(f_i)$ represents the weight of features.

$$o(d) = \frac{\sum_{f_i \in d} s(f_i) * wh(f_i)}{|d|} \qquad (3)$$

3.2 Time-Series-Based Multi-dimensional Anomaly Detection

When fake reviewers push online comments and ratings, the number of reviews maybe increases sharply and the score series fluctuates suddenly over a period of time. The earliest work for detecting fake reviews with time series is proposed in reference [6]. However, it establishes evaluation indicators only based on scores, rather than scores and comments. Therefore, we propose a detection method for fake reviews and ratings by using multi-dimensional time series.

Time Series Structure
The detection method is based on time series, including the number of reviews and the average rating in ascending order. As show in Eqs. (4–6), $R(s)\{r_1, \ldots, r_{n_s}\}$ and $TS(s) = \{ts_1, \ldots, ts_{n_s}\}$ represent the review series and its corresponding time sequence respectively, n_s is the number of reviews of the store, ts_i is the time of the review r_i, $ts_i \le ts_j$ and $1 \le i < j \le n_s$. The score of each review is denoted by ro_i, the time window size (defined as Δt), the review interval (defined as $I = [t_0, t_0 + T]$) and the n_{th} window time represented by I_n. Given a time window, the average score f_2 is the ratio of the total score ro_i to the number of comments f_1

$$I_n = [t_0 + (n-1)\Delta t, t_0 + n\Delta t], I = \bigcup_{n=1}^{N} I_n \qquad (4)$$

$$f_1(I_n) = |\{r_j : ts_j \in I_n\}| \qquad (5)$$

$$f_2(I_n) = \sum_{ts_j \in I_n} ro_j / f_1(I_n) \qquad (6)$$

Anomaly Detection Algorithm

The anomaly pattern detection algorithm based on multi-dimensional time series is shown in Algorithm 1.

Algorithm1. Detection algorithm in multi-dimensional time series

1. **Input:** Multidimensional-curves C , window size Δt ,time span I
2. **Output:** Periods when correlated anomalies appear4.Detected time of spam activities
3. Initialize time set $S_0 = \{I\}$,scale $\eta = 0$
4. n =length of C , w =time frame length
5. $S = \phi$ //set of periods to return
6. **for** $b = 1 \rightarrow n - w + 1$ **do**
7. $S = S \cup \{[b, b + w - 1]\}$ if
8. $|\{x \in L_i : i = 1,2, x \in [b, b + w - 1]\} = 2|$
9. **end for**
10. **While** Δt not small enough **do**
11. $\eta = \eta + 1, S_i = \phi \cdot$
12.   **for** $I \in S_{\eta-1}$ **do** fit a curve $F(I, \Delta t)$
13. $S_\eta = S_\eta \cup C$
14.   **end for**
15. **end while**
16. **Return** S_η

3.3   Feature Selection for Fake Reviews

Feature selection is to select feature subsets with the largest contribution rates from the original features. Therefore, we select eleven features that are most likely to affect fake reviews, as shown in Table 1.

Table 1. Selected feature

Feature	Feature	Feature	Feature
F0: Emotionality	F3: Negative Words	F6: Turning word	F9: Relativity
F1: User reputation	F4: Consistency	F7: The length of the text	F10: Text copy
F2: Review time	F5: Mage	F8: Terminology	

4   Experimental Results Analysis

4.1   Dataset

The experimental data are the same as Xie [7]. The data contain 12402 reviews, in which including 6492 real reviews and 5910 fake reviews. As shown in Table 2, among them, there are sudden surges in time series.

Table 2. Data statistics

Item	Period between 2010.5.15 to 2010.7.15	Other 3 months
The number of reviews	912 rise to 7512	4890
Average rating	2.4 rise to 4.83	3.1
Similar text	34%	5%

4.2 Independent Variable Selection

This paper calculates the information gain (IG) value of each feature in order to select the independent variables, as they have significant impact on detecting fake reviews. The results are shown in Table 3.

Table 3. Candidate features and information gains

Feature	F_0	F_1	F_2	F_3	F_4	F_5	F_6	F_7	F_8	F_9	F_{10}
IG	0.43	0.39	0.41	0.40	0.47	0.35	0.60	0.19	0.16	0.20	0.17

4.3 Detection Model

This paper calculates the approximate score of each review by emotional intensity and feature weight, then compare with the rating of the review show as in Fig. 1(a). The experimental results show that the score is basically consistent with the rating within the first 30 days. But in 30–90 days, the review score and the rating are inconsistent because the store hires a large number of water troops for the benefit. Therefore, there exists negative correlation. So, based on multi-dimensional time series, we detect more bursts detail from the review data. While, when the window size is set to 15 days, a sharp increase in the number of scores is found, which means a large number of fake reviews appeared during the time period, shown as in Fig. 1(b).

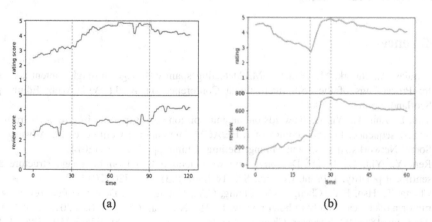

(a)   (b)

Fig. 1. Review-rating and reviews-scoring time consistency results

4.4   Experimental Analysis

Fake reviews are detected by using sentiment polarity, multi-dimensional time series and logistic regression model. The most common indicators including accuracy, recall rate and F1 value are used to evaluate the fake review detection model. We compare our model with Shao [8] and Feng [9]. It can be seen from Fig. 2(a–c) that the fake review recognition method based on rating-review consistency and multi-dimensional time series has achieved good results.

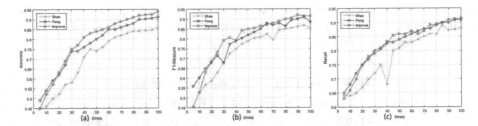

Fig. 2. Comparison of accuracy, F1 value and recall

5   Conclusion

With the development of e-commerce, researchers have made great efforts to detect fake reviews. Based on sentiment polarity and multidimensional time series, we establish a model to detect fake reviews. By comparing with other methods, our proposed method has achieved good results. But this method still needs to be improved. Firstly, there is no dynamic consideration of the review situation. Secondly, more important features maybe hid in the review text to be found.

Acknowledgments. This work is supported by Guangzhou scholars project for universities of Guangzhou (No. 1201561613).

References

1. Ntoulas, A., Najork, M., Manasse, M.: Detecting spam web pages through content analysis. In: Proceedings of the 15th International Conference on World Wide Web, Edinburgh, Scotland, pp. 83–92 (2006)
2. Yan, L., Zhu, T., Wu, H.: Towards online anti-opinion spam: spotting fake reviews from the review sequence. In: Proceedings of IEEE/ACM International Conference on Advances in Social Networks Analysis and Mining, Beijing, China, pp. 261–264 (2014)
3. Ren, Y., Yin, L., Ji, D.: Deceptive reviews detection based on Language structure and sentiment polarity. J. Front. Comput. Sci. Technol. **8**(3), 313–320 (2014)
4. Chang, T., Hsu, P.Y., Cheng, M.S., Chung, C.Y., Chung, Y.L.: Detecting fake review with rumor model—case study in hotel review. In: He, X., et al. (eds.) IScIDE 2015. LNCS, vol. 9243, pp. 181–192. Springer, Cham (2015). https://doi.org/10.1007/978-3-319-23862-3_18

5. Li, H., Chen, Z., Liu, B.: Spotting fake reviews via collective positive-unlabeled learning. In: Proceedings of IEEE International Conference on Data Mining, Washington, USA, pp. 899–904 (2014)
6. Dewang, R.K., Singh, A.K.: Identification of fake reviews using new set of lexical and syntactic features. In: Proceedings of the Sixth International Conference on Computer and Communication Technology, Allahabad, India, 115–119 (2015)
7. Xie, S., Wang, G., Lin, S.: Review spam detection via temporal pattern discovery. In: Proceedings of the 18th ACM SIGKDD International Conference on Knowledge Discovery and Data Mining, Beijing, China, pp. 823–831 (2012)
8. Shao, Z., Ji, D.: Spotting fake reviewers based on sentiment features and users' relationship. Comput. Appl. Softw. **33**(5), 158–161 (2016)
9. Feng, S., Banerjee, R., Choi, Y.: Syntactic stylometry for deception detection. In: Proceedings of the 50th Annual Meeting of the Association for Computational Linguistics, Jeju Island, Korea, pp. 171–175 (2012)

Fake Comment Detection Based on Time Series and Density Peaks Clustering

Ruitong Di[1,2], Hong Wang[1,2,3(✉)], Youli Fang[1,2], and Ying Zhou[1,2]

[1] School of Information Science and Engineering, Shandong Normal University,
Jinan 250014, China
1456029328@qq.com
[2] Shandong Provincial Key Laboratory for Distributed Computer Software
Novel Technology, Jinan 250014, China
[3] Institute of Biomedical Sciences, Shandong Normal University,
Jinan 250014, China

Abstract. This paper proposes a fake comment recognition method based on time series and density peaks clustering. Firstly, an anomaly recognition model based on multi-dimensional time series is constructed. Secondly, according to the idea of multi-scale features, seven benchmark-scale and corresponding subdivision-scale features are extracted hierarchically, and further, 49 features are finally obtained. At last, an optimized detection model based on density peaks clustering is proposed for identifying the fake comments, so as to improve the anti-noise ability of our method. The effectiveness of our proposed method is verified by several experiments, with the AUC value reaching 92%.

Keywords: Fake review · Time series · Multi-scale · Noise
Density peaks clustering

1 Introduction

In modern society, online shopping has become a trend, thus making the online review become an important way for customers to understand goods and stores. In general, purchasers decide whether to buy products by referring their ratings and comments. However, it can also provide opportunities for sellers to fake. For example, they employ the water army to praise their own products in order to improve the reputation of his store, and meanwhile, they hire the water army to depreciate products for dropping their competitors' reputation. It seriously affects the health development of e-commerce. In order to effectively identify the fake comment, this paper proposes a fake comment recognition method based on time series and density peaks clustering. The main innovations are as follow.

(1) The performance of detecting fake reviews in time dimensions is studied.
(2) We extract benchmark-scale features and the related subdivision-scale features hierarchically, according to the idea of the multi-scale feature fusion.
(3) We use the improved density peaks clustering(DPC) algorithm to remove noise comments, thus making our detecting model for fake comments more robust.

T. Hu et al. (Eds.): ICA3PP 2018 Workshops, LNCS 11338, pp. 124–130, 2018.
https://doi.org/10.1007/978-3-030-05234-8_15

2 Related Work

In recent years, domestic and foreign scholars have done a lot of work on the detection of the fake review. Professor Liu first proposed the fake comment recognition in 2008 [1]. Based on his work, Chang [2], Li [3] and Li [4] identify fake comments using information contained in comment texts. Song [5], Gao [6] and Husna [7] turn the issue of identifying fake reviews into identifying fake reviewers.

In a word, previous researchers mainly extract single-level features, without considering the impact of time and noise. This paper first constructs a time-series-based model to detect abnormal reviews by extracting multi-scale features hierarchically, and removes noise with the idea of density peaks clustering.

3 Feature Models

As mentioned above, in order to get more effective fake review detection model, we should extract multi-modal features.

3.1 Anomaly Detection Based on Time Series

When merchants hire water army to push fake ratings, the rating distribution may change, which makes the center of the distribution be high or low over time. Therefore, we focus on extracting useful information by using sample mean and sample entropy from all ratings. Firstly, the ratings for all customers of a store is sorted in ascending order according to the time, that is, for all $1 \ll i < j \ll n$, there is $ts_i < ts_j$, expressed as (1) and (2).

$$R(s) = \{r_1, r_2, \cdots, r_n\} \tag{1}$$

$$TS(s) = \{ts_1, ts_2, \cdots, ts_n\} \tag{2}$$

Where, $R(s)$ is the score series corresponding to the sorted time sequence of $TS(s)$, ts_i is the moment corresponding to the rating r_i, and s represents a store. For a store's rating, we select the rating time span, denoted as T, then we get the time window Δt, $I_n = [t_0 + (n-1)\Delta t,\ t_0 + n\Delta t]$, $I = \bigcup_{n=1}^{N} I_n$. For each time window, the average rating and the sample entropy is calculated respectively as formulas (3) and (4). Since both of them should be asymptotically normal [8], we use z-score to normalize them.

$$f_1(X_{I_n}) = \left(\sum_{i=1}^{r_{max}} n_i \times i\right)/S \tag{3}$$

$$f_2(X_{I_n}) = -\sum_{i=1}^{r_{max}} \left(\frac{n_i}{S} \log_2 \frac{n_i}{S}\right) \tag{4}$$

Where, $X_{I_n} = \{n_i,\ i = 1, 2, \cdots, r_{max}\}$, r_{max} indicates the maximum rating, n_i is the occurrence of the i-th possible rating, and $S = \sum_{i=1}^{r_{max}} n_i$. The corresponding algorithm which judges whether an abnormal rating occurs in an abnormal time period is shown as follows.

Algorithm1. Anomaly Patterns Detection Based on Time Series
1: **INPUT**: reviews of a store, window size Δt, threshold δ ,time span I
2: set $S = \phi$ // set of anomaly windows to return
3: construct time series $F(I, \Delta t) = \begin{bmatrix} f_1(X_{I_1}) & \cdots & f_1(X_{I_n}) \\ f_2(X_{I_1}) & \cdots & f_{12}(X_{I_n}) \end{bmatrix}$
4: **for** $i = 1 \to \frac{T}{\Delta t}$
5: **if** $\left(\left[z - score\left(f_1(X_{I_i})\right) > \delta \,\&\&z - score\left(f_2(X_{I_i})\right) > \delta \right] \right)$ **do**
6:    $S = S \cup I_i$
7: **end for**
8: **RETURN** S

3.2   Multi-scale Features

We extract benchmark-scale features and related subdivision-scale features hierarchically. The subdivision-scale feature is obtained based on the benchmark-scale feature.

Fake Comment Features

We propose 11 candidate features that are most likely to affect the fake comments detection results as the original features. The detailed features are in Table 1.

Table 1. Candidate comment feature

Item	Implication	Item	Implication
F0	Persistence with other comments		
F1	User Reputation	F6	Terminology
F2	Buyer's Show Pictures	F7	Personal pronoun proportion
F3	The number of adversative	F8	Consistency between reviews and ratings
F4	Emotional intensity	F9	The number of thumb up
F5	Comment text length	F10	Correlation

Benchmark-Scale Feature Extraction

Eleven features above have different importance for fake review detection, so we should select the most important features as the benchmark-scale features. For this objective, we propose a random forest model for selecting the most important features from features above. We first calculate the Feature Importance (FI) for each feature. Then, we sort the FI values in descending order. Finally, the features with lower FI values are deleted.

Subdivision-Scale Feature Extraction

In order to further define the dissimilarity between reviews, the distance between each pair of reviews is calculated on the benchmark-scale features above. After that, with each comment as a center and the cut-off distance $dc^{[17]}$ as a radius, we compute statistic values of every benchmark-scale features, and keep them as the corresponding subdivision-scale features of reviews. These statistic values include the mean, the standard deviation, the maximum, the minimum, the mode and the ratio of the number of reviews having the mode value to the total number of reviews. The subdivision-scale features are expressed as $V = \{mean,\ std,\ max, min, mod, r - mod\}$.

3.3 Feature Dimension Reduction

We get abundant features above. Considering the correlation among these features, we use the Principal Component Analysis(PCA) method to extract the most representative principal component factors. Before doing PCA, we do KMO (Kaiser Meyer Olkin) test to confirm whether the data are suitable for dimension reduction. When the KMO value higher than 0.6 and the significance value less than 0.05, the data are suitable for PCA. Therefore, we only extract the principal component factors whose eigenvalues are higher than one, which forms a feature vector.

4 Fake Comment Recognition Based on DPC

In June 2014, fast search and find of density peaks clustering (DPC) [9] was published. It has strong anti-noise performance through eliminating outliers. We improve it to identify fake comments. The density peaks clustering algorithm for detecting fake reviews is shown in Algorithm 2. After doing this algorithm, we identify the fake comment cluster.

Algorithm2. Density Peaks Clustering for detecting fake reviews

---

1: **INPUT:**   review data , cutoff distance d_c
2: compute dissimilarity between reviews
3: compute the local density of the comment
4: sort the local density
5: compute distance from nearest larger density review
6: draw decision graph
7: select the cluster center
8: **for** each review
9:    **if** (review $\notin$ the cluster center) **do**
10:      review is assigned to the same cluster as its nearest review of higher density.
11: **end for**
12: divide the border region
13: compute average local density
14: compute the largest average local density
15: divide noise
16: **RETURN CS**

---

5 Experimental Analysis

5.1 Feature Abstraction

The experimental data of this article are obtained from www.dianping.com/. We get 13142 reviews which contain 9764 real reviews and 3378 fake reviews.

First of all, we use time series to detect anomaly ratings. We set the Δt with 20 and the δ with 2. Seen from Fig. 1, the anomaly ratings occur in the thirteenth time window, as its z-score's absolute values of the mean and the sample entropy are higher than δ. Through verification, this phenomenon conforms to the real situation.

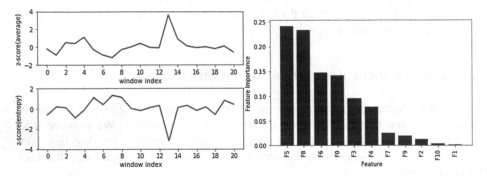

Fig. 1. Time series detecting anomaly   **Fig. 2.** Feature importance ranking

Then, we use random forests model to select 6 benchmark features. Figure 2 shows the feature importance ranking obtained by random forests. It can be seen that features of F5, F8, F6, F0, F3 and F4 are of great importance. After that, PCA is used to reduce the feature dimension. As the KMO test value is 0.897, and the significance value of the Bartlett's spherical test is 0.001, the data is suitable for reducing dimension by PCA. Finally, we extract principal component factors whose eigenvalues are higher than one.

5.2 Model Verification

This article uses ROC curve and AUC value to evaluate the model. We design three comparison experiments. The comparison between my method with all selected features and the method with only benchmark-scale features is shown in Fig. 3, and the comparison between my method and the method without time series is shown in Fig. 4. It can be seen my method has higher AUC value. The comparison between my method and the current popular methods (Ren et al. [10], Shao et al. [11]) is shown in Table 2, we can see that the TPR of my method is slightly higher than Ren et al. [10] and Shao et al. [11] while FPR is lower than the other two methods. So my method has a good effect.

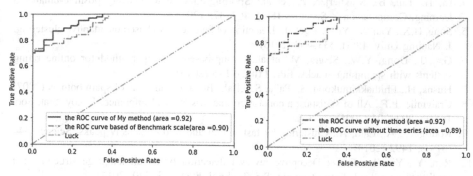

Fig. 3. Comparison between my method and the method with only benchmark-scale features

Fig. 4. Comparison between my method and the method without time series

Table 2. Comparison of my method with references [10] and [11]

Method	Number of features	Model	TPR	FPR
Ren [10]	5	Soft and hard clustering	74.84%	27.31%
Shao [11]	8	Heterogeneous graph	87.43%	22.52%
My method	49	Density peaks clustering	89.90%	15.44%

6 Conclusion

Aiming at effectively detecting fake comments, we build a multi-dimensional time series model, and use the density peaks clustering algorithm to identify fake comments. Through experimental comparison, our method has higher true positive rate and lower false positive rate. However, it still needs to be improved. Firstly, there is not a strict definition to divide multi-scale features. Secondly, there is still a demand to seek a better way rather than PCA for reducing the feature dimension.

Acknowledgments. This work is supported by the National Nature Science Foundation of China (No. 61672329, No. 61373149, No. 61472233, No. 61572300, No. 81273704), Shandong Provincial Project of Education Scientific Plan (No. ZK1437B010).

References

1. Jindal, N., Liu, B.: Opinion spam and analysis. In: International Conference on Web Search and Data Mining, pp. 219–230. ACM (2008)
2. Chang, T., Hsu, P.Y., Cheng, M.S., Chung, C.Y., Chung, Y.L.: Detecting fake review with rumor model—Case study in hotel review. In: He, X., et al. (eds.) IScIDE 2015. LNCS, vol. 9243, pp. 181–192. Springer, Cham (2015). https://doi.org/10.1007/978-3-319-23862-3_18
3. Li, J., Ott, M., Cardie, C., et al.: Towards a general rule for identifying deceptive opinion spam. In: Meeting of the Association for Computational Linguistics, pp. 1566–1576 (2014)

4. Li, H., Liu, B., Mukherjee, A., et al.: Spotting fake reviews using positive-unlabeled learning. Computacion Y Sistemas **18**(3), 467–475 (2015)
5. Song, H.X., Yan, X., Yu, Z.T., et al.: Detection of fake reviews based on adaptive clustering. J. Nanjing Univ. **49**(4), 433–438 (2013)
6. Gao, J., Dong, Y.W., Shang, M., et al.: Group-based ranking method for online rating systems with spamming attacks. EPL **110**(2), 1–6 (2015)
7. Husna, H., Phithakkitnukoon, S., Palla, S., et al.: Behavior analysis of spam botnets (2007)
8. Craigmile, P.F.: All of statistics: a concise course in statistical inference. J. Roy. Stat. Soc. **168**(1), 203–204 (2005)
9. Rodriguez, A., Laio, A.: Clustering by fast search and find of density peaks. Science **344** (6191), 1492 (2014)
10. Ren, Y., Yin, L., Ji, D.: Deceptive reviews detection based on language structure and sentiment polarity. J. Front. Comput. Sci. Technol. **8**(3), 313–320 (2014)
11. Shao, Z., Ji, D.: Spotting fake reviewers based on sentiment features and users' relationship. Comput. Appl. Softw. **33**(5), 158–161 (2016)

Towards Android Application Protection
via Kernel Extension

Tuo Wang[1], Lu Liu[1], Chongzhi Gao[2], Jingjing Hu[1],
and Jingyu Liu[3(✉)]

[1] School of Computer Science and Technology, Beijing Institute of Technology,
Beijing 100081, China
[2] School of Computer Science, Guangzhou University, Guangzhou, China
[3] School of Artificial Intelligence, Hebei University of Technology,
Tianjin 300401, China
liujy@hebut.edu.cn

Abstract. As an integral part of Android system security, Android application protection has always been favored by researchers. The current popular protection schemes include the source code confusion, anti-debugging technology, and confusions of executable files. However, these schemes modify the applications more or less undoubtedly, and that causes inconvenience while these applications are running. This article proposes a kernel-level Android application protection scheme which can eliminate the need for additional application modifications and protect all application data. Therefore, we designed an encryption system and implemented a prototype system Godzilla on the basis of the Linux kernel 3.18.14 in order to verify the validity of the design. Experiments show that the system can achieve our goals well. Compared to non-protected applications, protected ones will have corresponding time loss during installation and startup, but they are all within acceptable limits.

Keywords: Android application · Kernel · Encryption system

1 Introduction

The Android [1] system has been gradually developed since its introduction in 2007. It is used in smart phones, tablet computers, automotive systems, smart TVs, smart watches and other fields [2], and becomes the most popular embedded system.

However, the open source policy makes it serious for the Android system to suffer security problems [3], for instance, code and data leakage [4] once the device is rooted [5]. At present, researchers have made some attempts in this regard to protect code and data [6], such as Code obfuscation [7]. Some techniques achieve the purpose of stopping being reversed via anti-debugging and anti-interception [8].

These schemes can protect Android applications to a certain degree. However, there is no doubt that these solutions require some modifications per application. Therefore, we want to implement an application protection scheme that does not need to modify the application. Finally, we focus on the kernel [9] layer.

© Springer Nature Switzerland AG 2018
T. Hu et al. (Eds.): ICA3PP 2018 Workshops, LNCS 11338, pp. 131–137, 2018.
https://doi.org/10.1007/978-3-030-05234-8_16

At present, some mature encryption solutions are implemented in the Linux kernel. Dm-crypt [10] mechanism, introduced from 2.6 release, creates a virtual encryption layer on the abstract block device, providing transparent encryption for block devices. Although dm-crypt can protect data well, there are some problems to be solved. For example, in Linux system, if you want to encrypt a disk partition or file, you need to use tedious instructions. A slight carelessness may cause configuration errors. Since kernel 4.2, Linux has added the Ext4 Encryption [11] mechanism. It uses a directory-based encryption scheme. After setting the encryption policy for the target directory, the files or directories created in the target directory will use this encryption policy to encrypt their own data. In this way, bulk data encryption can be performed on a directory basis, and only sensitive data can be selectively encrypted. However, there are some issues when the scheme is applied directly to the Android system. For example, the encryption [12] and decryption process is very cumbersome and the mechanism requires the target directory to be empty.

Based on the attempts above, we hope to implement an encryption system in the kernel layer, which has features as follows: (1) Encryption by directory; (2) The encryption and decryption process are as simple as possible; (3) When the application is installing, the kernel can automatic encrypt all files including executable files, dependencies. The main contributions of this article are as follows:

(1) An encryption system is designed in the Linux kernel layer which implements encryption and decryption operations in a directory unit.
(2) According to the above, Godzilla, a prototype system which is applied to the protection of Android applications, is implemented in the Linux kernel version 3.14.18.
(3) In order to verify the performance of Godzilla, we applied the prototype system to the Samsung S7 edge mobile phone and did some tests. The result shows that the Godzilla system can achieve the goal of protecting Android applications.

In Sect. 2, we specifically describe the problems that need to be solved, and implement a prototype system Godzilla. Finally, we conducted a series of experiments (Sect. 3) to verify the feasibility of our design.

2   Design and Implementation

In this section, we will present solutions to the challenges we face and realize a prototype system, **Godzilla**, on the basis of the Linux kernel 3.18.14.

2.1   Managing Encrypted Files in Directory Units

In order to implement this function, we have to answer two questions: (1) how to distinguish between encrypted and ordinary files; (2) how to manage files in directory.

Mark the Encrypted File. By means of a flag, we can achieve the goal. For each file, there will be a unique inode structure corresponding to it. In the inode structure, there is an i_flags member that identifies the states of the file. There are four reserved states for this variable and we select the EXT4_INODE_ECOMPR (reserved for compression error) state to represent that the file/folder is encrypted.

Inherited Encryption Properties. When the file B is created in the directory A, it first determines whether the parent directory A is encrypted, that is, whether the corresponding bit of the inode(A)-> i_flags is set to 1. If it is, file B will automatically inherit the encrypted attribute of parent directory A, the corresponding position of inode(B)-> i_flags is set to 1.

2.2 Data Protection

File Encryption. When discussing file encryption, the most important thing is to consider where to "encrypt" without significantly affecting the performance of the original system.

In the Linux system, the page caching mechanism, which is between the virtual file level (VFS) and the file system layer, may give us some inspiration. When a write operation occurs, the kernel first checks whether the page to be written is already in the page cache. If it is not, add a new page and fill the page with the data to be written to the disk, then set the page as a dirty page. When the system reaches a certain mode, all dirty pages will be written back. In ext4_bio_write_page() method, the data page will be added to the bio structure before writing into the disk. In our method, page A is first copied to a new page A', then decrypt A', and finally replace A with A' added to the bio structure.

File Decryption. When performs a reading operation, it eventually maps to the do_-generic_file_read() method in the virtual file system layer. Due to the existence of page cache, the kernel buffer is first looked for a cached page that stores data. If the data page is found, a read-ahead operation will be triggered. if it not exists in kernel buffer, the kernel will go to the process of reading data from disk. In our method, before the page B returns to user space, we use a new page B' to store the data which is decrypted from B and return the B' to user space.

2.3 Application Protection

In the Android environment, the application's installation package is an APK (Android Package) file which contains application data and resource files. In the process of installing applications, a large number of IO operations are involved, and the application resolution operation applies the memory mapping [13] technology. When disk file maps to the memory area, the contents are not loaded into the memory immediately. When first accessing the file, the kernel will generate a page fault interrupt. In the filemap_map_pages() method, after data is read into the page cache, it will query related data pages and set new page table entries for the page. Therefore, we use a new page D' to store the data which is decrypted from D, then replace D with the new page D' before setting the page table entry.

3 Evaluation

In order to prove that the design scheme is effective and feasible, the prototype system Godzilla was modified and a switch was added. When the switch is turned on, the system can perform data encryption and decryption operation; and when it is closed, the system stops the mechanism. For the sake of convenience, we refer to the state in which the switch is turned on as an encrypted state, and the state when the switch is turned off as the normal state.

3.1 Data Protection Testing and Analysis

Encryption Validity Verification. We set/data/app as an encrypted directory. In normal state, we copy the file packages.xml to the directory/data/app. From the binary view tool we can see that the content is clear and unarguable, then enter encrypted state, write packages.xml to the directory again, at this time, the contents is still clear. Finally, we return to the normal state, the details of the file are very confusing. This indicates that the content has been encrypted and is currently in an unreadable state.

3.2 Application Protection Evaluation

We have randomly selected 12 applications from the top 50 applications in the google play store ranking list [14]. These applications cover social networking, payment, shopping, streaming media, and blogging.

Application Installation Time Assessment. *Setup.* We install the above 12 applications in the normal state and the encrypted state respectively, compared the time spent in the installation within the two states. Here we use an open source automated testing tool, AutomatorX [15], that records the time at which the application was installed and the time takes to complete the application.

Result. By comparison, it can be seen that the cost time of installing applications in the encrypted state is generally higher than that in the normal state (Fig. 1). This also shows that the data protection process extends the file write time. But for most applications, the time does not increase too much, generally within 4 s.

Application Launch Time Assessment. We used the built-in "am" command when starting the android application. We define the start-up time in the encrypted state as Te, Tn in the normal state, the difference between them is Td, $Td = Te - Tn$, defining the time loss $Tl = (Td/Tn) * 100\%$.

Result. It can be seen from Table 1 that the time loss fluctuation is very large, but through the value of Td, we found that the time difference is actually very small. This is acceptable to users.

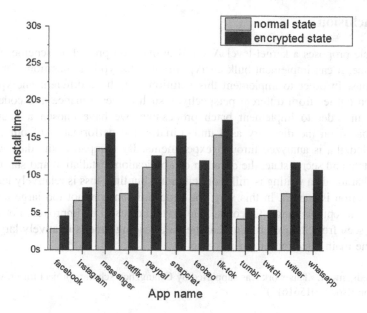

Fig. 1. Application installation time. The installation time in the encrypted state is generally longer than in the normal state.

Table 1. Application startup time

Application name	Start time		Time difference (Td)	Time loss (Tl)
	Encrypted state (Te)	Normal state (Tc)		
Facebook	0.808 s	0.588 s	0.220 s	37.41%
Instagram	1.181 s	0.446 s	0.735 s	164.80%
Messenger	1.043 s	0.357 s	0.686 s	192.16%
Netflix	2.445 s	1.202 s	1.243 s	103.41%
Paypal	3.307 s	1.610 s	1.697 s	105.40%
Snapchat	1.675 s	1.170 s	0.505 s	43.16%
Taobao	2.318 s	0.354 s	1.964 s	554.80%
Tik-tok	2.461 s	1.002 s	1.459 s	145.61%
Tumblr	0.987 s	0.862 s	0.125 s	14.50%
Twitch	1.347 s	1.037 s	0.310 s	29.89%
Twitter	1.555 s	0.446 s	1.109 s	248.65%
WhatsApp	1.177 s	0.629 s	0.548 s	87.12%

4 Conclusion

This article proposes a kernel-level Android application protection scheme. Based on this scheme, it can implement bulk encryption and decryption operations for Android applications. In order to implement this solution, we chose different encryption and decryption entries from different perspectives such as performance and code size. In addition, in order to implement batch processing, we have chosen a management scheme based on the directory as a unit. Finally, the performance of our prototype system Godzilla is analyzed through experiments. By comparing the data writing in normal state and secret state, the duration of application installation and startup, it can be seen that the data writing is still more efficient, but time loss is relatively large when the application is started. In this way, the time difference is not too large and is still within the acceptable range. Of course, the system can still be improved. For example, it can be seen from the experiment that the data reading time is relatively large, which will be the main direction of our next work.

Acknowledgement. This work was supported by Guangzhou scholars project for universities of Guangzhou (No. 1201561613).

References

1. Developers, Android. What is android (2011)
2. Wikipedia. https://en.wikipedia.org/wiki/Android_(operating_system). Accessed 29 May 2018
3. Hur, J.B., Shamsi, J.A.: A survey on security issues, vulnerabilities and attacks in Android based smartphone. In: 2017 International Conference on Information and Communication Technologies (ICICT), pp. 40–46. IEEE (2017)
4. Xue, Y., Tan, Y., Liang, C., Li, Y., Zheng, J., Zhang, Q.: RootAgency: a digital signature-based root privilege management agency for cloud terminal devices. Inf. Sci. **444**, 36–50 (2018)
5. Tan, Y., et al.: A root privilege management scheme with revocable authorization for Android devices. J. Netw. Comput. **107**(4), 69–82 (2018)
6. Xue, Y., Tan, Y., Liang, C., Zhang, C., Zheng, J.: An optimized data hiding scheme for deflate codes. Soft. Comput. **22**(13), 4445–4455 (2018)
7. Kovacheva, A.: Efficient code obfuscation for Android. In: Papasratorn, B., Charoenkitkarn, N., Vanijja, V., Chongsuphajaisiddhi, V. (eds.) IAIT 2013. CCIS, vol. 409, pp. 104–119. Springer, Cham (2013). https://doi.org/10.1007/978-3-319-03783-7_10
8. Wan, J.: Android app protection through anti-tampering and anti-debugging techniques. Ph. D. dissertation, Queen's University (Canada) (2018)
9. Love, R.: Linux kernel development. System **66**(66), 69–70 (2005). Author, F.: Article title. Journal 2(5), 99–110 (2016)
10. Saout, C.: dm-crypt: a device-mapper crypto target (2007). http://www.saout.de/misc/dm-crypt (2014)
11. Corbet, J., LWN.net Weekly: Ext4 encryption. Lwn.net (2015)
12. Zhang, X., et al.: Cryptographic key protection against FROST for mobile devices. Clust. Comput. **20**(3), 2393–2402 (2017)

13. Gorman, M.: Understanding the Linux Virtual Memory Manager. Prentice Hall, Upper Saddle River (2004)
14. Google Play Store. https://play.google.com/store/apps/collection/topselling_free. Accessed 29 May 2018
15. AutoMatorX. https://github.com/NetEaseGame/ATX. Accessed 29 May 2018

Threats and Coping Strategies Under the IOT

Zeping Li[1], Huwei Liu[1], and Ning Cao[2(✉)]

[1] School of Information, Beijing Wuzi University, Beijing, China
2953270587@qq.com
[2] College of Information Engineering, Qingdao Binhai University,
Qingdao, China
ning.cao2008@hotmail.com

Abstract. The development of the Internet of things (IoT) is fast and practical. It has developed and focused on a wide range of development in the world. IoT technology is a huge technological innovation in the field of information technology. The technology is considered to be the most promising information technology in the future and has applications in all aspects. There is a certain risk and hidden when the IoT in the application. The IoT will also impede its own development because of security problems, and the application of its wide range will also be reduced. In the face of the security threat of intelligence, systematization and generalization, a kind of network architecture of the network is proposed. Articles from the IoT security architecture of analysis network security threats, and security problems of IoT of rescue, put forward the corresponding solution strategy, to analyze IOT security model.

Keywords: The internet of things · Security threats · Coping strategies

1 Introduction

With the development of social science and technology, the IoT is based on the concept of modern technology and technology to realize the transmission and transportation of information express in modern society. And the rapid transmission and transportation of information can be realized. The exchange of information is bound to have the corresponding potential risks and many security threats. The problem is that equipment damage, the key to the login, the information disclosure and the computer intrusion behavior. These threats have caused serious damage to the construction of information security in our lives and countries, and have also hindered development under the framework of the IoT. High Qualcomm forecasts that the number of devices in the IoT will reach more than 25 billion in 2020. And Ali cloud predicts that the IoT will be more than 20 billion, so the development of the IoT will continue to be a hot spot in the future. Therefore, the problem of security under the framework of IoT is also a very important research point. This paper analyzes the problems existing in the IoT. Based on the research of former scholars, the author adds the public service layer and puts forward corresponding solutions. The security model of IoT can be analyzed for reference of relevant researchers.

© Springer Nature Switzerland AG 2018
T. Hu et al. (Eds.): ICA3PP 2018 Workshops, LNCS 11338, pp. 138–144, 2018.
https://doi.org/10.1007/978-3-030-05234-8_17

2 Domestic and Overseas Research Status

Consulting the relevant literature, we can understand the development of the IoT, and analyze the architecture of the IoT. According to the related analysis, the research and development of the architecture of the IoT are expounded from two aspects of software and hardware.

2.1 IoT Architecture

The IoT forms the connection between people and objects, objects and objects, and realizes information, remote management, control and intelligent network [1]. The architecture of the IoT is shown in Fig. 1, which can be divided into four parts: perception layer, network layer, application layer and public technology. The perception layer is the foundation of the whole security architecture. The external data is collected by the camera or sensor. The network layer is mainly used for the external data collected by the perceptual layer. The IoT in the Internet is a professional network with its unique properties at the network level. The transmission process of data and the equipment and network construction of the IoT and the way of intervention are the main points of the various security problems [2]. The application layer is the core of the whole IoT security system. The public technology is based on the overall management of the perception layer.

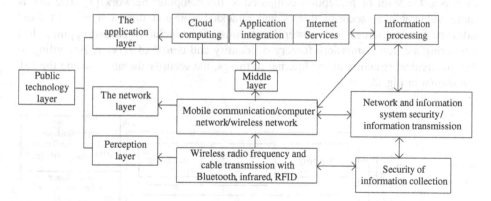

Fig. 1. Architecture diagram of IoT security architecture

2.2 Internet of Things Development

The development of the IoT, it is possible to consider both hardware and software. The hardware enhancement is better than the security performance of software optimization. Through the strengthening of network authentication and strict control of resource usage rights, it can avoid the occurrence of information without reason [3]. Zhong Xing microelectronics and the ministry of public security jointly launched a national standard security monitoring digital video encoding and decoding technology standard (SVAC). On the basis of semiconductor chip technology, the standard has the ability to harden the hard solution. It can improve the safety of the product by the chip coding and decoding.

Considering the security of the IoT from the software, the Internet based IoT is designed by the improvement, and there is a heterogeneous network. When the security measures are lacking and the data is interlinked, the data will be lost and the network will be disconnected [4]. However, the threat has been extended to software, and some hackers have extended their hands to silicon level in order to destroy the security of the system [5]. In 2016, large numbers of users in North America found that important sites, such as Twitter, Netflix, Paypal and Git Hub, were inaccessible. In the US internet paralysis event, Krebs on Security, a foreign security analysis website, pointed out that the infected DVR and camera devices mainly came from Hangzhou China Xiong Mai Information Technology Co, Ltd. and Zhejiang Dahua Technology Limited by Share Ltd [6].

3 Threats and Coping Strategies

3.1 Existential Threat

With the development of economy, technology and Internet, the IoT has many security problems, and may even cause new problems because of some security technology. We need to develop appropriate responses to specific security threats. The IoT has increased the level of perception compared to the computer network [7]. The IoT is more vulnerable to security threats and attacks because it does not rely on fixed infrastructure resources and power limitations. This includes eavesdropping, data tampering and retransmission, forgery of identity and denial of service. According to the hierarchical structure of the Internet of things, the security threats is facing the IoT are shown in Fig. 2.

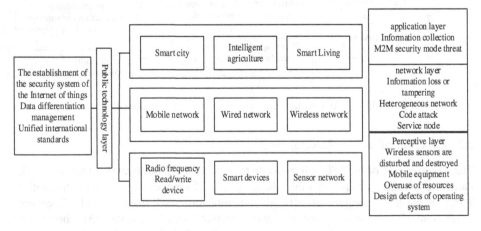

Fig. 2. Security threats under the IOT architecture

3.2   Coping Strategies

Application Layer. At this time we need to set different access rights to different customers can effectively improve the security of the customer group. Designing access data, the system can automatically organize when access data changes. Standardize the design pattern of the corresponding M2M, avoid the corresponding design loopholes, as far as possible to reduce the defect of the pattern.

Network Layer. Before information transmission, users are encrypted with different encryption methods, which can improve user information security. The security protection software of the network layer can be designed to improve its own defense capability. Strengthen the authentication management of key.

Perception Layer. The methods of physical or cryptographic mechanism are commonly used to ensure the security of RFID devices. We should also improve laws and regulations, establish a reasonable legal system, and increase penalties for criminals.

Public Technology Layer. The network has its own management mode, and the unified management method provides the illegal operation for the unlawful elements. We need to deepen the integration based on the network layer, the perception layer and the application layer.

4   Internet of Things Security Analysis Model

In order to improve the security of the IoT, in addition to the above security strategies, this paper proposes a model of IOT security analysis based on support vector machines (SVM). The SVM aggregate the collected data sets for aggregation classification. Finding the optimal linear hyperplane transformation to solve the two programming problem. We judge the situation of things according to the results of the final classification. A random set of data is first generated, in which a training sample set.

$$G_0 = \{(x_i, y_i) : x_i \in R^n, y_i \in \{-1, 1\}\}$$

The generated sample set is learned in Python. Model is divided into x_i^+ and x_i^-. You can look for a discriminant function, "f".

$$sgn(f(x_i)) = \begin{cases} +1, & x_i \in x_i^+ \\ -1, & x_i \in x_i^- \end{cases}$$

If the above function can be set up, the data set is linearly separable, otherwise the data set cannot be linearly divided. The SVM is in the space generated by all the selected eigenvalues. We can find the optimal hyperplane and maximize the classification interval as much as possible. By solving the problem of planning, two classifiers are finally obtained.

$$u(x) = \sum_{j=0}^{i} \alpha_i y_i \left(\phi(x_j), \phi(x) \right) - b$$

$$y(x) = \text{sgn}(u(x))$$

The upper equation requires the inner product operation on the high dimensional feature space, but it is usually unknown. But the inner product of the characteristic space can be calculated using one called kernel function. As shown in Fig. 3, the data set to be classified should be collected first. Then the data sets are classified, and the classification data is analyzed and the corresponding analysis results are obtained.

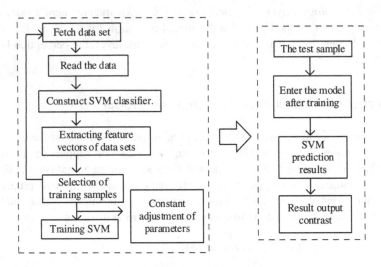

Fig. 3. SVM model flowchart

The SVM is applicable to the security analysis of the IoT in small quantities. The state of the IoT is divided into two states: abnormal and normal. When the data is obtained, the normal state is 1 and the abnormal state is 0. We select the appropriate characteristic parameters according to the state data of the IoT, and select the data set of the characteristic parameters. The flow of the specific security analysis model of the IoT, in Fig. 4.

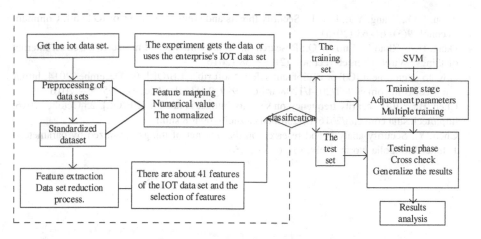

Fig. 4. Flow chart of IOT security analysis model

5   Summary

A wide range of applications, but also for the development of IoT technology has buried a lot of security risks. The leakage of customer's private information and the network threat caused by the expired network and protocol have caused some obstacles to the development of the Internet of things. This paper studies the literatures of scholars and sums up the corresponding security threats of IoT. And it puts forward corresponding countermeasures. The last part of the paper puts forward a security problem relative to the IoT, and puts forward a method to detect the security of the IoT. The method of SVM is used to classify the state data of the IoT and determine the security status of the Internet of things. It helps to further understand the algorithm of the SVM. Due to the limited ability and time, the data of the Internet of things cannot be obtained, and it is not perfect in the experimental simulation part. This is also the part that needs to be improved.

Acknowledgement. The study is supported by the National Nature Science Foundation of China "Research on the warehouse picking system blocking influence factors and combined control strategy" (No. 71501015), Beijing the Great Wall scholars program (No. CIT &TCD20170317), the Beijing Collaborative Innovation Center, the 2018 Major project of China society of logistics: "Research on the connectivity of modern logistics network system" (2018CSLKT2-004), and the project of Beijing Wuzi University Yunhe River scholar.

References

1. Dong, X.: Research progress on the privacy protection of the Internet of things. Comput. Res. Dev. **52**(10), 2341–2352 (2015)
2. Chen, Y.Y.: Analysis on the security threats and countermeasures of Internet of things. Cyber Space Secur. **8**(Z2), 17–20 (2011)

3. Zhou, C.Q., Wang, Y.J., Liu, T.: Security threats and countermeasures of IOT. Inf. Commun. Technol. **9**(5), 61–65 (2015)
4. Dang, H.E., Zhao E., Luo, W.Q.: Research on security threats and measures based on Internet of things. Wirel. Internet Technol. (2), 37–38 (2016)
5. How to overcome a IOT of equipment safety "soft rib" [EB/OL], 08 December 2014. http://www.eeworld.com.cn/IoT/2014/1208/arti-cle_999_2.HTML. Accessed 05 Nov 2016
6. Chen, B.L.: IOT security frequency on security budget is not 1% [EB/OL], 25 October 2016. http://tech.sina.com.cn/t/2016-10-25/docifxwzuci9469408.shtm
7. Chen, Y.: Security analysis and research on the internet of things optimized by parameters. J. Inner Mongolia Norm. Univ. (5), 666 (2016)

Framework Design of Financial Service Platform for Tobacco Supply Chain Based on Blockchain

Huwei Liu[1], Zeping Li[1], and Ning Cao[2(✉)]

[1] School of Information, Beijing Wuzi University, Beijing, China
liuhuwei@outlook.com, 2953210587@qq.com
[2] College of Information Engineering, Qingdao Binhai University,
Qingdao, China
ning.cao2008@hotmail.com

Abstract. In the development of tobacco supply chain finance, the imperfection of the credit system and financial service platform has become a major issue. With this issue as the starting point, we elaborated how these issues affect the development of the tobacco supply chain, and introduced blockchain technology on the basis of this issue. We reviewed previous research results and theoretical basis and analyzed the development process of the tobacco supply chain and the characteristics of blockchain technology. Based on the above, a framework of tobacco supply chain financial service platform based on blockchain technology is constructed, and corresponding solutions are given.

Keywords: Blockchain · Tobacco supply chain · Supply chain finance

1 Introduction

Blockchain technology is an innovative, forward-looking technology that is still in the development stage. Its consensus mechanism, encryption algorithms, and transaction capacity need to be further improved. In the field of supply chain finance at home and abroad, it is only gradually trying to apply blockchain technology. The portability and security of existing supply chain finance are all factors that blockchain technology has not yet been universally applied to. Tobacco supply chain financial service platform is for the credit of each participant in the whole supply chain. The credit rating is closely related to the credit of the core company. The credit rating of each participant is the strong support of the entire supply chain financial credit rating, and the real trade of tobacco supply chain is the core of the supply chain credit system. In order to solve the problem of tobacco supply chain finance, domestic scholars have conducted a lot of research on the issue of China's tobacco supply chain finance. From the existing research results and research process, we will find that the essence of the tobacco supply chain finance is that the tobacco supply chain finance problem is the credit issue of the tobacco supply chain participants, but the implementation process of these credit systems is difficult to control, and there are often unsatisfactory problems in the implementation process. At present, the popularization and application of Internet

T. Hu et al. (Eds.): ICA3PP 2018 Workshops, LNCS 11338, pp. 145–150, 2018.
https://doi.org/10.1007/978-3-030-05234-8_18

technologies, and the emergence of more information frontier technologies such as big data, Internet+, and blockchain, provide good conditions for the cracking of tobacco supply chain financial credit issues.

2 Literature Review

In 2015, the People's Bank of China and other countries defined Internet finance as a new type of financial business model in which traditional financial institutions and Internet companies used Internet technology and information and communication technologies to realize financing services, payment, investment, and information intermediary services [1]. Chaofeng Jiang [2] described supply chain finance as using the concepts and methods of supply chain management to provide financial services to related companies. The essence of this approach is to provide financial services to enterprises on the supply chain chain. Interspersed in the supply chain, it is also a trade-driven financial and logistics services. Hua Song [3] believes that the application of blockchain technology in Internet supply chain finance can be achieved at both financial activities and industrial activities. The blockchain application at the financial level is mainly for payment settlement and digital bills. At the industrial activity level, the blockchain technology can be used for proof of interest and proof of logistics operations. Tanshunzi Jin [4] pointed out in his article that the current financial transaction process in the supply chain is complex and the business process is highly dependent on labor, and there are problems such as high labor costs, high operational risks, and low returns. Supply chain finance can reduce labor costs, improve security, and achieve point-to-point transparency by applying blockchain technology. Iansiti and Lakhani [5] pointed out that in complex supply chains, companies started to use blockchain technology to track items; in the diamond industry, using blockchain technology, gems can be traced from mine to consumers. Guo and Liang [6] pointed out that supply chain finance involves a large number of manual inspections and paper records transactions. In the process, there are a large number of middlemen, which have large transaction risks, high costs, and low efficiency. Blockchain technology can significantly reduce manual intervention and digitize programs that rely heavily on paperwork with smart contracts. This will greatly increase the efficiency of supply chain finance and reduce the risk of manual operations. For suppliers, buyers, and banks of major players, and shared contract information scattered on distributed ledgers, smart contracts can ensure that payments are automatically made after a predetermined time and condition have been reached. Korpela, Hallikas, Dahlberg [7] pointed out in his article that the digitized, integrated supply chain is becoming more and more dynamic. The needs of customers need to be effectively shared, and products and services must be tracked in order to achieve visibility and transparency of the supply chain. Integration of business processes, standards and specification systems based on the point-to-point integration of product data, these blockchain technologies are considered as ways to improve security and efficiency. Overall, there is a lack of research on supply chain financial system application models based on blockchain technology at home and abroad. The financial principles, core technologies, core processes, and module models of blockchain supply chains have not been systematically proposed, and studies in this area need to be strengthened.

3 Tobacco Supply Chain Finance and Blockchain Technology

From the perspective of the supply chain's financial credit demand and blockchain characteristics, the two have a foundation for integration. Tobacco supply chain finance is mainly expressed in the form of real economy. The real economy is a system composed of many parties involved in enterprises, society, financial institutions, and government. In the end, it is all done by people. Therefore, it is difficult to avoid credit problems caused by human intervention. The blockchain is mainly an intelligent protocol that automatically executes system smart contracts without human intervention, avoiding credit issues caused by human involvement.

From the perspective of the cost and risk of the financial operation of the tobacco supply chain, the two have the necessity of integration. The tobacco supply chain is characterized by complexity, seasonality, high cost, etc. It is bound to increase the cost of tobacco supply chain finance (such as financing, loans, etc.) and increase the credit risk of tobacco supply chain participants. Applying blockchain technology to the tobacco supply chain, the blockchain platform can automatically confirm the transaction process according to the smart contract of the system. This transaction process is also a process of retrospection and certification of the future financial clearing and auditing of the system. Compared with the traditional supply chain operation process, it not only saves people, money, and goods, but also can optimize the system's process and improve the system's operating efficiency; in addition, the open nature of the blockchain system makes the system participants participate freely according to the pre-defined system rules. Participate in the event as a block broadcast system and linked to the system chain, stamped with a time stamp to form a distributed ledger. The account records the event in a true and complete manner. It is protected by encryption technology and time stamps. The data in the account book cannot be tampered with, unless more than 51% of the node's account book data in the system is modified (which cannot be done in reality). Otherwise, the data is true and complete, and the parties to the transaction cannot be denied.

From the perspective of financial sharing of the tobacco supply chain and flexible architecture of blockchain, the integration of the two can reduce the credit crisis caused by information asymmetry. Sharing finance will help reduce the transaction costs of the tobacco supply chain, achieve a reasonable flow of finance and its derivatives, enhance the scientific and optimal allocation of tobacco supply chain resources, and enhance the development capacity of the tobacco supply chain. The application of blockchain in the tobacco supply chain is the process of achieving the transfer of financial information of tobacco supply chain to value. At the same time, the flexible framework of the blockchain provides different application requirements for participants in the tobacco supply chain, and can achieve different types of public blockchains, private blockchains, and alliance blockchains. Tobacco supply chain participants can choose according to different needs.

4 Framework Design of Tobacco Supply Chain Financial Service Platform

Participants in the tobacco supply chain include suppliers, tobacco growers, professional cooperatives, logistics companies, processing companies, wholesale retailers, and consumers. From a deeper point of view, various participants are inextricably linked with core companies and financial institutions, and even each participant has business or financial contacts, resulting in a more complex system for the entire tobacco supply chain as that shown in Fig. 1.

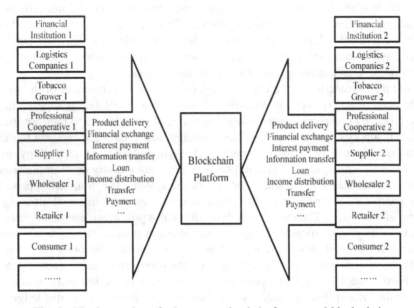

Fig. 1. The integration of tobacco supply chain finance and block chain

Take the example of the supplier 1 loan to the financial institution 2 in Fig. 1 as an example. In order to minimize the risk of participating in the event, the participating parties must abide by the smart contract in the blockchain platform, and the event information is fully disclosed and transparent to the participants. Take the example of the supplier 1 loan to the financial institution 2 in Fig. 1 as an example. In order to minimize the risk of participating in the event, the participating parties must abide by the smart contract in the blockchain platform, and the event information is fully disclosed and transparent to the participants. If a financial institution 2 proposes a smart contract for a loan, it is (1) whether the macroeconomic conditions of the main tobacco supply chain of the supplier 1 satisfy the loan demand; (2) the substitutable nature of the main product of the tobacco supply chain; (3) The stability of the cooperation relationship between supplier 1 and the core company of the tobacco supply chain; (4) Record of compliance of the supplier 1 in the historical loan event; (5) The rate of return in the historical sales record of the supplier 1; (6) The actual background of the supplier 1 loan event; (7) Whether the supplier 1 loan is paid according to the contract amount; (8) The legality of the supplier 1 loan application; (9) The average sales profit rate of the supplier 1; (10) Whether suppliers' collateral can compensate for financial risks; (11) Whether the volatility of the price of collateral materials market is fierce, etc. The blockchain platform uses intelligent algorithms to evaluate whether the supplier 1 meets the loan requirements based on the minimum standard values of the smart contract indicators. The blockchain platform will provide feedback based on the results of intelligent algorithm calculations. If the assessment allows vendor 1 loans, the blockchain platform automatically encapsulates the event (supplier 1 loans to financial institution 2) in a block fashion and automatically broadcasts the packaged blocks throughout the network to all participants on the tobacco supply chain. The event is valid on the basis of the participant's consent on the tobacco supply chain and is automatically time stamped and permanently recorded on the platform's chain, resulting in a permanent and transparent transaction record. The loan event is completed. Obviously, the blockchain is a basic technology, it has the potential to create a new technological foundation for the economic and trading systems of the tobacco supply chain finance industry. To be sure, blockchain technology will profoundly change the commercial operations of the tobacco supply chain finance industry. This change is far greater than the change in the tobacco supply chain industry. Blockchain applications are not only a challenge to traditional business models, but also an important opportunity to create new businesses and simplify internal processes.

5 Countermeasures and Suggestions

At present, some foreign developed countries or enterprises are concentrating their efforts on the development and application of smart contracts. Although some Chinese enterprises are also committed to the study of blockchain (such as the People's Bank of China, Wanxiang blockchain, etc.), but universities and scientific research institutions have studied less, it is suggested that China's scientific research institutes and universities pay attention to the development and research of blockchain technology, master the latest research progress of blockchain technology, and learn from the achievements of foreign blockchain technology research, build China's blockchain framework with independent knowledge and application in different industries, and study the function of mutual recognition of smart contracts in different industries, and improve the application results in various fields such as finance, logistics, and transportation in China.

Study the application of blockchain technology and its ideas in the tobacco supply chain finance field. At present, the foreign financial sector and bank owners are all seizing blockchain research in the financial and related fields. The People's Bank of China is also conducting related research. Therefore, it is recommended that local governments, related industries, and research institutes pay close attention to and pay attention to the research and application of blockchain technology in relevant fields, and timely master the latest research progress and lessons learned from blockchain technology. In addition, local governments and related departments should establish more projects in the field of blockchain research and strive for the support of national and local government funds.

Forward-looking research results should be used to formulate a blockchain credit system in the tobacco supply chain finance sector and form the basis of a financial services platform. The construction of the tobacco supply chain financial service platform should be developed in accordance with the blockchain technical standards. It should draw on the latest research results in international and related fields, and combine with senior researchers such as local governments, finance, law, related industries, and science and technology to formulate tobacco supply chain financial service platform standards based on blockchain technology, standardize the responsibilities and obligations of relevant entities in the tobacco supply chain financial market, and promote the application and development of blockchain technology in tobacco supply chain finance.

Acknowledgement. The study is supported by the National Nature Science Foundation of China "Research on the warehouse picking system blocking influence factors and combined control strategy" (No. 71501015), Beijing the Great Wall scholars program (No. CIT &TCD20170317), the Beijing Collaborative Innovation Center, the 2018 Major project of China society of logistics: "Research on the connectivity of modern logistics network system" (2018CSLKT2-004), and the project of Beijing Wuzi University Yunhe River scholar.

References

1. People's Bank of China, et al.: Guiding Opinions on Promoting Healthy Development of Internet Finance, Beijing (2015)
2. Chaofeng Jiang, S.: Service innovation in supply chain finance. China Bus. Market **1**, 64–67 (2017)
3. Hua Song, S.: Innovation and trend of supply chain finance based on industrial ecology. China Bus. Market **12**, 85–91 (2016)
4. Tanshunzi Tan, S., Ting Lei, F.: Bank application blockchain: prospects, challenges and countermeasures. New Finan. **7**, 36–40 (2017)
5. Iansiti, M.F., Lakhani, K.R.S.: The truth about blockchain. Harvard Bus. Rev. **1**, 118–127 (2017)
6. Guo, Y.F., Liang, C.S.: Blockchain application and outlook in the banking industry. Finan. Innov. **1**, 24 (2016)
7. Korpela, K.F., Hallikas, J.S., Dahlberg, T.T.: Digital supply chain transformation toward blockchain integration. In: Proceedings of the 50th Hawaii International Conference on System Sciences (2017)

Research on Application of Logistics Service Quality Management Based on Blockchain

Lili Sun[1], Zhaochan Li[1], Ning Cao[2(✉)], and Li Zhou[1]

[1] School of Information, Beijing Wuzi University, Beijing, China
sunlilibjwy@126.com, zhaochanlibwz@126.com,
zhoulibit@126.com
[2] College of Information Engineering, Qingdao Binhai University,
Qingdao, China
ning.cao2008@hotmail.com

Abstract. With the advent of emerging technology "blockchain", its characteristics such as decentralization, consensus mechanisms, traceability, and high trust have attracted attention. It can solve the problem of information tracing in the process of collecting, transferring and sharing information to prevent information from being tampered by using the distributed accounting technology, asymmetric encryption algorithm and intelligent contract. Blockchain protects digital life safety in the cyberspace. Nowadays, the blockchain technology is not only applied in the field of finance, but also has great potential in logistics. In the environment of building a country strong on quality, logistics service quality has been paid more and more attention. Based on this, the concept, core technology and characteristics of block chain technology are expounded in this paper. We build a logistics information management model based on blockchain to ensure the source of service quality data. What's more, we further discuss the application of blockchain technology in logistics service quality management in order to promote the application of block chain technology in the field of logistics.

Keywords: Blockchain · Token · Service quality · Logistics

1 Introduction

Blockchain technology is regarded as another disruptive technology after cloud computing, Internet of things and big data, which is received high concern by governments, financial institutions and enterprises. Since Satoshi Nakamoto proposed the concept of "Bitcoin" in 2008, the digital encrypted currency system represented by bitcoin began to enter the financial field, and blockchain came into being [1]. In 2016, China's Ministry of Industry and Information Technology released "White Paper on China Blockchain Technology and Application Development". It is pointed out that blockchain technology has been applied to many areas such as IoT, smart manufacturing, and supply chain management. People from all walks of life actively explore the use of this technology to promote development of the industry.

© Springer Nature Switzerland AG 2018
T. Hu et al. (Eds.): ICA3PP 2018 Workshops, LNCS 11338, pp. 151–157, 2018.
https://doi.org/10.1007/978-3-030-05234-8_19

In the field of IoT, Zhao and Xing [2] mentioned that the blockchain can provide a consensus mechanism to ensure the privacy security of the data transmitted between IoT devices. In the field of energy, foreign enterprises have started the energy block chain project. Li et al. [3] designed a framework of supply and demand interaction system of smart grid based on block chain. With the improvement of blockchain, many people have begun to explore the application of blockchain in logistics. It mainly focuses on information traceability, cross-border logistics, and finance in logistics [4]. There is less research on logistics service quality management.

In the environment of building a country strong on quality, we have put forward higher requirements for service industries. At present, there are many problems in the information data security and enterprise service quality management in the entire logistics industry process. Based on this, the concept and characteristics of block chain are expounded in this paper. We build a logistics information management model based on blockchain to ensure the source of service quality data. What's more, we further discuss the application of blockchain in logistics service quality management to promote the application of blockchain technology in logistics.

2 Blockchain Overview

The concept of blockchain originates from bitcoin, which is a digital currency. It is a data structure that combines blocks together in a chain, as shown in Fig. 1.

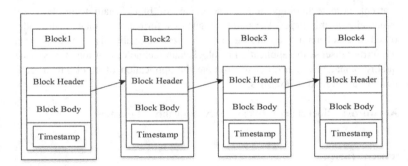

Fig. 1. Blockchain structure

In a narrow sense, blockchain is a chain-type data structure that combines data blocks in sequential order according to time sequence. Broadly speaking, it is a new distributed infrastructure and computing method. In addition, blockchain uses cryptographic methods to secure data transmission and access, and uses intelligent contracts to program and manipulate data.

In general, blockchain is a new application mode of computer technology. The core technologies include distributed accounting technology, asymmetric encryption algorithm and intelligent contract. Blockchain has four features. The first feature is decentralization. The rights and obligations of all computing and storage nodes in the system are equal. The second feature is consensus mechanism. The consensus mechanism mainly refers to how to achieve consensus among all nodes in the network. Data transactions can occur only if more than 51% of node members agree, to ensure consistency of each copy of information. The third feature is traceability. All data information is stored in a chain block with a timestamp. The fourth feature is high trust. According to the established rules of the system, ensure that the data information has high credibility. This reduces the system's trust risk.

3 Framework of Logistics Information Management Model Based on Blockchain

Big data has gradually become a national basic resource, but its development faces some challenges. The safety and authenticity of data issues are attracting more and more attention [5]. The blockchain technology can ensure the time-series data is not arbitrarily tampered with and counterfeited, which makes it be applied to the supply chain logistics and other fields. The overall framework of the logistics information management model based blockchain is shown in Fig. 2.

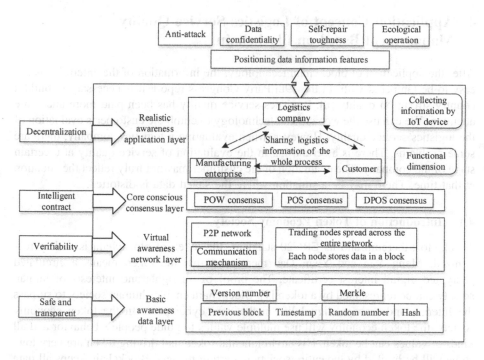

Fig. 2. The logistics information management model based on blockchain

Blockchain can be used to solve the security problems laying the data foundation for logistics service quality management. The application of blockchain can more realistically record logistics information from the following functional dimensions.

In intelligent warehousing and distribution dimension, it uses BeiDou Navigation Satellite System to provide high-precision positioning and navigation for logistics activities [6]. The blockchain can realize full-process block chaining from shipping, receiving, and ultimately the goods and funds can be traced back. In safe delivery dimension, blockchain utilizes asymmetric encryption mechanism and digital signature technology to ensure information security. For example, a logistics courier point has its own private key, and the express delivery needs to be signed by both parties' private keys. The receipt or delivery can be checked through the blockchain [7].

In traceability and anti-counterfeiting dimension, the timestamp function and traceability technology of blockchain can effectively solve the problem of traceability and anti-counterfeiting of items. For example, retail giant Wal-Mart, in collaboration with IBM and Tsinghua University, tracked the circulation of pork products through blockchain. Food source information, storage temperature, and transportation information is stored in blockchain to effectively prevent and detect fraud and errors. The same technology can be used to guarantee the traceability of logistics enterprise items.

4   Application Concept of Logistics Service Quality Management Based on Blockchain

After the application of blockchain technology, the information of the enterprise is not easy to be tampered with. In the 19th Party Congress report, it is necessary to build a country strong on quality [8]. Logistics service quality has been paid more and more attention. We can use the web crawler technology to climb the customer's evaluation of the logistics service quality. However, when evaluating a logistics company, there are some problems. There is a certain lag in the evaluation of service quality at a certain stage of the company. The evaluation of the customer may not truly reflect the situation at that time. There may be a situation where the saved data is distorted.

4.1   Introduction of Token Economy Society

Thanks to Ethereum and its ERC20 standard, the token of blockchain is widely recognized. Meng Yan and Yuan Dao mentioned that the token means a circulated encrypted digital interest certificate. The proof of all rights and interests of human society can be represented by a token [9]. Blockchain enables human society to surpass the Internet and reshape digital life in the new cyberspace. In the token economy society, the token economy will use multiple values to guide people's behavior and all kinds of values can be token. His environmental token and driving token are very low, so he will be limited by the entire society in certain matters. Blockchain keeps all data in its original archive, it is easy to retrospect and cannot be denied. Combining artificial intelligence and big data analysis technology, the token economy will be extremely conducive to national supervision and micro-social management. Through the ability of "Code is Law", many specifications can be written directly into intelligent contract.

4.2   Framework of Application Concept

Considering the multiple value-scale characteristics on the token economy society, we use blockchain technology to change the service quality management of logistics, as shown in Fig. 3. Blockchain technology, it can ensure that the data in the system is not easily tampered with. What we need to solve is that the information entered by all parties is true. For logistics companies and customers, the benefits and constraints of completing logistics service quality evaluation are different.

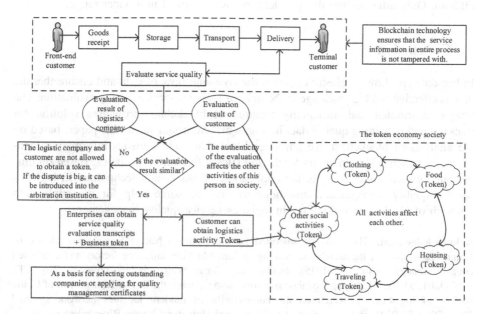

Fig. 3. Application concept of logistics service quality management based on blockchain

Logistics Company. The evaluation of service quality after the end of business is the transcript of the exam. In the token economy society, enterprises have business tokens which may be issued to facilitate the enterprise's other activities. For example, if the perfect score is 10 points, token can be obtained when the difference between the two scores is within 3 points. Otherwise, there is nothing. As the authorized party of this business activity can see the situation of each link through blockchain, the company will focus on strengthening the quality management of internal processes. We store important information such as business results and award certificates on the blockchain to prevent information loss or malicious modification. We build a credible quality management system to help optimize the current status of quality management.

Customer. There are front-end customers and end customers. The front-end customer is the client of goods in the logistics business, and the end customer is the receiving party. No matter which one is in the token economy society, as long as involved in logistics activities, they are responsible for their own evaluation. After the customer completes the evaluation of the transaction, if there is little difference between the self-assessment of the enterprise service quality, the logistics activity token may be obtained by the customer. If you make a malicious evaluation and it is examined by the arbitration institution, your logistics activity token will be cancelled.

There are existing problems in the application process. In terms of security, blockchain asymmetric encryption algorithms will gradually become vulnerable. It will be easier to crack asymmetric encryption algorithms [10]. We must increase the research of advanced technologies to ensure data security. In terms of efficiency, when there are large-scale logistics business transactions, data storage at each link will be difficult. Only after solving this problem can it be applied in a wider range.

5   Conclusion

In big data era, how to effectively track the dynamic flow of data and ensure that the data is effective is a big challenge in the field of logistics service quality evaluation. The unique distributed and traceability features of blockchain provide a solution for tracking and managing quality data in a network environment. In this paper, based on the analysis of blockchain, we introduce blockchain into logistics information management, which will help us master the logistics information resources. Based on this, we put forward some ideas for the application of blockchain technology in logistics service quality management, and hope to provide some help for the application research of blockchain technology in logistics service quality management.

Acknowledgement. The study is supported by the National Nature Science Foundation of China "Re-search on the warehouse picking system blocking influence factors and combined control strategy" (No. 71501015), Beijing the Great Wall scholars program (No. CIT &TCD20170317), the Beijing Collaborative Innovation Center, the 2018 Major project of China society of logistics: "Research on the connectivity of modern logistics network system" (2018CSLKT2-004), and the project of Beijing Wuzi University Yunhe River scholar.

References

1. Nakamoto, S.: A peer-to-peer electronic cash system. J. Gen. Philos. Sci. **39**(1), 53–67 (2008)
2. Zhao, K., Xing, Y.: An overview of internet of things security driven by blockchain technology. Inf. Netw. Secur. (5), 1–6 (2017)
3. Li, B., Zhang, J., Qi, B.: Blockchain: supporting technology for demand-side resources participating in grid interaction. Electric Power Constr. **38**(3), 1–8 (2017)
4. Zhang, X.: Analysis of blockchain technology and its application in logistics field. Sci. Technol. Econ. J. (18), 19–20 (2017)
5. Kim, H.M., Laskowski, M.: Towards an Ontology-Driven Blockchain Design for Supply Chain Provenance. Social Science Electronic Publishing (2016)
6. Kersten, W., Seiter, M., See, B.V., et al.: Trends and Strategies in Logistics and Supply Chain Management – Digital Transformation Opportunities (2017)
7. Wang, C., Wan, Y., Qin, Q.: Blockchain-based supply chain logistics information ecosystem model. Inf. Theory Pract. **40**(7), 115–121 (2017)

8. Mei, Y., Zhou, L.: Construction of powerful country with blockchain technology in big data era. Qual. Certification (1) (2016)
9. The token is the key to the next generation Internet digital economy. http://blog.csdn.net/myan/article/details/78712506. Accessed 28 Feb 2018
10. Wang, M.: Application of blockchain technology and its application in logistics express delivery. Logistics Technol. 36(3), 31–34 (2017)

Research on the Application of RFID Technology in Logistics Warehousing Management System

Jing Liu[1], Zhaochan Li[1], Lili Sun[1], Jinlong Wang[1], and Ning Cao[2(✉)]

[1] School of Information, Beijing Wuzi University, Beijing, China
liujingbjwzxy@126.com, zhaochanlibwz@126.com,
sunlilibjwy@126.com, wangjl2105@163.com
[2] College of Information Engineering,
Qingdao Binhai University, Qingdao, China
ning.cao2008@hotmail.com

Abstract. With the rapid development of Internet of Things technology matures, the application of Internet of Things technology in logistics warehousing management can effectively improve the efficiency of warehousing management. This paper introduces the warehouse management and RFID technology, and analyses problems of the RFID technology used in logistics warehousing management. Aiming at solving the problem, a new type of RFID system based on EPC system, ONS service, PML service, GIS technology and GPS technology is put forward. In addition, it was successfully applied to the warehouse management of WT enterprise, and the workflow of the system was introduced in detail. The key to build the cargo in-out warehouse dynamic mathematical model of distribution based on the corresponding algorithm was improved to solve the problem of cargo distribution. The system can realize the intelligent management of the warehouse, to further promote the application of Internet of things technology in logistics warehousing management.

Keywords: RFID · EPC · Warehousing management

1 Introduction

In recent years, with the rapid development of logistics management in China, warehousing operations management has become increasingly important. The application of RFID, GIS, GPS and other Internet of things technologies in logistics warehouse management system provides a new impetus for the further development of logistics industry.

1.1 Logistics Warehousing Management Overview

Logistics warehousing is an important part of enterprise logistics system, which plays an important role in regulating, coordinating and balancing in the whole system of logistics [2]. Logistics warehousing management refers to the planning, organization, leadership and control of all resources in the enterprise logistics warehousing.

T. Hu et al. (Eds.): ICA3PP 2018 Workshops, LNCS 11338, pp. 158–164, 2018.
https://doi.org/10.1007/978-3-030-05234-8_20

1.2 Overview of RFID Technology

RFID system is a non-contact automatic identification system, and it automatically identifies the target object through the radio frequency wireless signal, to obtain the relevant data [7]. RFID system uses electronic tags to identify an object. The electronic tags through the radio exchange data with the reader. The reader can be transferred to the host command to the electronic label, and then return the electronic tag data to the host [5] (Fig. 1).

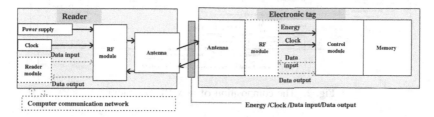

Fig. 1. RFID system composition.

2 Introduction to New RFID System Technology

In the 1980s and 1990s, the logistics warehousing field introduced RFID tags based on RFID technology development, RFID reader and RFID software operating system, logistics and warehousing management opened a new chapter [4].

The new RFID system, which integrates bar code technology with RFID technology by establishing EPC system. It uses bar code technology to identify the material and uses RFID tags to categorize the total storage through the classification of materials. In the EPC overall system, enterprises in the logistics and warehousing management only need to rely on the radio frequency identification system and information network system can complete the entire system of cargo coding and data tracking business. EPC integrated service software in the data processing software and network data system constitutes the Internet of Things [1].

3 Construction of New RFID System

3.1 The Working Principle of the System

The new RFID system uses the ONS and PML services based on the concept of cloud server into the RFID system, with the help of ONS server to store the information of each RFID tag to meet the management of cargo information requirements. While the separation of information management, to ensure the stability of information and security [3].

3.2   System Structure Diagram

The new RFID system takes advantage of the complementary form of RFID tags and barcode labels. It uses a flexible structure of demand for the encoding of goods. However, it uses RFID tags to label for the use of small, complex information products. The specific system components show in Fig. 2.

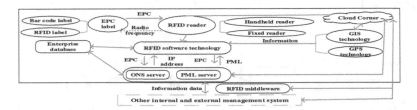

Fig. 2. The composition of new RFID system.

4   Dynamic Allocation Optimization Model and Simulation

The inventory frequency of the goods is dynamically changing with the market changes, so the position of the goods needs to be dynamically changed according to the inventory status of the goods [6].

4.1   Dynamic Allocation of Cargo Model

Dynamic allocation of cargo model establishment rules:

(1) The principle of proximity. For the high frequency of goods out of the warehouse, the nearest distribution of goods principle is the delivery rate of the cargo space, give priority distribution of goods from the exit port.

$$\min f_1(x, y) = \sum_{x=1}^{x} \sum_{y=1}^{y} \sqrt{(x - x_0)^2 + (y - y_0)^2}$$

(2) The principle of priority in warehousing and delivery.

$$\min f_2(k, x, y) = \sum_{k=1}^{k} \sum_{x=1}^{x} \sum_{y=1}^{y} f_k \times \left(\frac{x}{v_x} + \frac{y}{v_x} \right).$$

Among them, k: reservoir conditions under the conditions of the reservoir; f_k: the storage of goods access frequency; v_x: automatic car speed in the horizontal X direction; v_y: automatic car level Y direction of the speed of travel;

(3) The principle of uniform storage of cargo. That is, the same variety of goods placed adjacent or close to the seat, so you can save the goods out of the library to find a lot of time wasted goods, assuming that the first batch of similar goods distribution coordinates (a_k, b_k), the objective function Can be expressed as:

$$\min f_1(x, y) = \sum_{x=1}^{x} \sum_{y=1}^{y} \sqrt{(x - a_k)^2 + (y - b_k)^2}.$$

$$\min f(w, x, y) = \sum_{i=1}^{i} w_i \times f_i.$$

Among them, $w_1 + w_2 + \ldots + w_i = 1$.

4.2 Improve Adaptive Genetic Algorithm

Chromosome Coding Design. In this paper, an improved adaptive genetic algorithm [8] to solve the above model, based on the layout of the warehouse and the division of goods using binary encoding, the layout shown in Fig. 3, before entering the best cargo search and distribution to the corresponding goods, we must first consider the cargo and cargo one-to-one correspondence.

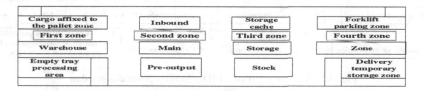

Fig. 3. The warehouse layout

For a binary chromosome decoding operation, just the opposite of the encoding here, the use of 1:3:5:5 way to decode, a chromosome is divided into 4 segments to solve, as follows: chromosomeX:00101100110010 decoding order; chromosomeX1:0 that the cargo space is empty, you can redistribute; chromosomeX2:010 converted to decimal is 2; that the cargo in the second district; chromosomeX3:11001 into decimal is 25; that the cargo abscissa is 25; chromosomeX4:10010 into decimal is 18; that the vertical axis of the goods is 18; The resulting cargo corresponding to the chromosome is: 022518, which is represented as two regions of the warehouse with coordinates of (22,51) and the cargo is an empty cargo.

Taking the reciprocal of the objective function as the fitness value of the improved genetic algorithm, in order to avoid the overflow of the function value to the processed single-objective function value plus the constant and the reciprocal, the fitness function of the population is

$$F(w, x, y) = \frac{1}{\min f(w, x, y) + 1}$$

This paper proposes an improved probability of adaptive crossover mutation as follows:

$$P_C = \begin{cases} P_{c1} + \dfrac{k_1\left(f_{max}-f'\right)}{\sqrt{\frac{1}{n}\sum_{i=1}^{n}\left(f_i-f_{avg}\right)}}, & f' \geq f_{avg} \\ P_{c1}, & f' < f_{avg} \end{cases}$$

$$P_m = \begin{cases} P_{m1} + \dfrac{k_2\left(f_{max}-f'\right)}{\sqrt{\frac{1}{n}\sum_{i=1}^{n}\left(f_i-f_{avg}\right)}}, & f \geq f_{avg} \\ P_{m1}, & f < f_{avg} \end{cases}$$

Where $P_{c1} = 0.8$, $P_{m1} = 0.1$, f_{max} is the maximum fitness value of the population, f' is the fitness of two individuals that crosses larger, f_{avg} population average fitness value. f is the individual fitness value to be mutated. The improved method is to use the standard deviation of the population instead of $f_{max}-f_{avg}$ to measure the diversity of the population and to improve the effect of the discrete group point on the solving process. Algorithm flow is shown in Fig. 4.

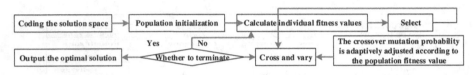

Fig. 4. The flow chart of RFID adaptive genetic algorithm

4.3　Simulation Results Analysis

According to the warehousing model established above and the design of the improved adaptive algorithm, a group of goods that have not been directly assigned to the optimization are redistributed and simulated through the following steps. Without

Table 1. The table about the distribution of cargo location before optimization.

Cargo code	Turnover rate	Cargo location	Coding
T010110	0.25	020816	00100100110000
T010103	0.09	021110	00100101101010
T010122	0.17	031703	00111000100011
T010213	0.11	031612	00111000001100
T010207	0.061	010514	00010010101110
T010320	0.013	010320	00010001110100
T010313	0.042	021824	00101001011000
T010319	0.052	010128	00010000111100

optimization the distribution of cargo location table is as follows (Table 1):

According to the above steps to simulate the cargo storage location, we get the following distribution (Table 2):

Table 2. The table about the distribution of cargo location after optimization.

Cargo code	Turnover rate	Cargo location	Coding
T010110	0.25	010406	00010001100101
T010103	0.09	011108	00010101100111
T010122	0.17	010809	00010011101001
T010213	0.11	011008	00010100101000
T010207	0.061	020108	00100101001000
T010320	0.013	021609	00100100001001
T010313	0.042	021012	00101000001110
T010319	0.052	010406	00100011001000

By comparing the table before and after optimization about the distribution of cargo location, we can learn that the allocation of cargo space has changed. After optimizing the allocation table, you can see that the cargo space with large turnover rate has been adjusted to a convenient exit near the exit. Without human intervention in the entire distribution process, the distribution of cargo location directly related to the warehousing turnover rate. The optimal allocation of cargo not only makes the cargo to meet the needs of their respective outbound, but also ensures the orderly and efficient cargo-inbound at the same time improving the efficiency of the warehouse.

5 Conclusion

In this paper, a new type of RFID system is proposed, taking WT enterprise as an example to study its practical application. We study the dynamic distribution of cargo location in and out of warehouses in the enterprise warehouse management system. We used the IOT technology in logistics and warehousing management. It will improve storage management efficiency, enhance the overall level of logistics management, and effectively reduce the cost of logistics management. What's more, the storage management will become more scientific and efficient.

Acknowledgements. The study is supported by the National Nature Science Foundation of China "Research on the warehouse picking system blocking influence factors and combined control strategy" (No. 71501015), Beijing the Great Wall scholars program (No. CIT &TCD20170317), the Beijing Collaborative Innovation Center and the 2018 major project of China Society of Logistics: "Research on the connectivity of modern logistics network system" (2018CSLKT2-004), the project of Beijing Wuzi University Yunhe River scholar.

References

1. Chelloug, S.A.: Energy-efficient content-based routing in internet of things. J. Comput. Commun. **3**(12), 9–20 (2015)
2. Fei, F.: Application of bar code technology in warehouse management. Logistics Eng. Manag. **36**(12), 64–66 (2014)

3. Fu, X.: Research and designing about application of RFID technology in logistics and warehousing. Anhui University of Science and Technology, Published master's thesis, Anhui, China (2015)
4. Hong, F.: Design and implementation of warehouse logistics monitoring system based on RFID. J. World **9**, 1–2 (2016)
5. Luo, A., Yi, B., Shen, C.: Design of food digital ID and its application in electronic receipt of wine logistics. Trans. Chin. Soc. Agric. Eng. **10**(20), 262–268 (2013)
6. Yang, Y.: Research on digital warehousing based on RFID technology, Zhejiang Technology University, Zhejiang, China (2016)
7. Zhao, J., Tao, L., Gao, S.: Study on the design and application of live pig electronic tag. Anim. Feed Sci.: Engl. **1**, 12–16 (2013)
8. Zhao, C.: Optimization of logistics distribution routing based on improved genetic algorithm. Knowl. Econ. **6**, 48–49 (2016)

A DRDoS Detection and Defense Method Based on Deep Forest in the Big Data Environment

Ruomeng Xu[1] , Jieren Cheng[1,2(✉)], Fengkai Wang[3] ,
Xiangyan Tang[1], and Jinying Xu[4]

[1] School of Information Science and Technology, Hainan University,
Haikou 570228, China
cjr@hainu.edu.cn
[2] State Key Laboratory of Marine Resource Utilization in South China Sea,
Haikou 570228, China
[3] Rossier School, University of Southern California,
Los Angeles, CA 90089, USA
[4] Zhejiang Science and Technology Information Institute,
Hangzhou 310006, China

Abstract. Distributed denial-of-service (DDoS) has developed multiple variants, one of which is distributed reflective denial-of-service (DRDoS). Within the increasing number of Internet-of-Things (IoT) devices, the threat of DRDoS attack is growing, and the damage of a DRDoS attack is more destructive than other types. Many existing methods for DRDoS cannot generalize early detection, which leads to heavy load or degradation of service when deployed at the final point. In this paper, we propose a DRDoS detection and defense method based on deep forest model (DDDF), and then we integrate differentiated service into defense model to filter out DRDoS attack flow. Firstly, from the statistics perspective on different stages of DRDoS attack flow in the big data environment, we extract a host-based DRDoS threat index (HDTI) from the network flow. Secondly, using the HDTI feature we build a DRDoS detection and defense model based on deep forest, which consists of 5 estimators in each layer. Lastly, the differentiated service procedure applies the detection result from DDDF to drop the identified attack flow in different stages and different detection points. Theoretical analysis and experiments show that the method we proposed can effectively identify DRDoS attack with higher detection rate and a lower false alarm rate, the defense model also shows distinguishing ability to effectively eliminate the DRDoS attack flow, and dramatically reduce the damage of DRDoS attack.

Keywords: DRDoS · Deep forest · IoT · Big data · Differentiated service

© Springer Nature Switzerland AG 2018
T. Hu et al. (Eds.): ICA3PP 2018 Workshops, LNCS 11338, pp. 165–176, 2018.
https://doi.org/10.1007/978-3-030-05234-8_21

1 Introduction

The service providers, security practitioners are struggling to eliminate numerous information security threats that against modern organizations in the era of big data. With the rapid development of network-based systems and lowered marginal cost of learning skills about cyber-attacks, it is totally foreseeable that the number, the frequency and the magnitude of the attacks, will grow faster than ever. One out of many DRDoS methods is that, attackers send request packets to many open domain name servers (DNS) or network time protocol (NTP) servers with source IP set as intended victim's IP, then those servers respond to the intended victim, which amplifies the effect of attack. By injecting a huge number of worthless access requests, and the internal server or devices reflecting more packets, the DRDoS attack brings the danger of congestion effectively, and the high accessibility of conducting such attacks is achieved due to the easy-use tools and relatively low cost.

The rest of the paper is organized as follows. Related work is discussed in Sect. 2. In the Sect. 3, we analyze the feature of general type DRDoS attack as the base theorem for the method we proposed in Sect. 4. And in Sect. 4, we'll detail the calculation method of the DRDoS detection method and characterized each part of it. We'll then introduce deep forest model for classification and apply differentiated service in the defense method. In Sect. 5, we simulate the DNS DRDoS attack, and then evaluate the proposed method with different parameters to verify that both detection and defense method are effective and could effectively distinguish normal network flow and DRDoS attack flow. And lastly comes the Sect. 6, we conclude the advantage of the method we proposed, and discuss some further work for the enhancement of this method.

2 Related Works

In 1999, CERT published the first report to warn the Internet about the threat of DDoS attacks, with concrete preventive actions to mitigate the threat in their articles [1]. After a few months, the first massive DDoS attack was witnessed, and many years after that, the style of attacks were not changed as much [2]. Since the first DDoS attack, researchers had begun to disassemble, study and analyze some DDoS attack tools, measuring their impact on the Internet [3]. We proposed a DDoS attack detection method using IP address feature interaction in 2009 [4]. Then we proposed a DDoS attack detection using three-state partition based on flow interaction [5]. Given previous work, we proposed a DDoS detection method based on multi-feature fusion [6]. And a better method was presented based on IP flow interaction [7]. And an adaptive DDoS attack detection method based on multiple-kernel learning was also proposed [8]. And a change-point DDoS attack detection method based on half interaction anomaly degree was presented [9]. We've presented an abnormal network flow based DDoS detection method [10], which shows a better performance among other existing methods.

Currently, the security detection can be classified as host-based security detection and fusion-based security detection. For the host-based detection, using local information collected from the node or its neighbors, every network node can monitor itself, and therefore the decisions are provided separately within the system; as for the fusion-based detection, the method focused on the global information, making the decisions in variable ways [11, 12]. With processor centered collecting all of the data from every node, the decision can be made from fused information.

However, these years, due to the proliferation of new attack strategies such as Slowloris attacks and DRDoS attacks, the interest in defending against complicated DDoS attacks has been increased. Li, Wang and Wang, they proposed a verifiable chebyshev maps-based chaotic encryption schemes with outsourcing computations in the cloud/fog scenarios [13]. Li, Chen and Chow proposed multi-authority fine-grained access control with accountability approach for cloud computing [14].

According to the real DRDoS attack record on the Internet, there was a DNS DRDoS targeted Spamhaus used 30,956 open DNS servers, and the attack flow reached 300Gbps. For comparison, the largest NTP DRDoS attack flow was 400Gbps with 4,529 NTP servers. Liu, Li and Wei et al. proposed the SF-DRDoS attack, which used the peer-to-peer network such as Kad and BT-DHT. The SF-DRDoS attack could further push the amplification as large as 2,400 [15], making it one of the most destructive attacks in the net.

3   Analysis of General Type DRDoS Attack

The purpose of security detection is detecting the attacks with high efficiency, high reliability and low cost, by implementing accessible, available and applicable detection mechanisms. Based on the theory and our consideration, this paper is going to focus on host-based detection, as every node could respond to the suspicious network flow independently and efficiently. The features our detection implementation needs are from request packets and response packets passing through each node.

The UDP amplification attack is one out of many DRDoS attack methods, it begins with a server controlled by attacker allowing IP address spoofing. Attackers would send request packets to many open DNS or NTP servers with source IP set as intended victim's IP. Figure 1 shows a possible means conducting a DRDoS attack.

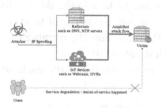

Fig. 1. DRDoS attack

One of the most commonly used means for attackers to hide themselves is IP spoofing. With this trick, attackers could fabricate any source IP in the packet. Meanwhile, attackers could control many zombie computers and IoT devices to initiate a DRDoS attack. Both means would result in the changes of the distribution of the source IP, especially the former scheme. When attacker initiates a DRDoS attack, the router near to the attacker would be able to detect massive unique source IPs, and merely a few destination IP addresses, which shows an one-to-many relationship. Also, the many-to-one relationship can be witnessed near victims side. These could be used as a feature value in our proposed method, as detailed description as follows.

During the DRDoS attack, the number of request packets sent per second is unusually large near the attacker side. This leads to the high bandwidth usage and the wide distribution of the source port being occupied. Correspondingly, on the way from the reflectors to the victim, the high bandwidth can still be observed, whereas the wide distribution of the destination port can be seen.

4 The Proposed Method

To construct a valid detection and defense methods meets the needs of the big data environment, we will face two main issues of availability and time complexity. These issues relied on high velocity and large volume of big data. the detection algorithm must be efficiently enough to handle the large amount of data as well as the network of IoT devices.

4.1 Extract Features at Different Layers

Given a network flow A with n sample packets to be detected, we define each IP packet as $IP_i = (S_i, D_i, T_i, P_{si}, P_{di})$, where we define S_i as the source IP, D_i as the destination IP, P_{si} as the source port, P_{di} as the destination port, and T_i as the payload. We will take Δt as the parameter for sampling time. And we define vulnerable service for DRDoS as VSD. In each sample interval, we merge all the source IP and destination IP into one single set M. And we suggested extracting features for the k-th IP in the set M by $\left(C_{qk}, V_{qk}, P_{qk}, C_{rk}, V_{rk}, P_{rk}\right)$. C_{qk} represents the amount of request packets of VSD s by the k-th source IP through the node in a fixed period of time; V_{qk} is the volume per unit time of these VSD request packets with the k-th source IP, and P_{qk} represents the number of unique port numbers of these packets going through from k-th source IP; C_{rk} represents the amount of response packets to the destination IP through current node in a fixed period of time; V_{rk} is the volume per unit time of these response packets with the k-th destination IP; also, P_{rk} represents the number of unique port numbers of those packets designated to each destination IP.

These features are going to be calculated for each IP in each sample interval, as follows:

1. When attacker initiates the DRDoS attack, for some S_i, there would be a large number of request packets and response packets from the reflectors. Thus we count the number of request packets and response packets for each source IP and destination IP respectively. And for request packets to the VSD, we use a dictionary W_q with its key denotes the source IP, and $W_q[S_i]$ denote the corresponding number of

request packets declared from the S_i. Similarly, we define W_r for response packets from the VSD.

$$\forall_{(S_i, D_i, T_i, P_{si}, P_{di})} \begin{cases} W_q[S_i] = W_q[S_i] + 1 & \text{if } T_i \text{ is a request packet to VSD} \\ W_r[D_i] = W_r[D_i] + 1 & \text{if } T_i \text{ is a response packet from VSD} \end{cases} \quad (1)$$

At the end of each sample interval, we calculate the amount of request and response packets respectively for each IP

$$\forall_{M_k \in M} \begin{cases} C_{qk} = W_q[V_k], & \text{if } M_k \text{ exists in } W_q \\ C_{qk} = 0, & \text{otherwise} \end{cases} \quad (2)$$

$$\forall_{M_k \in M} \begin{cases} C_{rk} = W_r[V_k], & \text{if } M_k \text{ exists in } W_r \\ C_{rk} = 0, & \text{otherwise} \end{cases} \quad (3)$$

If there is any C_{qk} with an abnormally large value, it's highly possibly that this M_k is under DRDoS attack in current network. Because one of the key factors of the DRDoS attack in big data environment is the velocity, attackers generate enormously large amount of request packets to reflectors, so that the final response flow could be as large as possible. Therefore, a boom value of C_{rk} also suggests the M_k is under DRDoS attack.

2. For request and response packets, we calculate the volume per unit time of these packets with the same source IP and destination IP separately. We define the length of each packet as L_i, and for request packets, we use a dictionary Q_q with source IP as its key, the corresponding total length from that source IP as its value. Meanwhile, for the response packet, a dictionary Q_r is defined with destination IP as its key.

$$\forall_{(S_i, D_i, T_i, P_{si}, P_{di})} \begin{cases} Q_q[S_i] = Q_q[S_i] + L_i & \text{if } T_i \text{ is a request packet to VSD} \\ Q_r[D_i] = Q_r[D_i] + L_i & \text{if } T_i \text{ is a response packet from VSD} \end{cases} \quad (4)$$

Then we could calculate the volume per unit time for each IP in M as Eqs. (5) and (6).

$$\forall_{M_k \in M} \begin{cases} V_{qk} = \frac{Q_q[M_k]}{\Delta t}, & \text{if } M_k \text{ exists in } Q_q \\ V_{qk} = 0, & \text{otherwise} \end{cases} \quad (5)$$

$$\forall_{M_k \in M} \begin{cases} V_{rk} = \frac{Q_r[M_k]}{\Delta t}, & \text{if } M_k \text{ exists in } Q_r \\ V_{rk} = 0, & \text{otherwise} \end{cases} \quad (6)$$

An abnormally gigantic value of V_{qk} shows that there's possibly a DRDoS attack, because some VSD requires a larger size of request packets to gain more amplification for response flow from reflectors, thus we extract this basic feature from the request packets to VSD. And for V_{rk}, it's obviously that this is the key point of the DRDoS attack. If V_{rk} is an abnormally large value, it indicates that this M_k is under DRDoS attack.

3. Because each IP packet occupies one source or one destination port of a machine at a time, we are also taking the amount of ports into consideration. Likely, we use a dictionary J_q with source IP as its key, the corresponding value $J_q[S_k]$ is a set which represents the unique source port from S_k. Meanwhile, for the response packet, a dictionary J_r is defined similarly.

$$\forall_{(S_i, D_i, T_i, P_{si}, P_{di})} \begin{cases} J_q[S_i] = J_q[S_i] \cup \{P_{si}\} & \text{if } T_i \text{ is a request packet to VSD} \\ J_r[D_i] = J_r[D_i] \cup \{P_{di}\} & \text{if } T_i \text{ is a response packet from VSD} \end{cases} \quad (7)$$

Then we could calculate P_{qk} and P_{rk} as Eqs. (8) and (9).

$$\forall_{M_k \in M} \begin{cases} P_{qk} = ||J_q[M_k]||, & \text{if } M_k \text{ exists in } J_q \\ P_{qk} = 0, & \text{otherwise} \end{cases} \quad (8)$$

$$\forall_{M_k \in M} \begin{cases} P_{rk} = ||J_r[M_k]||, & \text{if } M_k \text{ exists in } J_r \\ P_{rk} = 0, & \text{otherwise} \end{cases} \quad (9)$$

We use P_{qk} and P_{rk} as another two basic features in the HDTI, because when attacker initiate the DRDoS attack, and to make the DRDoS attack effective and valid, the attacker would send request packets to VSD as much as possible, which leads to that there are many request packets been sent the same time, and each packet requires a unique source port number, thus the P_{qk} would be an abnormally large number. And based on the principles of TCP/IP, a response packet's destination port number is the same source port number of the corresponding request packet, which suggests that P_{rk} would be an abnormally large number as well if M_k is under DRDoS attack.

4.2   Analysis of the Feature Value

We characterized each part of the proposed six-tuple feature value with real-world observation to explain why it is effective for both detection and defense. Based on the phenomena during different stages of a DRDoS attack, the validity on the feature components can be discussed into three situations.

1. **Attack Source.** A relatively abnormal growth among C_q, V_q and P_q can be observed. By applying the features to the deep forest's classifier, we would be able to detect the upstream of the attack flow.
2. **Intended Victim.** An abnormally enormous value among C_r, V_r and P_r can be observed. Moreover, the closer to the intended victim, the larger these components extracted in the nodes are, as the attack flow clustering from reflectors to the intended victim.
3. **Internal Nodes in the Internet.** The nodes in the internet can obtain both upstream from attack flow and send downstream attack flow, which means that both streams can be observed and extracted. We are calling the flow with these features

mentioned as mixed upstream and downstream or MUD in short. When attack flow lies in the MUD, we can still recognize the threats by classifying this with normal flow with random forest.

Given the consideration and assumptions above, we can classify the feature proposed into 4 classes illustrated in Fig. 2. We defined 0 as a relatively low value, and 1 stands for a relatively large value in the corresponding position in the 6-tuple feature $(C_{qk}, V_{qk}, P_{qk}, C_{rk}, V_{rk}, P_{rk})$.

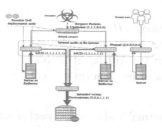

Fig. 2. Description of 4 classes features

With the definitions above, the status for any node in a network where under potential threat of a DRDoS attack could be revealed by our proposed detection method, and an efficient defense method could be deployed upon any node in the Internet.

4.3   Deep Forest Based DRDoS Detection and Defense Method

With features gathered from the network flow based on our proposed method above, a valid deep forest model can be trained by HDTI in order to determine if a certain IP was under a DRDoS attack. If the model classified the IP is under threat, i.e., downstream, upstream or MUD type, the differentiated service procedure will be introduced and activated to achieve the elimination of DRDoS attack flow in early, middle and post stages.

Detection Model. To implement this, firstly, we gathered the 6-tuple feature, HDTI, by online sampling from normal network flow and DRDoS simulation. The normal network flow contains the packets of VSD. Then we take 30 s of normal network and 30 s of simulated DRDoS attack to form a 60-s training set for the deep forest modeling. The model of our deep forest contains 5 estimators, including an XGBoost classifier, 2 random forest classifiers and 2 completely-random tree forest classifiers, as shown in Fig. 3.

Defense Model. Within the trained deep forest model, we could identify the type for each IP in the network flow which needs detection, and make corresponding process against different attack packets by differentiated service.

In the actual setting up of the defense method, in order to make the differentiated service wise enough, in other words, demolishing attacks where letting normal network

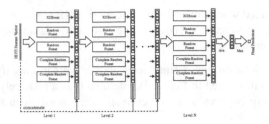

Fig. 3. Deep DRDoS detection model based on HDTI

flow, a set of applicable thresholds H should be applied. We define both VSD request and response packet that exceeded the thresholds H as abnormal packets. And if an IP was classified as MUD, then we will tag it as both upstream and downstream. The differentiated service will drop an abnormal packet when the following condition meets.

1. If the source IP of an abnormal VSD request packet was identified as upstream, the differentiated service drops it.
2. If an abnormal VSD response packet with its destination IP identified as downstream, it would be also getting filtered.

To get a set of applicable thresholds H, we could learn from the normal and legitimated corresponding VSD request and response packets separately with the statistics method applied. And in real-world, experts could change their experience into empirically rules for identifying whether a packet is abnormal of not.

5   Experiment

Our experiment was based on the WRCCDC 2018 [16], which contains a small company with more than 50 users, 7 to 10 servers, and common Internet services such as a web server, a mail server, and an e-commerce site. Inside this dataset, the typical overall, including all unrelated packets, bandwidth is around 166Mbps. We will mainly conduct following experiment to validate the method we proposed with DNS DRDoS.

1. Directly inject response packets into the network to validate the differentiated service in the victim side. The bandwidth of our injected response packets is configured as $b = [100, 200, 500, 1000]$ Mbps.
2. Inject attacker's request packets to validate the detection method and differentiate service near the attacker side. If there is any DRDoS request packet passed through our detect method, corresponding response packet will be sent to the victim side. And the bandwidth of our injected request packets is configured as $b = [1, 10, 20, 50, 100]$ Mbps.
3. Inject both request packets and response packets into the network to validate the proposed method when deployed at any node in the network. The bandwidth of our injected response packets is configured as $b_r = [100, 200, 500, 1000]$ Mbps, and for the request packets, $b_s = [1, 10, 20, 50, 100]$ Mbps.

And we take another 30 s of normal network flow and 30 s of DRDoS attack flow, where the first 10 s contains only request packets, i.e., upstream, the following 10 s is consisted of response packets, i.e., downstream, and the final 10 s is mixed with both upstream and downstream. Then we compare the method we proposed to support vector machine (SVM), k nearest neighbor (kNN) and pure random forest approaches with the same dataset and experiment settings.

5.1   Experiment Result

The result of our experiment consists of two parts, the first part is DRDoS attack detection between these methods, and the second part demonstrates the DRDoS attack elimination rate of our proposed method. We will discuss the experimental results at the end of each part.

DRDoS Attack Detection Comparison. We conduct various experiments and the representative results are gathered and illustrated in Figs. 4 and 5 for comparison. The rest of the results are shown in Tables 1 and 2.

Among these experiment results, we could see that when given a short Δt, all the methods shows a great detection rate. However, the missing rate of SVM approach is relatively high compared to HDTI and kNN means. And for HDTI and kNN, when given a fixed Δt, the larger the upstream and downstream are, the better the detection rate is. But the false alarm rate of kNN are also getting larger and larger. When take this into real-world consideration, a higher false alarm rate is more likely to cause the service interruption for legitimated users. Although the detection rate of kNN approach reached 100 almost in all experiments, and it could indeed identify the DRDoS attack flow, the high false alarm rate would also cause service degradation or interruption. The HDTI approach we proposed shows relatively higher detection rate and lower false alarm rate, which could detect near all DRDoS attack flow without causing service interruption for legitimated users.

As the information shown above, we finished cross comparison with traditional SVM and kNN classification algorithms to test the efficiency and validity of the three methods under differentiated conditions. It is obvious that the detection method we proposed can be adopted to different situations better than SVM and kNN classifier.

We noticed the relatively high value among false alarm rate and missing rate by SVM method, whereas the low accuracy on detecting real threats, as the traditional SVM didn't provide neither multi-classifier nor solution to the non-liner problems, this also contributed to the poor performance of the SVM classifier in our experiment.

Although upcoming theories and implementations based on rough set provided the combinative SVM for multi-classifying, the time cost of training such classifiers goes up. Besides, the vector processed in an SVM depends on the size of samples, the memory and time a SVM take towards a large training set could be explode. In short, the traditional SVM classifiers may not meet the needs of host-based DRDoS attacks in big data environment.

Table 1. Crossed comparison with DRDoS detection methods of $b_r = 1$, $b_q = 1000$

Method	Detection rate/Missing rate/False alarm rate			
	$\Delta t = 0.01$	$\Delta t = 0.1$	$\Delta t = 0.5$	$\Delta t = 1.0$
HDTI	100.0/0.0/0.0	99.2/0.8/0.0	97.3/2.7/0.0	99.5/0.5/0.0
SVM	94.4/5.6/10.4	92.3/7.6/12.6	93.7/6.3/15.6	94.3/5.6/10.3
Random forest	100.0/0.0/9.2	100.0/0.0/3.2	23.1/76.9/2.4	27.3/72.7/0.4
kNN	99.9/0.1/10.5	100.0/0.1/2.7	75.0/25.0/3.0	100.0/0.1/0.5

As for the velocity, attacker sends malicious VSD request at a very high speed to reflectors like DNS servers and IoT devices, and the accumulated response packets from distributed reflectors leads to even higher speed near the victim. So the HDTI feature we designed and the detection method we proposed show higher detection rate, lower missing rate and false alarm rate compared to other detection methods.

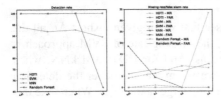 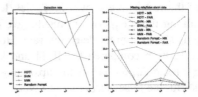

Fig. 4. Experiment result of $b_r = 1$, $b_q = 100$

Fig. 5. Experiment result of $b_r = 20$, $b_q = 500$

Table 2. Crossed comparison with DRDoS detection methods of $b_r = 10$, $b_q = 1000$

Method	Detection rate/Missing rate/False alarm rate			
	$\Delta t = 0.01$	$\Delta t = 0.1$	$\Delta t = 0.5$	$\Delta t = 1.0$
HDTI	100.0/0.0/0.0	100.0/0.0/0.0	99.8/0.2/0.0	100.0/0.0/0.0
SVM	93.4/6.5/10.4	86.9/13.1/19.4	88.4/11.6/23.1	91.4/9.5/17.1
Random forest	100.0/0.0/12.0	100.0/0.0/0.8	100.0/0.0/3.0	100.0/0.0/0.7
kNN	100.0/0.0/15.0	100.0/0.0/1.2	100.0/0.0/0.6	100.0/0.0/0.3

DRDoS Attack Defense Comparison. The experiment results of our DRDoS attack defense method could be evaluated by the attack elimination rate, we conduct the experiment with $\Delta t = 0.1$, and the results are illustrated in Figs. 6 and 7, where the $b_r = 1000$ and $b_q = 10$ were set.

We could see that after applied the defense method we proposed, the DRDoS attack flow showed a gigantic drop, which suggests that the method is valid and could effectively relieve the network load for the intended victim, avoiding service degradation or denial of service for normal users as much as possible.

As we can see in the Fig. 8, after applied the method we proposed, the DRDoS attack flow could be reduced a lot in early, middle and post stages, which suggests that

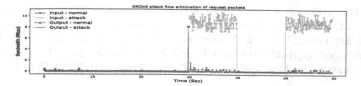

Fig. 6. The proposed defense method when eliminate the upstream and MUD

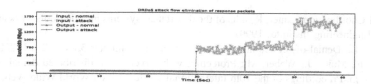

Fig. 7. The proposed defense method when eliminate the downstream and MUD

this method could be deployed at somewhere near the attack source, any internal node in the Internet, such as the router or switch in ISP, or deployed at the victim side.

6 Conclusion and Future Direction

In this paper, we developed an novel method to detect and defense DRDoS attacks with increasing IoT devices in big data environment. To the part of detecting threats, we analyzed the statistical features of the DRDoS request and response packets through nodes in the network, uniqueness ports, packet lengths, and IP information lied in them. By our new definition upon those features processed and combined, the host-based DRDoS threat index, HDTI, is proposed. The evaluation and experiments had been confirmed the validity, efficiency and accuracy of our proposed detection method. With the high accessibilities applying to the nodes inside the modern network environment by the proposed method, we are confident to put the detection model and take the HDTI as the main factor in host-based detection scheme and the trigger of the defense method upcoming in this paper.

As for the DRDoS defense method we proposed, it build the on top of a deep forest model, which consists of 5 estimators in each layer. Together with the differentiated service procedure, a high effective defense method with low cost and false alarm rate or missing rate can be expected. More importantly, as our method is focusing on the most harmful and representative attack among different DDoS attacks, picking universal features which don't need to be sophisticating preprocessed, therefore our detection and defense method can be used against other kinds of DRDoS attacks.

Our upcoming tasks lie in the classification in the host-detection method, and the introduction of fusion-based detection and defense method. An universal evaluation of network status can be made by fusion-based methodology, with gathered information from the hosts, the macroscopic threat evaluating system by fusion of the cluster can be achieved afterwards, which could optimize our proposed method in a new conventional mean.

Funding. This work was supported by the National Natural Science Foundation of China [61762033, 61702539]; The National Natural Science Foundation of Hainan [617048, 2018CXTD333]; Hainan University Doctor Start Fund Project [kyqd1328]; Hainan University Youth Fund Project [qnjj1444]. This work is partially supported by Social Development Project of Public Welfare Technology Application of Zhejiang Province [LGF18F020019].

References

1. CERT Coordination Center: Results of the distributed-systems intruder tools workshop. Software Engineering Institute (1999)
2. Garber, L.: Denial-of-service attacks rip the Internet. Computer **33**(4), 12–17 (2000)
3. Kargl, F., Maier, J., Weber, M.: Protecting web servers from distributed denial of service attacks. In: Proceedings of the 10th International Conference on World Wide Web, pp. 514–524. ACM (2001)
4. Jieren, C., Yin, J., Liu, Y.: DDoS attack detection using IP address feature interaction. In: International Conference on Intelligent Networking and Collaborative Systems, pp. 113–118. IEEE Computer Society (2009)
5. Jieren, C., Zhang, B., Yin, J.: DDoS attack detection using three-state partition based on flow interaction. Commun. Comput. Inf. Sci. **29**(4), 176–184 (2009)
6. Jieren, C., Yin, J., Liu, Y.: Detecting distributed denial of service attack based on multi-feature fusion. In: Security Technology - International Conference, pp. 132–139 (2009)
7. Jieren, C., Xiangyan, T., Zhu, X.: Distributed denial of service attack detection based on IP flow interaction. In: International Conference on E -Business and E -Government, pp. 1–4. IEEE (2011)
8. Jieren, C., Chen, Z., Xiangyan, T.: Adaptive DDoS attack detection method based on multiple-kernel learning. Security and Communication Networks (2018)
9. Jieren, C., Ruomeng, X., Xiangyan, T.: An abnormal network flow feature sequence prediction approach for DDoS attacks detection in big data environment. Comput. Mater. Contin. **55**(1), 95–119 (2018)
10. Manikopoulos, C., Papavassiliou, S.: Network intrusion and fault detection: a statistical anomaly approach. IEEE Commun. Mag. **40**(10), 76–82 (2002)
11. Aleroud, A., Karabatis, G.: Contextual information fusion for intrusion detection: a survey and taxonomy. Knowl. Inf. Syst. **52**(3), 563–619 (2017)
12. AlEroud, A., Karabatis, G.: Beyond data: contextual information fusion for cyber security analytics. In: 31st ACM Symposium on Applied Computing (2016)
13. Li, J., Wang, L., Wang, L.: Verifiable Chebyshev maps-based chaotic encryption schemes with outsourcing computations in the cloud/fog scenarios. Concurr. Comput.: Pract. Exp. (2018). https://doi.org/10.1002/cpe.4523
14. Li, J., et al.: Multi-authority fine-grained access control with accountability and its application in cloud. J. Netw. Comput. Appl. https://doi.org/10.1016/j.jnca.2018.03.006
15. Bingshuang, L., Jun, L., Tao, W.: SF-DRDoS: the store-and-flood distributed reflective denial of service attack. Comput. Commun. **69**(1), 107–115 (2015)
16. WRCCDC 2018. https://archive.wrccdc.org/pcaps/2018/

An Improved Authentication Protocol in Telemedicine System

Lijuan Zheng[1(✉)], Yunjia Zhang[1], Rui Zhang[2], Jianyou Chen[3],
Meng Cui[1], and Chunlei Song[1]

[1] School of Information Science and Technology,
ShiJiaZhuang TieDao University, Shijiazhuang 050043, China
zhenglijuan@stdu.edu.cn, zhangyunjiaa@163.com,
1084324590@qq.com, 1358523654@qq.com
[2] State Key Laboratory of Information Security (SKLOIS),
Institute of Information Engineering, Chinese Academy of Sciences,
Beijing 100093, China
zhangrui@iie.ac.cn
[3] Hebei Coal Safety (Security) Training Center, Qinhuangdao 066100, China
chenjy9898@163.com

Abstract. Telemedicine is an effective way to solve the imbalance in the distribution of medical resources. However, since related medical privacy data needs to be transmitted over the Internet, it will be exposed to the attacker. Therefore, designing a corresponding authentication protocol to protect users' privacy has practical significance. For the security problems existing in telemedicine systems, an improved telemedicine system authentication protocol is proposed. This authentication protocol has indistinguishability and forward security, it can effectively resist attacks such as retransmission, tracking, eavesdropping, man-in-the-middle and denial of service. The relevant security performance analysis proves that this protocol can have higher efficiency and security.

Keywords: Telemedicine · Authentication · Hash function · Digital signature

1 Introduction

With the increasing demand for medical services and the rapid development of information technology, the speed of telemedicine development is very rapid. In these years. In short, the scale of telemedicine services is increasing at a very fast rate.

Telecare Medicine Information Systems (TMIS) is a system that combines EMR [1], network and medical institutions to help patients and medical institutions to quickly obtain electronic medical records or health reports. Reference [2] proposed a highly efficient and secure certificateless authentication protocol, but it can't resist eavesdropping attack. In reference [3], a TMIS authentication scheme is proposed. The scheme can't resist impersonation attacks and man-in-the-middle attacks, so a more secure authentication scheme is proposed in reference [4]. The scheme in reference [5] can't resist password guessing attack [6]. In reference [7], a remote rural medical information system model is proposed. In reference [8] a medical system with

© Springer Nature Switzerland AG 2018
T. Hu et al. (Eds.): ICA3PP 2018 Workshops, LNCS 11338, pp. 177–184, 2018.
https://doi.org/10.1007/978-3-030-05234-8_22

emergency treatment and rescue function is proposed. However, authentication protocols are not used in these two studies to ensure the security of data transmission. In reference [9] and [10] two medical data exchange and authentication protocol based on the cloud environment are proposed. However, the data exchange and authentication protocol proposed in reference [9] can't resist the impersonation attack and does not satisfy the anonymity of the patient. However, these schemes can't ensure the anonymity of the patients. In reference [11], the trust level of the network management department in this protocol is difficult to guarantee, so the unsafe factors of the protocol are also increased.

In order to solve the problems existed in current authentication protocols in telemedicine system, an improved authentication protocol is proposed in this paper. Through security and performance analysis, it has good efficiency and security.

2   Communication Model of Authentication Scheme

The communication model of authentication scheme in telemedicine system is shown as in Fig. 1. The authentication scheme has four parts: medical server MS, patient P, doctor D and key distribution center KDC. Among them, the role of MS is to complete the legal verification of the identity of the doctor and the patient, and to store and forward their communication data as the third party. The role of KDC is to assign key pairs to the remaining three parties, to distribute their respective public keys, and to assign a shared key to the patient and the doctor respectively.

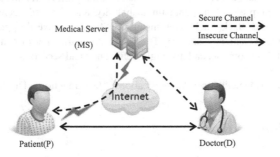

Fig. 1. Authentication communication mode

3   The Description of the Protocol

3.1   The Definition of Symbols

The definition of the symbols in the protocol is shown in Table 1.

3.2   Process of the Authentication Scheme in Telemedicine System

The authentication process is shown in Fig. 2, and the specific process is as follows:

Table 1. Symbol definition

Symbol	Definition	Symbol	Definition
PK_X/SK_X	Public/private key of X	S_X	Digital signature results of X
ID_X	Identity of entity X	S'_X	Digital verification results of X
m_X	Message digest of X	t_X	Time stamp of X
$H(X)$	MD5 operation to message X	$E_k(X)$	Encryption to message X with key k
$Sig_k(X)$	Signature to message X with key k	$V_k(X)$	Verification to message X with key k
C_X/P_X	Encryption/decryption results of X	$D_k(X)$	Decryption to message X with key k
key_X	Shared key between X and medical server	M	Medical treatment/diagnosis information

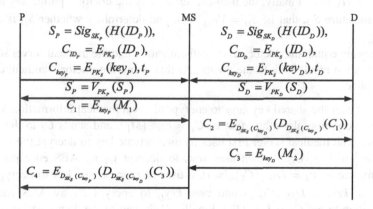

Fig. 2. Authentication process in telemedicine system

First, KDC distributes key pairs for patients, doctors and medical server, and releases the public key of all users. Patients and doctors obtained a shared key key_x from KDC.

(1) The patient uses the MD5 hash function to generate a message digest $m_{ID_P} = H(ID_P)$, then uses own private key SK_P to digitally sign m_{ID_P}, that is, $S_P = Sig_{SK_P}(m_{ID_P})$. Next, the patient uses the medical server public key PK_s to encrypt ID_P, that is, $C_{ID_P} = E_{PK_s}(ID_P)$. Finally, the patient sends t_p, S_p and C_{ID_P} to the medical server. The patient uses the medical server public key to encrypt the key_P obtained from KDC, gets $C_{key_P} = E_{PK_s}(key_P)$, and sends C_{key_P} to the server. After receiving t_p, S_p and C_{ID_P}, medical server first verifies the timeliness of messages, then decrypts the C_{ID_P} with its own private key, that is, $ID'_P = D_{SK_s}(C_{ID_P})$. Next, it uses the MD5 hash function to generate a message digest $m'_{ID_P} = H(ID'_P)$. Finally, the medical server uses the patient public key to

verify the signature S_p, that is, $S'_P = V_{PK_P}(S_P)$, and determines whether S'_P is equal to m'_{ID_P}.

If they are equal, the patient passes authentication and medical server sends verification result back to the patient.At this point, the patient's authentication is completed.

(2) The doctor uses the MD5 to generate $m_{ID_D} = H(ID_D)$, then uses own private key SK_D to digitally sign m_{ID_D}, that is, $S_D = Sig_{SK_D}(m_{ID_D})$. Next, the doctor uses the medical server public key PK_s to encrypt ID_D, that is, $C_{ID_D} = E_{PK_S}(ID_D)$. Finally, the doctor sends t_D, S_D and C_{ID_D} to the medical server.

The doctor uses PK_s to encrypt the key_D obtained from KDC, gets $C_{key_D} = E_{PK_S}(key_D)$, and sends C_{key_D} to the server.

After receiving t_D, S_D and C_{ID_D}, the medical server first verifies the timeliness of messages, then decrypts the C_{ID_D} with its own private key, that is, $ID'_D = D_{SK_S}(C_{ID_D})$. Next, it uses the MD5 hash function to generate a message digest $m'_{ID_D} = H(ID'_D)$. Finally, the medical server uses the doctor's public key to verify the signature S_D, that is, $S'_D = V_{PK_D}(S_D)$, and determines whether S'_D is equal to m'_{ID_D}.

If they are equal, the doctor passes authentication and the medical server sends the verification result back to the doctor. At this point, the doctor's authentication is completed.

(3) Patient uses the shared key key_P to encrypt his own medical information M_1 using AES encryption algorithm, that is, $C_1 = E_{key_P}(M_1)$, and sends C_1 to the medical server. The medical server first uses its own private key to decrypt the C_{key_P}, that is, $key'_P = D_{SK_S}(C_{key_P})$, then uses key'_P to decrypt C_1 by AES encryption algorithm, that is, $P_1 = D_{key'_P}(C_1)$. Next, it uses its own private key to decrypt C_{key_D}, that is, $key'_D = D_{SK_S}(C_{key_D})$ and uses key'_D to encrypt P_1 by AES encryption algorithm to get $C_2 = E_{key'_D}(P_1)$. Finally, C_2 is sent to the doctor. After receiving C_2, the doctor used key_D to decrypt C_2 to get $P_2 = D_{key_D}(C_2)$.

(4) The doctor gives diagnostic message M_2, and encrypt it by using key_D and AES encryption algorithm to get $C_3 = E_{key_D}(M_2)$. Then, the doctor sends C_3 to the medical server. The medical server uses key'_D to decrypt C_3 to get $P_3 = D_{key'_D}(C_3)$ and uses key'_P to encrypt P_3 to get $C_4 = E_{key'_P}(P_3)$. Next, the medical server sends C_4 to the patient. After receiving the C_4, the patient uses key_P to decrypt C_4 to get $P_4 = D_{key_P}(C_4)$, which is the diagnostic message that given by the doctor.

At this point, an authentication process and secure data communication have been completed.

4 Performance Analysis

This section evaluates the performance of the protocol APTS proposed in this paper in these two aspects, and compares it with the three schemes of SHAP [11], ESCAP [2] and TMAS [1].

4.1   Authentication Delay

Authentication delay of protocol APTS, SHAP [11], ESCAP [2], TMAS [1] is as follows respectively:

$$D_{APTS} = 11P + 12(2M_W + t_W) + 4M_L + 16T_{us} + 8T_{hash} + 8T_v \tag{1}$$

$$D_{SHAP} = 12P + 11(2M_W + t_W) + 6M_L + 2T_{us} + 3T_v + 14T_{hash} + 7T_n + 19T_e \tag{2}$$

$$D_{ESCAP} = 14P + 16(2M_W + t_W) + 27T_{hash} + 10T_n + 3T_v \tag{3}$$

$$D_{TMAS} = 15P + 29(2M_W + t_W) + 43T_{hash} + 4T_n + 9T_{us} + 14T_v \tag{4}$$

4.2   Authentication Cost

Authentication cost of protocol APTS, SHAP [11], ESCAP [2], TMAS [1] is as follows respectively:

$$C_{APTS} = 8C_S + 16C_{us} + 8C_{hash} + 8C_v \tag{5}$$

$$C_{SHAP} = 8C_S + 2C_{us} + 14C_{hash} + 3C_v + 7C_n + 19C_e \tag{6}$$

$$C_{ESCAP} = 10C_S + 27C_{hash} + 10C_n + 3C_v \tag{7}$$

$$C_{TMAS} = 11C_S + 43C_{hash} + 4C_n + 9C_{us} + 14C_v \tag{8}$$

4.3   Performance Analysis Results

Table 2 lists parameters for evaluating authentication delay and authentication cost, some of which are derived from reference [12].

Table 2. Evaluation parameters

Parameter	Value	Parameter	Value	Parameter	Value	Parameter	Value
P (ms)	0.5	T_n (ms)	1	C_{us}	1	C_{hash}	1
β_L (ms)	0.5	T_{hash} (ms)	1	C_v	10	b (B)	50
β_W (ms)	2	T_v (ms)	10	C_n	1	γ (ms)	0.5
B_L (Mbps)	100	T_e (ms)	2	C_S	10	t_w (ms)	2
B_W (Mbps)	11	T_{us} (ms)	1	C_e	2		

(1) The effect of authentication request arrival rate λ on authentication delay

Figure 3 is the curve of the authentication delay with the authentication request arrival rate λ. It can be seen that under the same authentication request arrival rate, the protocol APTS proposed in this paper is less than the proposed TMAS protocol and the ESCAP protocol, slightly larger than the SHAP protocol.

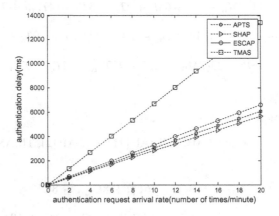

Fig. 3. The relationship between authentication delay and authentication request arrival rate λ

(2) The effect of authentication request arrival rate λ on authentication cost.

Figure 4 is the curve of the authentication cost with the authentication request arrival rate λ. It can be seen that the authentication cost of protocol APTS proposed in this paper is less than TMAS protocol, slightly larger than the ESCAP and SHAP protocols. But APTS has better security.

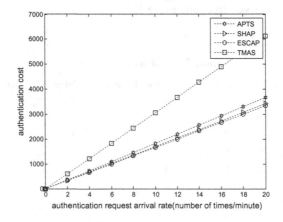

Fig. 4. The relationship between authentication cost and authentication request arrival rate λ

5 Security Analysis

The comparison of protocol security analysis is shown in Table 3.

Table 3. Protocol security analysis

Contrast parameters	APTS	SHAP	ESCAP	TMAS
Indistinguishability	√	√	√	√
Forward secrecy	√	√	√	√
Mutual authentication	√	√	√	√
Credible level of authority	High	Low	High	High
Anti-replay attack	√	√	√	√
Anti-man-in-the-middle attack	√	×	×	√
Anti-impersonation attack	√	√	√	√
Anti-eavesdropping attack	√	√	×	√
Anti-tracking attack	√	√	×	√
Flexibility	High	High	Low	Low

The authentication protocol proposed in this paper can not only ensure patients, but also guarantee anonymity of doctors, while ensuring the security of data transmission.

6 Conclusion

In order to solve several typical attacks in telemedicine system, a new authentication protocol used in telemedicine system is proposed. It realizes mutual authentication between the patient and the doctor. It can effectively resist replay attack, tracking, eavesdropping, impersonation attack, man-in-the-middle attack and so on, so as to ensure the security requirements of the telemedicine system.

Acknowledgment. This research was partially supported by Research and practice of higher education teaching reform of Hebei Education Department (No. 2016GJJG112).

References

1. Ying, Z.: Design and simulation of authentication scheme for telemedicine system. Zhejiang Gongshang University, Hang Zhou (2015)
2. Guo, R., Wen, Q., Jin, Z., Zhang, H.: An Efficient and secure certificateless authentication protocol for healthcare system on wireless medical sensor networks. Sci. World J. **2013**, 1–7 (2013)
3. Wu, Z.-Y., Lee, Y.-C., Lai, F., Chung, Y.: A secure authentication scheme for telecare medicine information systems. J. Med. Syst. **36**(4), 2609–2619 (2012)
4. He, D., Chen, J., Zhang, R.: A More Secure Authentication Scheme for Telecare Medicine Information Systems. Plenum Press, New York (2012)

5. Wei, J., Hu, X., Liu, W.: An Improved Authentication Scheme for Telecare Medicine Information Systems. Plenum Press, New York (2012)
6. Jiang, Q., Ma, J., Ma, Z., Li, G.: A privacy enhanced authentication scheme for telecare medical information systems. J. Med. Syst. **37**(1), 9897 (2013)
7. Padhy, R.P., Patra, M.R., Satapathy, S.C.: Design and implementation of a cloud based rural healthcare information system model. UNIASCIT **2**(1), 149–157 (2012). ISSN 2250-0987
8. Banerjee, A., Agrawal, P., Rajkumar, R.: Design of a cloud based emergency healthcare service model. Int. J. Appl. Eng. Res. **8**(19), 2261–2264 (2013)
9. Chen, C.-L., Yang, T.-T., Shih, T.-F.: A secure medical data exchange protocol based on cloud environment. J. Med. Syst. **38**, 112 (2014). https://doi.org/10.1007/s10916-014-0112-3
10. Chen, C.-L., Yang, T.-T., Chiang, M.-L., Shih, T.-F.: A privacy authentication scheme based on cloud for medical environment. J. Med. Syst. **38**, 143 (2014). https://doi.org/10.1007/s10916-014-0143-9
11. Deng, Y.: Research on privacy preserving authentication protocol in mobile medical care network. Anhui University, He Fei (2017)
12. Zheng, L.: Research and design of authentication protocol in identity and location separation network. Beijing Jiaotong University, Beijing (2014)

Improving the Security of a Public Auditing Scheme for Multiple-Replica Dynamic Data

Jing Lu[1], Yuxiang Chen[2], Hui Tian[2(✉)], Yonghong Chen[2],
Tian Wang[2], and Yiqiao Cai[2]

[1] Network Technology Center, National Huaqiao University,
Xiamen 361021, China
[2] College of Computer Science and Technology, National Huaqiao University,
Xiamen 361021, China
cshtian@gmail.com

Abstract. Cloud auditing is a significant technique for determining the security of data owners' data in cloud. However, multiple-replica places greater demands on cloud auditing, where not only the integrity of each data replica but also the number of replicas should be checked. Moreover, it is also significant to support dynamical updating for multiple-replica data. Therefore, how to achieve secure and effective multiple-replica dynamic data auditing is a cutting-edge issue for cloud auditing. Recently, an efficient multi-replica dynamic data auditing scheme (IEEE Transactions on Information Forensics & Security, DOI: 10.1109/TIFS.2014.2384391) was presented to address this issue. Unfortunately, there is a security defect in this protocol, as we demonstrate in this paper. Specifically, a dishonest cloud storage provider can store an aggregation of all data copies instead of each replica itself without being detected by an auditor. Accordingly, we suggest a solution to resolve the problem while preserving all the properties of the original protocol.

Keywords: Cloud storage · Multi-replica · Public auditing

1 Introduction

Cloud storage, which enables data owners (DOs, also called data users) to store and access their data in remote clouds cost-effectively and expediently, has attracted increasing attentions. Despite cloud storage's tremendous advantages, how to determine the security of DOs' data in the cloud remains one of the most challenging obstacles preventing its wider adoption [1]. To address this concern, the auditing technique, which is shown to efficiently verify data integrity remotely, is popularly employed. So far, many novel solutions for different cloud auditing requirements, such as, dynamic auditing [2, 3], privacy-preserving auditing [4, 5] and shared-data auditing [6, 7], have been proposed. More recently, research on multiple-replica data auditing has become a new hot topic in the cloud auditing field. Multiple-replica is a popular storage strategy adopted in the cloud to enhance the reliability and availability of cloud data [8–10]. As a common data storage strategy, multiple-replica places greater demands on cloud auditing. Specifically, the auditing scheme must check not only the

© Springer Nature Switzerland AG 2018
T. Hu et al. (Eds.): ICA3PP 2018 Workshops, LNCS 11338, pp. 185–191, 2018.
https://doi.org/10.1007/978-3-030-05234-8_23

integrity of each data replica but also whether the number of replicas in the cloud satisfies the requirement of a given DO. This problem can become even more complicated, if data dynamics is taken into consideration. Therefore, how to achieve secure and effective multiple-replica dynamic data auditing is still a cutting-edge issue for cloud auditing.

To overcome the problem, Liu et al. [9] extended Merkle Hash Tree (MHT) [2] to support multiple-replica, and accordingly presented a secure auditing for multiple-replica dynamic data based on the improved MRT (MR-MHT). However, their method induces relatively high storage costs for cloud storage providers (CSPs), and heavy communication and computation overheads while updating data information, due to the specific construct characteristic of the MR-MHT. Almost simultaneously, Barsoum and Hasan [10] presented another auditing protocol, called MB-PMDDP, which employs an authenticated data structure, map-version table (MVT), to record the data properties. Compared with the aforementioned MR-MHT based public auditing protocol, MB-PMDDP effectively reduces the communication and computation costs by placing the MVT in the third public auditor (TPA) instead of the CSP, and achieves effective verification with less storage overhead on the CSP and lower communication cost, due to the pre-computation of aggregation tags for the blocks at the same indices in each replica. However, through a careful review and analysis, we demonstrate that MB-PMDDP has a security flaw when facing an active attack. To be more specific, a dishonest CSP may only store the linear combination of all data replicas instead of each replica itself; accordingly, in the verification phase, the CSP can generate proofs by dividing the aggregation into required parts and pass the auditing without being discovered. To overcome this problem, we provide a simple and secure improved solution without sacrificing any desirable features of the original protocol.

The remainder of this paper is organized as follows. In Sect. 2, we briefly introduce the system model of multiple-replica data auditing and review the core algorithms of MB-PMDDP. In Sect. 3, we analyze the security of MB-PMDDP in detail, and present an improved solution. Finally, Sect. 4 concludes the whole paper.

2   Background and Review of MB-PMDDP

As shown in Fig. 1, a public auditing system for multiple-replica data consists of three main entities: **(1) Data Owner (DO)**, who wants to outsource his/her data files into cloud for secure and efficient storage. Particularly, he/she require multiple-replica storage for some highly important data; **(2) Cloud Service Provider (CSP)** manages the cloud service and provides scalable and on-demand storage services to users; **(3) Third Party Auditor (TPA)**, who is authorized to conduct public auditing, aims to provide credible verification result and accordingly build a bridge for trust between the DO and the CSP. As mentioned above, the integrity of multiple-replica cloud data may face the following challenges. First, the CSP, which suffers Byzantine failures occasionally, may hide the data security incidents from the DOs for their own self-interest [2, 3]. More seriously, a dishonest CSP might neglect to keep or even deliberately delete rarely accessed data [3, 4]. Second, some CSPs may not choose to store exact number of copies required by the service agreement [9, 10]. Third, some CSPs may ignore the data dynamics, i.e., neglect to keep updating of some or even all copies [10]. Therefore, a desirable public auditing protocol for multiple-replica cloud data should be able to verify both the copy number and integrity of multiple-replica data correctly, while efficiently supporting the data updating.

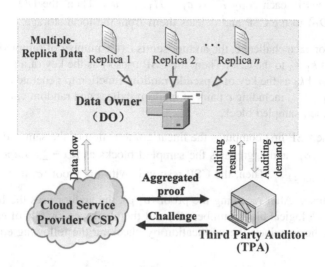

Fig. 1. System model of public auditing for multiple-replica data

Let G_1, G_2 and G_T be cyclic multiplicative groups with the same prime order p. g is a generator of G_2. e: $G_1 \times G_2 \to G_T$ denotes a bilinear pairing and $H(0, 1)^* \to G_1$ is a map-to-point hash function. F is a data file to be stored in the cloud, and composed of m blocks as $F = \{b_1, b_2, ..., b_m\}$. The verification phase of MB-PMDDP includes six steps: *Key Generation, Generation of Distinct Copies, Generation of Tags, Challenge, Response and Verify Response*. Because the aforementioned security flaw occurs in the verification phase and for the sake of length constraint of the paper, we will omit the updating phase, which can be referred to in the original paper [10] for details.

Key Generation: The DO generates a secret key $x \in Z_p$, and computes the public key y as $y = g^x \in G_2$.

Generation of Distinct Copies: For a file $F = \{b_j\}_{1 \leq j \leq m}$, the DO generates its i-th replica as $F'_i = \{b'_{i,j}\}_{1 \leq j \leq m}$, where each replica block $b'_{i,j}$ is encrypted from the original one b_j by an encryption scheme as $b'_{i,j} = E(i \| b_j)$. In such a way, n differentiable copies $\mathbb{F} = \{F'_i\}_{1 \leq i \leq n}$ are created. Further, an encrypted block $b'_{i,j}$ is split into s sector, i.e., $b'_{i,j} = \{b'_{i,j,k}\}_{1 \leq k \leq s}$, the file copies $\mathbb{F}$ can be accordingly denoted as $\mathbb{F} = \{b'_{i,j,k}\}_{1 \leq i \leq n, 1 \leq j \leq m, 1 \leq k \leq s}$.

Generation of Tags: The DO selects s random elements $(u_1, u_2, ..., u_s) \in G_1$. For the file copies $\mathbb{F}$, he/she generates a tag $\sigma_{i,j}$ for each block copy as $\sigma_{i,j} = (H(ID_F \| BN_j \| BV_j) \cdot \prod_{k=1}^{s} u_k^{b'_{i,j,k}})^x$, where BN_j is the logical number of the block at physical position j, BV_j is the current version of the block, and $ID_F = Filename\|n\|u_1\|$ $\dots\|u_s$ is a unique fingerprint for each file F comprising the file name, the number of all the data replicas, and the random values $\{u_k\}_{1 \leq k \leq s}$. In order to reduce the computation and storage costs of the CSP, the DO computes an aggregated tag σ_j for the blocks at the same indices in each copy F'_i as $\sigma_j = \Pi_{1 \leq i \leq n}\sigma_{i,j}$. Then, the DO sends $(\mathbb{F}, \Phi = \{\sigma_j\}_{1 \leq j \leq m}, ID_F)$ to the CSP and deletes them from the local storage.

Challenge: For each challenge, the auditor sends c (the number of sampled blocks) and two fresh keys k_1, k_2 to the CSP. Then, the CSP uses k_1 as the key of a pseudo-random permutation, and k_2 as the key of a pseudo-random function to generate a challenge set $Q = \{(j, r_j)_q\}_{1 \leq q \leq c}$, including c pairs of random indices and random values, where j is the index of each sampled block.

Response: The CSP first computes the linear combination of the sampled blocks' tags as $\sigma = \prod_{(j,r_j) \in Q} \sigma_j^{r_j}$, and aggregates the sampled blocks as $\mu_{i,k} = \sum_{(j, r_j) \in Q} r_j \cdot b'_{i,j,k}$, where $\mu = \{\mu_{i,k}\}_{1 \leq i \leq n, 1 \leq k \leq s}$. Then, the CSP responds with the proof (σ, μ) to the auditor.

Verify Response: After receiving the proof (σ, μ), the auditor uses the block indices $\{j\}$ to obtain the logical block number BN_j and the block version BV_j of each sampled block, and further conducts the verification by checking the following equation:

$$e(\sigma, g) = e\left(\prod_{(j,r_j) \in Q} [H(ID_F\|BN_j\|BV_j)^{r_j}]^n \cdot \prod_{k=1}^{s} u_k^{\sum_{i=1}^{n} \mu_{i,k}}, y\right). \tag{1}$$

If Eq. (1) holds, the CSP passes the verification; otherwise, he/she fails.

3   On the Security of MB-PMDDP

As mentioned above, in MB-PMDDP, a dishonest CSP is able to make the auditor believe that the expected data replicas are exactly stored by actually only keeping the aggregation of these replicas. This process can be formally described as follows.

Assume that a CSP computes an aggregated data block $\mathfrak{B}_{j,k}$ for the blocks at the same indices in each copy F'_i as $\mathfrak{B}_{j,k} = \prod_{i=1}^{n} b'_{i,j,k}$ and stores $\mathbb{F}^* = \{\mathfrak{B}_{j,k}\}_{1 \leq j \leq m, 1 \leq k \leq s}$ in the cloud instead of the original one. In the challenge step, the auditor sends a message (c, k_1, k_2) to the CSP, which is employed to generate the set Q by the CSP. In the response step, the CSP first computes the aggregation of the sampled blocks' tags as $\sigma = \prod_{(j,r_j) \in Q} \sigma_j^{r_j}$, and aggregates all the sampled blocks as $\mu_k^* = \sum_{(j, r_j) \in Q} r_j \cdot \mathfrak{B}_{j,k}$, where $\mu^* = \{\mu_k^*\}_{1 \leq k \leq s}$. To generate a proper proof to pass the verification, the CSP divides each μ_k^* into n parts as $\varpi^* = \{\varpi_{i,k}^*\}_{1 \leq i \leq n, 1 \leq k \leq s}$, where $\mu_k^* = \sum_{1 \leq i \leq n} \varpi_{i,k}^*$. Finally, the CSP responds by sending the proof (σ, ϖ^*) to the auditor. In the verify response step, the auditor checks the following equation:

$$e(\sigma, g) = e\left(\prod_{(j,r_j)\in Q} [H(ID_F||BN_j||BV_j)^{r_j}]^n \cdot \prod_{k=1}^{s} u_k^{\sum_{i=1}^{n} \omega_{i,k}*}, y\right), \qquad (2)$$

where

$$\sum_{i=1}^{n} \omega_{i,k}* = \mu_k* = \sum_{(j,r_j)\in Q} r_j \mathcal{B}_{j,k} = \sum_{(j,r_j)\in Q} \left(r_j \sum_{i=1}^{n} b'_{i,j,k}\right)$$

$$= \sum_{i=1}^{n} \left(\sum_{(j,r_j)\in Q} r_j b'_{i,j,k}\right) = \sum_{i=1}^{n} \mu_{i,k} \qquad (3)$$

Therefore, Eq. (2) can be changed into

$$e(\sigma, g) = e\left(\prod_{(j,r_j)\in Q} [H(ID_F||BN_j||BV_j)^{r_j}]^n \cdot \prod_{k=1}^{s} u_k^{\sum_{i=1}^{n} \mu_{i,k}}, y\right), \qquad (4)$$

which is identical to Eq. (1). In other words, the CSP is able to deceive the auditor into believing that he/she correctly stores n data replicas.

The main reason for this security flaw is the fact that the data proof of each replica is provided by the CSP and straightforwardly aggregated in the *response* step. Under this condition, to pass the verification, the CSP only needs to provide a data proof set (corresponding to each replica) with a correct combination, even if the elements in the proof set are incorrect or not actually stored in the cloud. To overcome this security vulnerability, we propose the following solution to avoid the pre-combination of data replicas by the CSP. In the *Key Generation* step, two additional parameters, sk_a and pk_a, are introduced as respectively the secret and public key of the auditor. In the *Generation of Tags* step, the DO generates a set of n random values, e.g., $T = \{t_i\}_{1 \leq i \leq n}$, and computes the aggregated tags σ_j with the help of T. That is to say, the original equation $\sigma_j = \prod_{1 \leq i \leq n} \sigma_{i,j}$ is replaced with $\sigma_j = \prod_{i=1}^{n} \sigma_{i,j}^{t_i}$. Further, the DO signs the set T with the public key pk_a (i.e., the signature $\psi = SIG(pk_a, (t_1||t_2||\dots||t_n)))$, and sends ψ to the auditor for archiving. In the *Verify Response* step, the auditor first obtains the set T with the help of the signature ψ and the secret key sk_a. Finally, the auditor verifies the proof by checking the following equation:

$$e(\sigma, g) = e\left(\prod_{i=1}^{n} \left(\prod_{(j,r_j)\in Q} H(ID_F||BN_j||BV_j)^{r_j}\right)^{t_i} \cdot \prod_{k=1}^{s} u_k^{\sum_{i=1}^{n} t_i\mu_{i,k}}, y\right). \qquad (5)$$

The correctness of this equation can be demonstrated as follows.

$$e(\sigma, g) = e(\textstyle\prod_{(j,r_j)\in Q} \sigma_j{}^{r_j}, g)$$

$$= e\left(\prod_{(j,r_j)\in Q}\left(\prod_{i=1}^{n}\left(H(ID_F||BN_j||BV_j) \cdot \prod_{k=1}^{s} u_k^{b'_{i,j,k}}\right)^{x \cdot t_i}\right)^{r_j}, g\right)$$

$$= e\left(\prod_{i=1}^{n}\left(\prod_{(j,r_j)\in Q} H(ID_F||BN_j||BV_j)^{r_j}\right)^{t_i} \cdot \prod_{k=1}^{s} u_k^{\sum_{i=1}^{n} t_i\left(\sum_{(j,r_j)\in Q} r_j b_{i,j,k}\right)}, g^x\right). \qquad (6)$$

$$= e\left(\prod_{i=1}^{n}\left(\prod_{(j,r_j)\in Q} H(ID_F||BN_j||BV_j)^{r_j}\right)^{t_i} \cdot \prod_{k=1}^{s} u_k^{\sum_{i=1}^{n} t_i \mu_{i,k}}, y\right)$$

Due to its complete lack of the knowledge of the set T, the CSP will not be able to obtain the aggregation of data replicas in advance, which can thereby remedy the aforementioned security flaw. In addition, it is easy to prove that the proprieties in the original protocol, such as support for data dynamics and multiple-replica auditing, are still well maintained in the revised version. From the perspective of performance, the improved protocol will induce slightly more computation overhead than the original one, for adding n exponentiations in the *Generation of Tags* step and n multiplications in the *Verify Response* step, while keeping the communication overheads nearly unchanged.

4   Conclusion

In this paper, we revisit a public auditing protocol for multiple-replica dynamic data, called MB-PMDDP, and demonstrate that it has a security flaw, namely, a dishonest CSP is able to pass the verification of the auditor using only the aggregation of data replicas instead of storing the expected data replicas exactly. Accordingly, we then provide a solution to remedy this security problem while preserving all the features of the original protocol.

Acknowledgments. This work was supported in part by National Natural Science Foundation of China under Grant Nos. U1405254 and U1536115, Natural Science Foundation of Fujian Province of China under Grant No. 2018J01093, Research Project for Young Teachers in Fujian Province (Program for High-Education Informationization) under Grant No. JAT170055, and Program for Science and Technology Innovation Teams and Leading Talents of Huaqiao University under Grant No. 2014KJTD13.

References

1. Ren, K., Wang, C., Wang, Q.: Security challenges for the public cloud. IEEE Internet Comput. **16**(1), 69–73 (2012)
2. Wang, Q., Wang, C., Ren, K., Lou, W., Li, J.: Enabling public auditability and data dynamics for storage security in cloud computing. IEEE Trans. Parallel Distrib. Syst. **22**(5), 847–859 (2011)

3. Tian, H., et al.: Dynamic-hash-table based public auditing for secure cloud storage. IEEE Trans. Serv. Comput. **10**, 701–714 (2017)
4. Wang, C., Chow, S.S.M., Wang, Q., Ren, K., Lou, W.: Privacy-preserving public auditing for secure cloud storage. IEEE Trans. Comput. **62**(2), 362–375 (2013)
5. Yu, Y., et al.: Identity-based remote data integrity checking with perfect data privacy preserving for cloud storage. IEEE Trans. Inf. Forensics Secur. **12**(4), 767–778 (2017)
6. Wang, B., Li, B., Li, H.: Oruta: privacy-preserving public auditing for shared data in the cloud. IEEE Trans. Cloud Comput. **2**(1), 43–56 (2014)
7. Wang, B., Li, B., Li, H.: Panda: public auditing for shared data with efficient user revocation in the cloud. IEEE Trans. Serv. Comput. **8**(1), 92–106 (2015)
8. Hao, Z., Yu, N.: A multiple-replica remote data possession checking protocol with public verifiability. In: Proceedings of the 2nd International Symposium on Data, Privacy and E-Commerce (ISDPE), pp. 84–89 (2010)
9. Liu, C., Ranjan, R., Yang, C., Zhang, X., Wang, L., Chen, J.: MUR-DPA: top-down levelled multi-replica merkle hash tree based secure public auditing for dynamic big data storage on cloud. IEEE Trans. Comput. **64**(9), 2609–2622 (2015)
10. Barsoum, A.F., Hasan, M.A.: Provable multicopy dynamic data possession in cloud computing systems. IEEE Trans. Inf. Forensics Secur. **10**(3), 485–497 (2015)

Feature Extraction of Dichotomous Equipment Based on Non-intrusive Load Monitoring and Decomposition

Fangping Li[1], Wei Zhang[1], Heng Liu[2(✉)], and Maosheng Zhang[1,3]

[1] Yulin Normal University, Yulin 537000, Guangxi, China
[2] Guangxi Medical University, Nanning 530021, Guangxi, China
liuheng@gxmu.edu.cn
[3] National Engineering Research Center for Multimedia Software,
Wuhan University, Wuhan 430079, Hubei, China

Abstract. Non-invasive load monitoring and decomposition technology plays a very important role in the process of intelligent power grid construction nowadays. This paper explores the feature extraction of transient and steady state by using the data of known binary single electrical equipment state. Regarding to the steady state characteristic parameter extraction, the method of Fourier series decomposition is used to calculate the average active power and reactive power, and then make a parameter table of steady state power and later analyze waveform characteristics. Regarding to transient characteristic parameters extraction, Mallat algorithm is used to make an extraction of the disturbance waveform, with its high frequency coefficient as the difference between the transient and steady-state characteristic value, so as to estimate the duration of the disturbance directly. By extracting the two-state characteristics, this paper explores the load marks that can be used to distinguish different devices. More over, this article combines with many measured data to verify the results, which has made a satisfy.

Keywords: Non-invasive load monitoring · Feature extraction
Fourier transform · Transient characteristics · Steady state characteristics
Mallat algorithm

1 The Introduction

In recent years, with the widespread uses of electricity, the users of electric power system reliability, safety, economy and stability of the proposed higher requirements, but as a result of current technology, manpower, material resources and financial resources, in the present stage of our country electric power operation monitoring system is not complete, it's growing power industry, there are some lag. Therefore, the traditional monitoring has been difficult to meet the needs of systematization, energy saving, fault detection and analysis. To solve the disadvantages of traditional load monitoring system, Hart [1] noninvasive load decomposition is put forward, the purpose is to reduce the cost, and implement more efficient to get more specific data capacity of electric power. Noninvasive monitoring load (non-intrusive load

© Springer Nature Switzerland AG 2018
T. Hu et al. (Eds.): ICA3PP 2018 Workshops, LNCS 11338, pp. 192–200, 2018.
https://doi.org/10.1007/978-3-030-05234-8_24

monitoring, NILM) is of the essence of decomposition, load the user information on total load is decomposed into each information of electrical equipment, and access to electricity equipment information of energy consumption of electricity, such as power law. In 2009, Niu proposed a bilateral accumulation and (CUSUM) transient time automatic monitoring algorithm based on sliding window [2]. In the same year, Li made an in-depth study of the non-invasive load decomposition in the steady-state system, and proposed the optimal solution method and table method [3]. In 2010, Wang proposed a short-term load forecasting method based on wavelet decomposition [4]. In 2013, Yu started with the load mark, and proposed a solution method based on non-intrusive load monitoring and decomposition [5]. In 2014, Lin puts forward the load identification method based on clustering fusion [6], in the same year, Liu for noninvasive power load monitoring and explore the decomposition, was proposed based on example of machine learning method, established a new look-up table method [7]; In 2015, Sheng studied the recognition algorithm of non-invasive electrical appliances, and proposed the identification algorithm of household electrical appliances [8]. In 2016, Xu and others proposed to improve the working status of the chicken group algorithm to identify the household appliances, and proved its feasibility and accuracy with examples [9]. In 2017, Tsui Can studies the key technologies of non-invasive load monitoring, and proposes the method of extracting features of non-active current harmonic load to improve the characteristics of similar electrical loads [10]. Cheng also discusses three key technologies in non-invasive load monitoring, namely event detection, feature extraction and load identification, and looking forward to the development of the smart grid [11].

This paper tries to mine data on Power consumption data for different electric equipment, and it is based on that non-invasive load monitoring and decompose, the data of the known bistate electric equipment single state data is studied, the mathematical model and the calculation method are combined, and the operational characteristics are summarized by extracting the transient and steady-state feature parameters, and the load stamp can be used to distinguish the different equipment. It can be used to identify a single piece of equipment, and to identify the use of electrical equipment, and to help the user to see the use of some of the electrical equipment, and make a reasonable plan of energy efficiency, and to use it in a targeted way to develop energy-saving methods, which has important research implications. According to the data of equipment data, weekly wave data, harmonic data and operation record, we will analyze the equipment data, data, harmonic data and operation record of different electrical equipment, and establish a model to extract characteristic parameters, namely, the extraction of load characteristic parameters. The load characteristic parameters are divided into two types: steady-state characteristic parameters and transient characteristic parameters. In order to make the difference of power difference power equipment more obvious, we extracted the steady-state characteristic parameters and transient characteristic parameters of the electric equipment. Based on the method of Fourier series decomposition, we used the method of calculating the active power and average reactive power to extract the characteristic quantity of the stable operation state of the power equipment, and the steady-state power parameter table and waveform characteristic analysis were made. The transient feature parameters are extracted, and the wavelet transform (Mallat algorithm) is used to extract the disturbance waveform, and then the image is analyzed according to the obtained image [12].

2 Monitoring Algorithm

2.1 Fast Fourier Transform

Fourier transform is an important tool of mutual transformations between the time domain and the frequency domain. The essence of Fourier transform is to decompose original waveform signal into many different frequency sine wave, and we can analyze the results in the further. The fast Fourier transform (FFT), proposed by Cooley and Tuke in 1965, aims to solve the problem of large computation in discrete Fourier transform (DFT). In this paper, the steady-state characteristics are extracted based on the fast Fourier transform. The principle of the FFT which are finite long discrete signals X(n), n = 0, 1, 2..., N − 1 is:

$$X(k) = \sum_{n=0}^{N-1} x(n) W_N^{kn}, \ k = 0, 1, \ldots, N-1, \ W_N = e^{-j\frac{2\pi}{N}} \tag{1}$$

$$x(n) = \frac{1}{N} \sum_{n=0}^{N-1} X(k) W_N^{-nk}, \ n = 0, 1, \ldots, N-1 \tag{2}$$

The steady-state characteristic parameters can be obtained by using the fast Fourier transform. The steady-state characteristic parameter is a characteristic quantity which can be extracted when the electrical equipment is in a steady state operation. In this paper, the steady-state characteristic parameters we mainly extract are active power, reactive power, power factor Angle, the similarity of the steady-state current waveform, and current odd harmonic relative fundamental wave phase difference. The former three are the fundamental information of electric equipment, and the latter two serve as basic characteristic parameters in identifying the type of electric equipment.

2.2 Wavelet Transform

The Fourier transform gets the global frequency spectrum, and does not analyze the frequency of the specific position, so the transient signal will be smoothed out and lose the extraction of the signal details feature. Facing the difficult in dealing with transient characteristics in the fast Fourier transform, scholars came up with an idea that they can replace the infinitely long trig functions with a finite length attenuated wavelet basis, and the wavelet transform can be obtained. As a new transformation, wavelet transform analysis method is a good analysis of transient characteristics of the algorithm. It has the ideology of localizing the short time Fourier transform (STFT), and overcomes the drawback of the window size which does not change in coordinate with the frequency. The wavelet transform has two variables, scale a(scale) and peace displacement (translation). And its formula is expressed as follows:

$$WT(a, \tau) = \frac{1}{\sqrt{a}} \int_{-\infty}^{+\infty} f(t) * \Psi\left(\frac{t - \tau}{a}\right) dt \tag{3}$$

In addition, the wavelet transform implementation has fast algorithm, namely the Mallat wavelet decomposition algorithm proposed by S. Mallat in 1986, which can greatly reduce the computation. Transient feature extraction based on this method in this paper. Due to the reason that the signal mutation is mainly produced by the high frequency signal, we use high-pass filter to remove the low frequency component in the signal, and exploit the high frequency coefficient acquired in the former procedure as the eigenvalues of the difference between the transient and steady state, disturbance of the time [13], and concrete analysis through waveform extraction.

In conclusion, this paper based on the fast Fourier transform and Mallat algorithm to establish a model to extract steady state and transient characteristics.

3 Model Introducing

3.1 Steady State Feature Extraction

First, the fast algorithm of discrete Fourier transform (DFT) and fast Fourier transform (FFT) was used to calculate the harmonic phase lag voltage (φ_h), namely the harmonic current phase lag behind the voltage at the beginning of the early phase of an Angle, principle as follows [14]:

$$X(k) = \sum_{n=0}^{N-1} x(n) W_N^{nk}, \ k = 0, \ldots, N - 1 \tag{4}$$

$$x(n) = \frac{1}{N} \sum_{n=0}^{N-1} X(k) W_N^{-nk}, \ n = 0, \ldots, N - 1 \tag{5}$$

Using harmonic data of measurement device, based on Fourier series decomposition algorithm to calculate the average active power(P) and the reactive power(Q), according to the active power equal to the average instantaneous power in a cycle of definition, can obtain:

$$P = \frac{1}{T} \int_0^T uidt = \sum_{h=1}^{\infty} V_h I_h \cos\varphi_h \tag{6}$$

φ_h is the phase of the h sub harmonic current hysteresis voltage.

$$Q = \sum_{h=1}^{\infty} V_h I_h \sin\varphi_h \tag{7}$$

Therefore, the power factor Angle can be defined as: $\varphi = arctg\left(\frac{P}{Q}\right)$ (Table 1).

Table 1. Steady-state characteristic parameters of four dual-state devices

Device ID	P	Q	φ
Joyoung hot water kettle	20617.44	7536.33	1.22035227
Incandescent lamp	13071.95	17661.23	0.637166903
Efficient lightbulb	35186.44	−21551.5	−1.02124033
SKYWORTH TV	−4583.25	−7278.9	0.561945064

Because some electrical components of electrical appliances or the working principle is same or similar, other parameters that can reflect the characteristics of electrical appliances need to be extracted. The power supply voltage is constant frequency voltage, and the current harmonic distortion rate can reflect all the harmonic amplitude characteristics of the current, and the mathematical parameters describing the distortion characteristics of current waveform are shown below.

① Effective value of current (I_{rms})

$$I_{rms} = \sqrt{\sum_{h=1}^{\infty} I_h^2} \tag{8}$$

② The current distortion rate (ITHD)

The distortion rate refers to the degree of deviation of the distortion waveform from the sinusoidal waveform. It is defined as the square root of the sum of the square root of each harmonic effective value and the percentage of its effective value. The expression is as follows (Table 2 and Fig. 1):

Table 2. The steady-state characteristic value of the electrical equipment

Device ID	I_{rms}	The fundamental wave virtual value	ITHD (%)
Joyoung hot water kettle	2.8794e+05	7.2034e+226	4.97
Incandescent lamp	3.7662e+03	6.5020e+228	5.54
Efficient lightbulb	4.0849e+03	−9.0330e+229	76.3
SKYWORTH TV	1.2872e+03	2.1462e+169	168.73

$$ITHD = \frac{1}{I_1} \sqrt{\sum_{h=2}^{\infty} I_h^2} = \sqrt{(\frac{I_{rms}}{I_1})^2 - 1} \times 100\% \tag{9}$$

It is known from the above that different electric devices have different waveform characteristics, and similar electric devices have similar waveforms. According to the steady-state current waveform of the electrical equipment measured by the experiment,

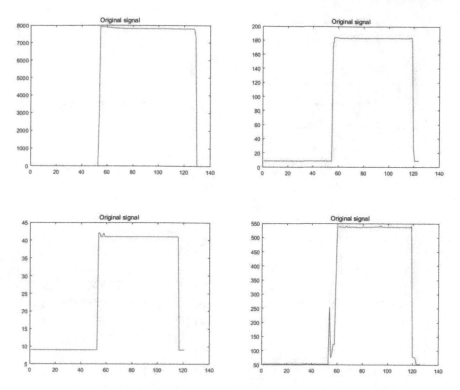

Fig. 1. The IC images of Joyoung hot water kettle, Incandescent lamp, Efficient lightbulb and SKYWORTH TV.

some devices have similar current waveform due to the same or similar working principle. At this time, the single parameter is prone to error, and the current harmonic distortion rate is obtained, the current harmonic distortion rate can reflect the characteristics of the harmonic amplitude of the current.

3.2 Transient Feature Extraction

For transient feature extraction, we use the fast algorithm of wavelet transforms—Mallat algorithm. That is used to extract high-frequency coefficients. Thus determining the instantaneous disturbance mutation point. Drawing high-frequency coefficient images through by MATLAB, and carry on the concrete analysis, the maximum modulus of each device's high-frequency coefficient will be used as the foundation of judgement. By using it, the four dual-state devices can be distinguished in a minute (Fig. 2).

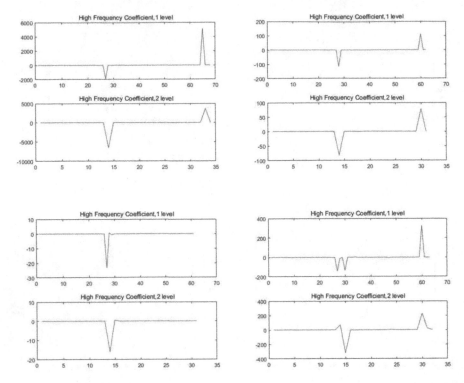

Fig. 2. The high frequency coefficient drew wave graph of the first and second layers of the Joyoung hot water kettle, Incandescent lamp, Efficient lightbulb, and SKYWORTH TV's data after passing the Mallat algorithm.

These figures obtained at this time can determine the modulus maximum of its high frequency coefficient from the vertical axis, based on this, four devices can be distinguished. As we can see, that the twists and turns occur in the figures is the place where transient changes occur. It can reflect the transient state of the input band directly. The following is the wave diagram of the four devices corresponding to the modulus maximum of the high-frequency coefficients (Fig. 3 and Table 3).

After the decomposition of the Mallat algorithm, the modulus maxima of the 4 measured equipment's high frequency coefficients can be obtained, we listed them in the above table, obviously, it is found that the modulus maximum of these four high frequency coefficients is different. Therefore, the modulus maximum of the high frequency coefficients obtained can be used as a transient characteristic value to distinguish different devices [15].

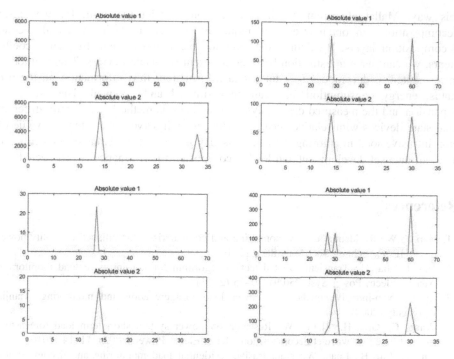

Fig. 3. The modulus maximum of the high frequency coefficients

Table 3. 1- & 2-layer modulus maxima for high-frequency coefficients for four devices

Device ID	The first layer modulus maximum value	The second layer modulus maximum value
Joyoung hot water kettle	5.1301e+03	6.5460e+03
Incandescent lamp	1.1455e+02	8.1000e+01
Efficient lightbulb	2.3334e+01	1.6000e+01
SKYWORTH TV	3.2739e+02	3.2000e+02

4   Conclusion

Through analyzing the data of electric equipment, like the electric current and the voltage at the measuring point, this paper extracts phase by Fourier Transform firstly, and then exploit Fourier series decomposition to analyze the harmonic data of the measured equipment, which bases on Fast Fourier Transform to extract the steady-state features of the two-state device. The active power, average reactive power, and the current waveform distortion rate can be calculated by the Fourier series decomposition. The magnitude of the current distortion reflects the degree of deviation of the waveform from the sine wave. We distinguish two-state devices by calculating the current distortion rate of four kinds of two-state devices. Extraction of transient characteristics, in this way, Mallat algorithm which is based on wavelet transform for waveform decomposition can obtain the high frequency coefficient of the first and second decomposition layers. By finding the modulus maximum of high frequency coefficients, we can make a distinction between different two-state devices. This method is implemented to decompose user total load information, thus information on the use status, energy consumption, etc. can be estimated and obtained. The user type expansion and the measured data analysis show that this method can identify different dual state devices with relative accuracy. The research serves as a reference value of Non-intrusive load monitoring data analysis. By using Fourier Transform calculation method, data set development and load decomposition performance is prospected.

References

1. Hart, G.W.: Residential energy monitoring and computerized surveillance via utility power flows. IEEE Technol. Soc. Mag. **8**(2), 12–16 (1989)
2. Niu, L., Jia, H.: Transient event detection algorithm for non-intrusive load monitoring. Autom. Electr. Power Syst. **35**(09), 30–35 (2011)
3. Li, P.: Non-intrusive method for power load disaggregation and monitoring. Tianjin University (2009)
4. Wang, C., Guo, H., Zhang, W.: Research on power system short term load forecasting method based on wavelet decomposition. Hebei Electr. Power **29**(02), 11–14 (2010)
5. Yu, Y., Liu, B., Luan, W.: Nonintrusive residential load monitoring and decomposition technology. South. Power Syst. Technol. **7**(04), 1–5 (2013)
6. Lin, J.: Application of recognition model for power load in cluster ensemble and deep learning. South China University of Technology (2014)
7. Liu, B.: Non-intrusive power load monitoring and disaggregation technique. Tianjin University (2014)
8. Sheng, M.: Algorithm research of non-intrusive household appliances recognition. Ocean University of China (2015)
9. Xu, Y., Li, W., Li, D., You, X.: Disaggregation for non-invasive domestic appliances based on the improved chicken swarm optimization algorithm. Power Syst. Prot. Control **44**(13), 27–32 (2016)
10. Cui, C.: Study on key technologies in non-intrusive residential load monitoring for intelligent power utilization. School of North China Electric Power University (2017)
11. Cheng, X., Li, L., Wu, H., Ding, Y., Song, Y., Sun, W.: A survey of the research on non-intrusive load monitoring and disaggregation. Power Syst. Technol. **40**(10), 3108–3117 (2016)
12. Huang, Y., Li, W., Liang, Z., Xue, Y., Wang, X.: Efficient business process consolidation: combining topic features with structure matching. Soft Comput. **22**(2), 645–657 (2016)
13. Bin, Z., Jing, S.: A power quality analysis method based on Mallat algorithm and fast fourier transform. Power Syst. Technol. **2007**(19), 35–40 (2017)
14. Lei, D.: The research on algorithm of the NILM in circuit fault detection and household appliances power consumption monitoring. College of Electrical Engineering of Chongqing University (2012)
15. Tan, W., Xie, D., Xia, J., Tan, W., Fan, L., Jin, S.: Spectral and energy efficiency of massive MIMO for hybrid architectures based on phase shifters. IEEE Access **6**, 11751–11759 (2018)

Author Index

Printed in the United States
By Bookmasters